NEWSPAPERS AND NAXALITE MOVEMENT
An Analysis

NEWSPAPERS AND NAXALITE MOVEMENT

An Analysis

DR. J. MADHU BABU

KANISHKA PUBLISHERS, DISTRIBUTORS
NEW DELHI-110 002

KANISHKA PUBLISHERS, DISTRIBUTORS
4697/5-21 A, Ansari Road, Daryaganj
New Delhi-110 002
Phones : 2327 0497, 2328 8285
Fax : 011-2328 8285
E-mail: kanishka_publishing@yahoo.co.in

Newspapers and Naxalite Movement:
An Analysis

First Published 2010

ISBN 978-81-8457-215-5

PRINTED IN INDIA

Published by Madan Sachdeva for Kanishka Publishers, Distributors, 4697/5-21A, Ansari Road, Daryaganj, New Delhi-110 002, Typeset by Sunshine Graphics, Delhi, and Printed at Rajdhani Printers, Delhi.

To

My **mother** and **sister**

Who are responsible for my

Birth and ***growth***

—Madhu Babu

Foreword

The first news about Naxalbari in the West Bengal appeared in the national press in late May, 1967. Consequently, the period 1968 and 1969 saw the outbreak of struggles of landless and poor peasants that stormed the rich people. The upsurge in Naxalbari had its impact in Andhra Pradesh. Srikakulam is one of the 23 districts in the state of Andhra Pradesh which was influenced by the movement although the district did not have a strong communist base in the past. The movement took a new turn in October, 1968 after an incident in Garudabhadra (Srikakulam), in which a demonstration of girijans was attacked by men of landlords. They never even spared women and did not hesitate to molest them. This angered the people of several neighbouring villages who assembled and forcibly cultivated the landlords' land which was followed by severe police repression.

Although Naxalite movement has completed more than 40 years, most of the studies only focussed on the genesis of the Naxalite movement and its impact on socio-economic aspects. Only one study in specific done in Andhra Pradesh by Dr. Stevenson of Osmania University, Hyderabad analyzed the role of newspapers in insurgency with particular reference to Andhra Pradesh. However, this study too did not analyze the newspapers quantitatively in relation to the coverage given to Naxalite issues. Thus, the present study undertaken by J. Madhu Babu is significant in this context as the study makes an attempt to content-analyze the English and Telugu newspapers by systematically and methodically by categorizing news contents, editorials, cartoons and edit page articles by drawing an appropriate sample during the eight-year study period (1999-2006). Despite the work is tedious, the researcher has painstakingly gone through the newspapers to capture the trend in media coverage of the Naxalite Movement. I appreciate the work undertaken by Dr. Madhu Babu and congratulate him on the occasion of publishing the work in the form of a book.

Dr. DVR Murthy
Associate Professor
Department of Journalism
Andhra University
Visakhapatnam-530 003

February 1, 2010

Acknowledgements

I am greatly indebted to many people for making the present study possible.

I am extremely grateful to Prof. B. Devi Prasad, Research Director and Professor of Social Work, Andhra University, Visakhapatnam for his valuable guidance and suggestions throughout the work.

I am extremely thankful and grateful to Dr. D.V.R. Murthy, Joint Research Director and Chairman, Board of Studies, Department of Journalism and Mass Communication, Andhra University, Visakhapatnam for his continuous help and supervision throughout the course of the study.

I take this opportunity to acknowledge my thanks to Dr. P. Bobby Vardhan, Head, Department of Journalism and Mass Communication and Member, Doctoral Committee, for his continous encouragement and cooperation throughout my research work. I am thankful to Dr. Challa Ramakrishna, Assistant Professor and Department of Journalism for his cooperation. Special thanks to Prof. K. Stevenson, Department of Journalism and Mass Communication, Osmania University, Hyderabad for his valuable suggestions and encouragement.

My thanks are due to Prof. B. Vijayalakshmi, Department of Social Work, Prof. U. Vindya, Department of Psychology, Dr. B. Ratna Kumari, Department of Women Studies, Dr. M. Prasada Rao, Department of Economics, Prof. K. Ravi, Department of Politics, Andhra University, Visakhapatnam, Dr. V. Satti Reddy, Associate Professor, Sri Potti Sree Ramulu, Telugu University, Hyderabad, Dr. K. Balagopal, Human Rights Forum, Hyderabad, S.R. Sankaran, IAS Retd., Convener, Committee of Concerned Citizens, Hyderabad and V.S. Krishna, State Secretary HRF.

I express my gratitude to my well-wishers C.S. Ranganayukulu, Smt. Sarada, A. Sudharsanamma, Botany Lecturer, Guduru, Nellore district, Ch. Vijayalakshmi Parameswar Rao, Law Officer, Visakhapatnam Port Trust, Smt. P. Bobby, Vijaya Kumar Kurra, Divya Mary, G. Salomi, M. Madhavi Kalpana, G. Sridevi, Dr. K. Madhu Babu (Economics), Dr. N.V. Prasad (Zoology), Dr. A. Jayaraj (Geology), Dr. T. Lakshmi Prasad (Geology), Dr. Veerendra (Bio-chemistry), Dr. Pridhviraj (Telugu), G. Ravi, Ch. Koteswara Rao, R. Tirupati Rao, D. Rajendhra, G. Leela Prasada Rao, G.K.D. Prasad and M. Nagaraju.

My friends and well-wishers Dr. C.M. Vinay Kumar, Dr. G. Anitha, Srinivas (Geophysics), helped me in the comparison of the draft. I sincerely thank them for their help.

I also thank all my journalist colleagues.

I am thankful to my bosomfriends P. Kesava Rao, B. Chakravarthy, M. Vasantha, Venu Kumba, Sai Satyanarayana, Vijay Srinivas, Padma Maddi, Neeraja, Afroz, K.V. Subrahmanyam, Ramachandra Reddy, Khaja Rahamantulla, John William, M. Rama Rao and Ms. Jayanthi.

I record my sincere thanks to the computer programmer N.V.N. Sharma and data entry operators Ms. Shaila Dimple.

Lastly I record my gratitude to my mother J. Ethalamma for her unstinted support and my sisters Ms. Sukhadakumari and Vidyullatha for their constant encouragement and support throughout my career and also during the doctoral work.

J. MADHU BABU

Contents

Contents

Abbreviations

AICC	:	All India Congress Committee
AICCCR	:	All India Coordination Committee of Communist Revolutionaries
AICCTU	:	All India Central Council of Trade Union
AIFTU	:	All India Federation of Trade Unions
AILRC	:	All India League for Revolutionary Culture
AIPRF	:	All India People's Resistance Forum
AOB	:	Andhra Orissa Border
APCCCR	:	Andhra Pradesh Coordination Committee of Communist Revolutionaries
APCLC	:	Andhra Pradesh Civil Liberties Committe
APPS Act	:	Andhra Pradesh Public Security Act
APSC	:	Andhra Pradesh State Committee
BJP	:	Bharatiya Janata Party
CC	:	Central Committee
CCC	:	Committee of Concerned Citizens
CCCRGU	:	Coordination Committee of Communist Revolutionary Group for Unity
CCOMPOSA	:	Coordination Committee of Maoist Parties and Organizations in South Asia
CMC	:	Central Military Commission
COC	:	Central Organizing Committee
CP	:	Chandra Pulla Reddy
CPB (M)	:	Communist Party of Bhutan (Maoist)
CPC	:	Communist Party of China

CPI	:	Communist Party of India
CPI (M)	:	Communist Party of India (Marxist)
CPI (ML)	:	Communist Party of India (Marxist Leninist)
CPN-M	:	Communist Party of Nepal – Maoist
CPUSI	:	Communist Party of United States of India
CRGU	:	Communist Revolutionary Group for Unity
CRPF	:	Central Reserved Protection Force
CRZ	:	Compact Revolutionary Zone
DV	:	Devulapalli Venkateswara Rao
FALN	:	Fuerzes Armadas de Liberations National
HRF	:	Human Rights Forum
JNM	:	Jana Natya Mandali
KS	:	Kondapalli Seetharamaiah
LWE	:	Left Wing Extremism
MCC	:	Maoist Communist Centre
MCCI	:	Maoist Communist Centre of India
MLA	:	Member of Legislative Assembly
MPTC	:	Mandal Parishad Territorial Constituency
NHRC	:	National Human Rights Commission
NTSZC	:	North Telangana Special Zonal Committee
OCCR	:	Organizing Committee of Communist Revolutionaries
OPDR	:	Organization for Protection of Democratic Rights
PCI	:	Press Council of India
PGA	:	People's Guerilla Army
PLGA	:	People's Liberation Guerilla Army
PLO	:	Palestinian Liberation Organization
POTA	:	Prevention of Terrorism Act
PSP	:	Praja Socialist Party
PU	:	Party Unity
PUCL	:	Peoples Union for Civil Liberties

PW	:	People's War
PWG	:	People's War Group
RCS	:	Rythu Coolie Sangham
RSU	:	Radical Students Union
RTC	:	Road Transport Corporation
RWA	:	Revolutionary Writers Association
RYL	:	Radical Youth League
SNS	:	Satyanarayana Singh
SSP	:	Samyukta Socialist Party
SZMC	:	Sub Zonal Military Commission
TADA	:	Terrorists and Disruptive Activities (Prevention Act)
TDP	:	Telugu Desam Party
TN	:	Tarimala Nagi Reddy
TRS	:	Telangana Rashtra Samithi
UCCRI	:	Unity Centre of Communist Revolutionaries of India
UPA	:	United Progressive Alliance
VM	:	Vinod Mishra
VV	:	Vara Vara Rao

1

Naxalite Movement: An Overview

The Naxalite movement owes its origin to the Communist Party of India (Marxist) in West Bengal. The group which was split from the CPI (M) led an armed struggle against the landed gentry at Naxalbari[1] in West Bengal. However, the uprising was crushed by the police in a few months by the United Front Government that was in power in the state. Thus the revolt which acquired the label of 'Naxalism' paved the way for waging struggles against the established feudal order by the oppressed masses in different parts of the country (Gupta, 2004). In fact, 'Naxalism' identifies with the fight against poverty and alienation. There are around 40 groups in the country professing the ideology of 'Naxalism' which is otherwise known as Marxism, Leninism and Maoism. About 11 groups have a predominant place in the Naxalite movement which has identified itself with the Left wing extremism in the country. The present chapter discusses the genesis of the Naxalite movement, splits of the movement, and the state policy towards the movement while reviewing the studies that deal with the relationship between the media and the Naxalite movement.

---

1. The Naxalite movement derives its name from a small village Naxalbari on the tri-junction of India, Nepal and East Pakistan (presently Bangladesh), where tribals took up arms against the oppression of the landlords in 1967. The movement spread to different parts of the country. The term 'Naxalite' came to symbolize an individual who took up arms in a bid to overthrow the entrenched status quo in favour of the downtrodden. There are close to 40 groups in the country professing adherence to the philosophy of Marxism, Leninism and Maoism.

Genesis of Naxalite Movement

Two Communist leaders–Charu Mazumdar and Kanu Sanyal ignited the first spark of Naxalite movement to achieve peasant rights at Naxalbari in West Bengal which appeared in the national press in late May, 1967. It was reported that a group of tribal peasants had taken control of the Naxalbari area under the leadership of the local unit of the Communist Party of India (Marxist). The first clash was triggered between peasants and landed gentry on May 22, 1967 when a landlord attempted to forcibly evict a poor tenant from his land in defiance of a court order. The next attack took place the following day when the tribals tried to occupy a land near a tea estate, protected by the private armed guards. On May 24 a small party of policemen went to the estate area and one officer was killed in the ambush. Consequent upon the attack, a bigger police force was sent to the village, which fired on the demonstrating women and children, killing nine in the absence of the men, who had fled (Dasgupta, 1974: 2-3). In June the struggle intensified further, particularly in the areas of Naxalbari, Kharibari and Phansidewa in West Bengal (Johari, 1972). Soon after the first incident in the last week of May, 1967, the leaders of the Naxalbari Unit of the CPI (M) declared the area as "liberated zone"(Dasgupta, 1974: 8). It meant that the police and the government officials would not be allowed to enter that area as the armed squads were formed to defend the area. Village Committees of CPI (M) were established under the leadership of Charu Mazumdar to take over the administration of schools and other public activities. These committees also performed the function of judicial bodies. Raids were organised on the houses of rich peasants and the stocks of hoarded rice were confiscated. The mortgage and loan documents in their possession were destroyed. Fire arms and ammunition were snatched away from the *jotedars* (Landlords). These incidents received unprecedented publicity in the national press. The rich peasant parties, particularly the Bangala Congress, the Praja Socialist Party (PSP) and the Samyukta Socialist Party, as well as the Congress Party, demanded immediate police action. Also, they took the initiative in forming 'Resistance Committees' in the areas adjoining the villages where the Naxalite guerillas were active. Within a few days, three tribals were killed by the 'defensive actions' of these Resistance Committees (Dasgupta, 1974: 9). In the ruthless cordon and search operations, hundreds were beaten up and over one thousand were arrested.

Some leaders like Jangal Santal were arrested, others like Charu Mazumdar went underground, yet others like Tribheni Kanu, Sobhan Ali, Gorkha Majhi and Tilka Majhi became "communist martyrs" (See Appendix-I).

Naxalbari-Type Upsurge

The period 1968 and 1969 saw the outbreak of struggles of landless and poor peasants that rebelled against the rich people. The upsurge in Naxalbari had its impact in Srikakulam, one of the 23 districts in the state of Andhra Pradesh. Unlike most other districts it had never been a strong communist base in the past. For instance, the communists failed to gain a single seat from this area in any of the first four general elections and their percentage of votes were 4.9, 12.7, 5.6 and 4.4 respectively for the CPI (M) and the CPI combined (Dasgupta, 1974: 46).

In Srikakulam district, two school teachers built up a mass base amongst the tribals since the late 1950s. Vempatapu Satyanarayana (popularly known as Satyam) together with Adibhatla Kailasam was finding the militancy of their struggle coming into direct conflict with the existing Communist Party state leadership. Forcible seizures of crops, land occupations, growing clashes with the landlords were developing into armed clashes with the police. These two teachers were soon joined by youth leader Panchadi Krishnamurthy. Added to this, the folk performances of Subbarao Panigrahi became the vehicle of revolutionary politics.

With the outbreak of the news of Naxalbari, Sathyam and others immediately embraced the politics of Naxalbari as in it they found the answers for which they were grouping and which the state leadership of the then CPI (M) and later Andhra Pradesh Coordination Committee of Communist Revolutionaries (APCCCR) was unwilling to provide. The spark was triggered on October 31, 1967 when two comrades 'Koranna' and 'Manganna' were shot dead by landlords at Levidi village in Srikakulam district on the way to the Girijan Sangam Conference. In response to this, the girijans (tribes) rose in a big way against the landlords. Seizure of the land of landlords, property and food grains spread from village to another which was organised by tribes moving in groups armed with traditional weapons. This continued for six months, which paralysed the local police forces. But in March, 1968, the government sent a special armed police to suppress the mass movement. Two persons were killed and 1500 others were arrested. Ironically, the police resorted to looting and destroying of tribal villages (Dasgupta, 1974: 48).

The movement took a new turn in October, 1968 after an incident in Garudabhadra, in which a demonstration of girijans was attacked by men of landlords. They did not spare women and did not hesitate to molest them. This angered the people of several neighbouring villages who assembled and forcibly cultivated the landlords' land which was followed by severe police repression.

This incident forced Naxalites to think about more effective ways of combating the repression unleashed by the police and the landlords' men. Panchadi Krishnamurthy, the leader of the Naxalites in the Srikakulam district, decided to make direct contact with Charu Mazumdar and other leaders of All India Coordination Committee of Communist Revolutionaries (AICCCR) ignoring the state leaders.

Mazumdar advised the Srikakulam leaders to forsake the line of building mass movements based on economic struggles and to start guerilla actions. He also suggested that the Srikakulam leaders should concentrate on action to annihilate "class enemies" and to destroy the police force in that context (Dasgupta, 1974, Banerjee, 1980). The first phase of the guerilla movement began on November 25, 1968, when 250 girijans from 25 villages attacked the houses of a moneylender in Parvathipuram and took over his accumulated rice and grains worth Rs. 20,000. This was the beginning of a series of raids on landlords, moneylenders and their agents in which the guerillas destroyed and burnt houses and decamped with money and other belongings (Appendix-II). Alongside these activities there took place several encounters with the police. In 1969, the number of functioning squads of Naxalites increased and so did the attacks. But, in October, 1969 the government sent 12,000 Central Reserved Protection Force (CRPF) and the battle went on for nearly six months. Major guerilla actions took place in the upper Aviri area, on the Bothili hills and near 'Sanjuvai', 'Vegulavada' and 'Inthamanugadda'; all in the district of Srikakulam. By January 1970, as many as 120 policemen were killed. Consequently, the leaders like Satyam, Adibhatla Kailasam, Panchadi Krishnamurthy, Panchadi

Nirmala, Dr. Chaganti Bhaskar Rao and Subba Rao Panigrahi died in police actions.

Revolutionary activities were launched by the Indian Maoists in several other areas besides Naxalbari and Srikakulam. Prominent among those areas were Debra-Gopiballavpore in West Bengal, Mushahari in Bihar, Lakhimpur-Kheri in Uttar Pradesh, Chamkaursahib in Punjab, Pulpalli, Tiruchelli in Kerala, Ganjam and Koraput in Orissa, Goalpura in Assam (See Appendix-II).

Splits in the Movement

The Communist Movement in India split several times in the 1960s, and a major feature of these splits was the role, the attitude and views of the Communist Party of China. The first split, in 1964, led to the formation of CPI (M), the second, in 1967, led to the birth of the Naxalite movement and CPI (ML), subsequently, the CPI (ML)* split into smaller groups because of conflicting interpretations of the Chinese line (See Figure-1).

The Birth of CPI (ML)

At a meeting on February 8, 1969, All India Coordination Committee of Communist Revolutionaries (AICCCR) gave a call for the formation of a Marxist Leninist Party. In a declaration it said, "Idealistic deviation on the question of party building arises as a result of the refusal to recognize the struggle that must be waged within the party. The idea that the party should be formed only after all opportunistic tendencies, alien trends and undesirable elements have been purged through class struggles is nothing but subjective idealism. To conceive of a party without contradictions, without struggle between the opposite, that is to think of a pure and faultless party, is indulging in mere idealist fantasy." (*Liberation*** March, 1969, Vol. 2, No. 5). Thus, the CPI (ML) was formed on April 22, 1969 after holding the birth anniversary of Lenin. Parimal Das Gupta, General Secretary of the State Electricity Board Employees' Union of West Bengal defected and formed a rival coordination

---

* CPI (ML) has been split into Asit Sen's Maoist Communist Center (MCC), Subdesh Mitra's Lal Jhanda Dal (Red Flag Party), Parimala Das Gupta's proletarian path, Amulya Ganguli's Communist group and Ashim Chatterji's Regional Committee (Johari, 1972).

** *Liberation*, is the monthly English organ of the CPI (ML).

Figure-1

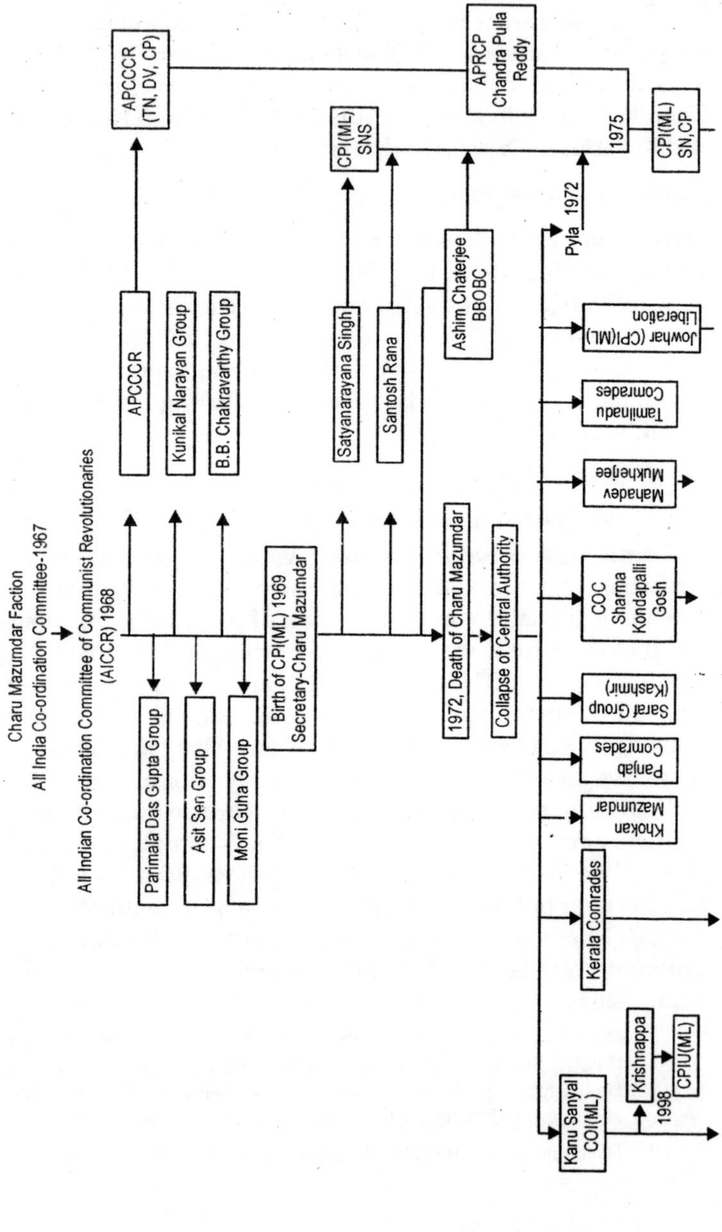
Charu Mazumdar Faction
All India Co-ordination Committee-1967
All Indian Co-ordination Committee of Communist Revolutionaries (AICCR) 1968
Parimala Das Gupta Group
Asit Sen Group
Moni Guha Group
APCCCR
Kunikal Narayan Group
B.B. Chakravarthy Group
APCCCR (TN, DV, CP)
Birth of CPI(ML) 1969 Secretary-Charu Mazumdar
Satyanarayana Singh
Santosh Rana
CPI(ML) SNS
Ashim Chaterjee BBOBC
APRCP Chandra Pulla Reddy
1972, Death of Charu Mazumdar
Collapse of Central Authority
Pyla 1972
1975
CPI(ML) SN,CP
Jowhar (CPI(ML) Liberation
Tamilnadu Comrades
Mahadev Mukherjee
COC Sharma Kondapalli Gosh
Saraf Group (Kashmir)
Panjab Comrades
Khokan Mazumdar
Kerala Comrades
Kanu Sanyal COI(ML)
1998
Krishnappa
CPIU(ML)

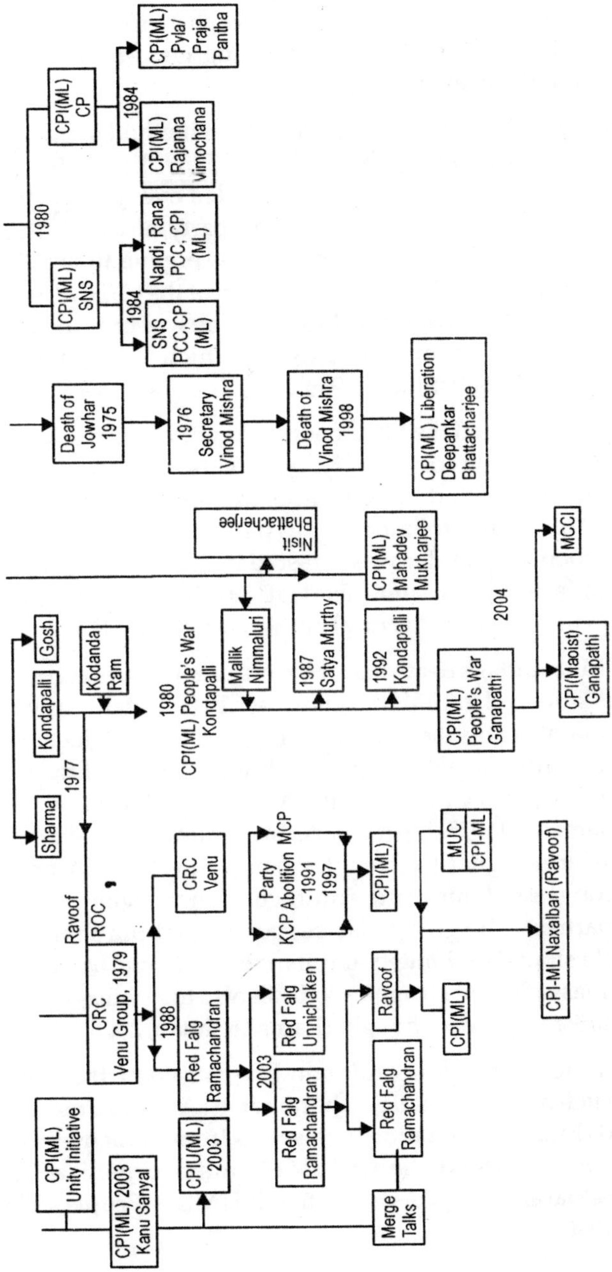
CPI(ML) Pyla/ Praja Pantha
CPI(ML) CP
1984
CPI(ML) Rajanna vimochana
1980
Nandi, Rana PCC, CPI (ML)
CPI(ML) SNS
1984
SNS PCC,CP (ML)
Death of Jowhar 1975
1976 Secretary Vinod Mishra
Death of Vinod Mishra 1998
CPI(ML) Liberation Deepankar Bhattacharjee
Nisit Bhattacharjee
CPI(ML) Mahadev Mukharjee
MCCI
2004
Gosh
Kondapalli
Kodanda Ram
Mallik Nimmaluri
1987 Satya Murthy
1992 Kondapalli
1980 CPI(ML) People's War Kondapalli
CPI(ML) People's War Ganapathi
CPI(Maoist) Ganapathi
Sharma
1977
Ravoof
ROC
CRC Venu
Party KCP Abolition MCP -1991 1997
CPI(ML)
MUC
CPI-ML
CRC Venu Group, 1979
1988
Red Falg Ramachandran
Red Falg Unnichaken
2003
Ravoof
CPI(ML)
CPI-ML Naxalbari (Ravoof)
CPI(ML) Unity Initiative
CPI(ML) 2003 Kanu Sanyal
CPIU(ML) 2003
Red Falg Ramachandran
Red Falg Ramachandran
Merge Talks

committee at the state level. In a document he criticized the CPI (ML) for choosing the cities, for refusing to participate in trade unions and for ignoring the task of building class-based mass organisations at village level.

This document also criticised the CPI (ML)'s method of guerilla warfare as "Cheguevarism." (*Liberation,* July 1969. Vol. 2, No. 9). Another important leader Asit Sen, who presided over the Calcutta rally, which announced the formation of a new party, also eventually broke away from the CPI (ML) and formed a new organisation called Maoist Communist Centre (MCC). His criticism of the CPI (ML) was similar to that of Parimal Dasgupta. Moreover he was critical of the "annihilation of class enemy campaign", which was formally launched after April, 1969 (Singh, 1969).

Both the CPI (ML) and the MCC continued with their respective forms of armed struggle for the next two years. In the process; Mazumdar acquired a kind of cult status among Naxalites. The negative aspect of the development of this personality cult revealed itself shortly when Mazumdar was arrested in Calcutta on July 16, 1972. Less than a fortnight later, his death in the police lock up, virtually led to the collapse of central authority in CPI (ML).

After the Mazumdar's death one of the major initiatives at course correction was launched in 1974 by a group of CPI (ML) activists who concentrated mainly in the then undivided state of Bihar. It included Jauhar (Subrata Dutt), Nagabhushan Patnaik and Vinod Mishra. This group renamed itself as CPI (ML)-Liberation in 1974, and in 1976 during the Emergency (1975-77), it adopted a new line. It called for the continuation of armed guerilla struggles along with efforts to form a broad anti-Congress democratic front, consisting even of non-Communist parties. The group also suggested that pure military armed struggle should be limited and that there should be greater emphasis on mass peasant struggles to Indianise the philosophy of Marxism-Leninism and Mao thought (Ramakrishnan, 2005).

During the next three years, this new line caused further splits with leaders such as Kondapalli Seetharamaiah (Andhra Pradesh) and N. Prasad (Bihar) dissociating themselves from the activities of the party. Prasad formed the CPI (ML) (unity organization) Kondapalli Seetharamaiah (KS) started the CPI (ML)—People's War on April 22, 1980.

People's War

The CPI (ML) – People's War was formed on Lenin's birth anniversary on April 22, 1980. The formation was part of a process to reorganize a centre for the all- India revolution after it went out of existence in 1972. A similar attempt was made in 1974 when the COC (Central Organising Committee) was formed. This was dissolved in May, 1977. In fact the AP State Committee had to function without a central committee from July, 1972 to January 1974 and again from May, 1977 to April 1980. The 1980 centre was formed on the basis of two issues: the first was the self-critical review and the second was the tactical line. (CPI-ML (PW) Report, 1988). The self-critical review was basically the same as that presented to the COC in 1975 with a few changes. The tactical line basically upheld the legacy of Naxalbari while rectifying the 'left' errors of that period. Both had enriched by the practice of the preceding eight years. Kondapalli Seetharamaiah was later expelled from the People's War in 1992. He died on April 12, 2002. People's War operations commenced in Karimnagar district, in the North Telangana region of Andhra Pradesh, and subsequently spread to other parts of the state and to other states also. (See Figure-2). Ideological differences led to splits and there was reunification of these splinter groups. At present, the CPI–ML People's War has a strong presence in eight states, and significant presence in another seven. The other major Naxalite group is the Maoist Communist Centre (MCC) of Bihar. According to an estimate, the Naxalite movement has a presence in 53 districts in about 15 states (Reddy, 2004). The People's War (PW) Movement has formed several guerrilla bases in Andhra Pradesh, Chhattisgarh, Orissa, Madhya Pradesh, Jharkhand, Bihar, Maharashtra and West Bengal. In states like Tamil Nadu, Karnataka, and Kerala in South India and Rajasthan, Uttar Pradesh, Haryana and Punjab in the north, the PW tried to expand its activities.

On August 11, 1998, CPI (ML) Party Unity merged with CPI (ML) People's War, popularly known as the People's War Group (PWG). The merger was the result of five years of negotiations between the two underground movements. The unified party retained the name CPI (ML) People's War (Ganapathy, 1998; Ramana, 2004; Saigal, 2005).

People's Guerilla Army

The military wing of the People's War Group (PWG), the People's Guerilla Army (PGA) was reportedly founded on December 2, 2000 in Bihar and Jharkhand and a month later, on January 2, 2001 in Andhra Pradesh, some where in dense Dandakaranyam in the North Telangana Region, by reorganizing its guerilla force (See Figure-3). The formation of the PGA coincided with the first death anniversary of three top PWG leaders, including central committee members.[1] It is styled on the pattern of similar guerilla forces in Turkey, the Philippines and Peru, the PWG said in a statement at the founding of the PGA. The PGA functions under the Central Military Commission, a single operational command. A Regional Military Commission supervises a group of State Military Commission or Zonal Military Commissions. Each Regional Military Commission reports to the Central Military Commission. The armed cadre of the PWG is organized by the PGA. The PWG announced that the PGA would consist of a three forces viz., main force, a secondary force and a people's militia. The understanding of the PW and the MCC resulted in forming a broad based united front on issues; Coordination Committee of Maoist Parties and organizations in South Asia (CCOMPOSA) four years ago, and the formation of the Compact Revolutionary Zone (CRZ) from the forest tracts of Adilabad (Andhra Pradesh) to Nepal travelling the forest areas of Maharashtra, Chhattisgarh, Jharkhand and Bihar (Gupta, 2004). The understanding between the PW and the MCC has not only paved the way for stopping internecine clashes, but also helped in the CRZ becoming a reality. The CCOMPOSA formation is significant because it established fraternal ties with revolutionary groups outside India. The coalition consists of the PW, the MCC, the Revolutionary Communist Centre of India (MLM), the Revolutionary Communist Centre of India (Maoist) all from India, the Purba Bangala Sarbhahara Party and the Bangladesh Sanajiwai Party (ML) from Bangladesh, the Communist Party of Nepal (Maoist) and the Communist Party of Ceylon (Maoist). (CCOMPOSA – 2001).

---

1. The Central Committee members are Shyam alias Nalla Adi Reddy, Mahesh alias Erram Reddy Santosh Reddy and Murali alias Seelam Naresh. All three were killed in an encounter on December 2, 1999 in the Koyyur forests, Karimnagar district, Andhra Pradesh.

Figure 2: CPI (ML) PW State, District and Divisional Committees in Andhra Pradesh

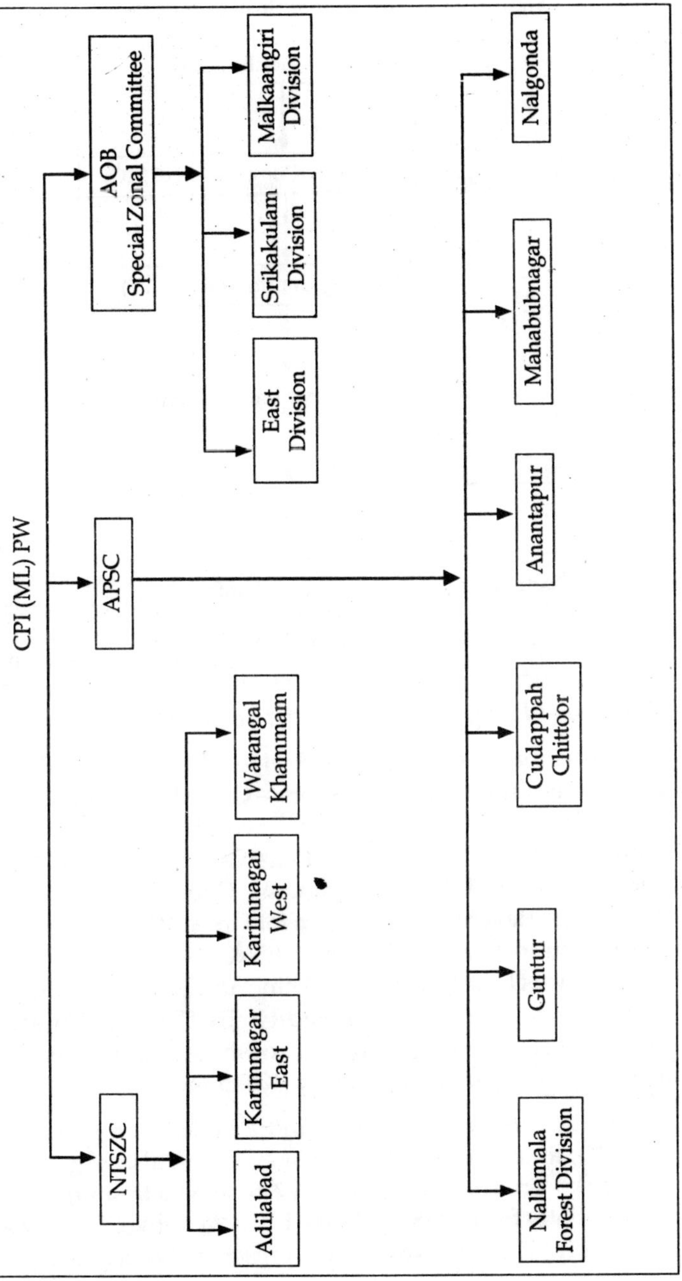

Figure 3: Organizational Structure of People's War

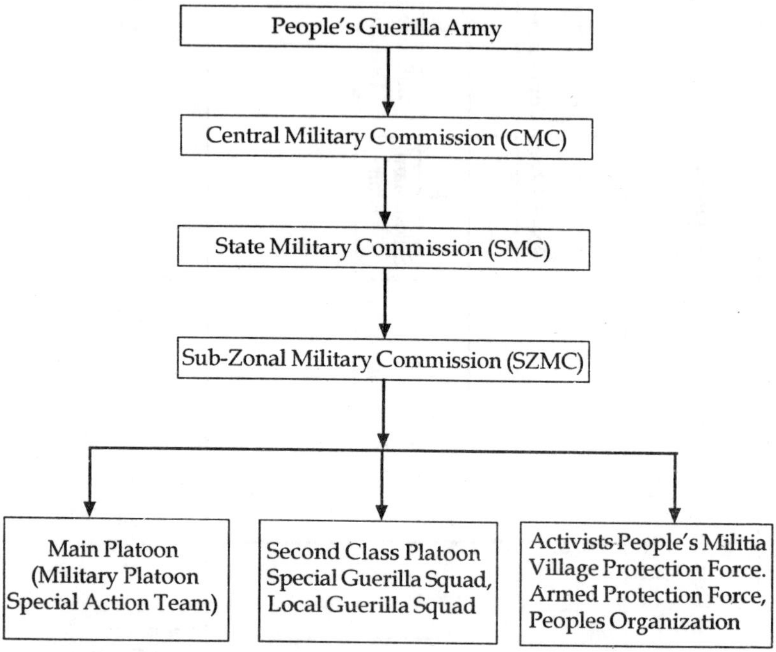

Communist Party of India (Marxist Leninist) Janashakti

CPI (ML) Janashakti was formed on July 30, 1992 with the merger of seven Communist groups. They are – CPI (ML) Resistance, one group of the unity centre of Communist Revolutionaries of India (Marxist Leninst), CPI (ML) Agami Yug, Paila Vasudeva Rao's CPI (ML), CPI (ML) (Khokan Mazumdar Faction), Coordination Committee of Communist Revolutionary Group for Unity (CRGU) and Communist Revolutionary Group for Unity (CRGU). CPI (ML) Janashakti's ideology was based on the 'mass line' developed by Chandra Pulla Reddy and Tarimila Nagi Reddy. In 1994, it contested in 13 constituencies of the Andhra Pradesh Legislative Assembly and won only in Illendu constituency (Khammam).

A trade union namely All India Federation of Trade Unions (AIFTU), and a peasant's movement were also organized by the Janashakti group. However, in 1996, one faction broke away and subsequently formed the CPI-ML Unity Initiative. The same remains as CPI (ML) Kanu Sanyal faction, presently. Soon the main body got split into seven more factions, which included among others the K. Rajanna faction. This settled on a strategy of guerilla warfare, a tactical line similar to the erstwhile People's War Group (PWG). It is this faction that became a united front with the PWG, which merged with the Maoist Communist Center to form the Communist Party of India-Maoist in September, 2004. The present day CPI-ML Janashakti (alternatively known as Rajanna faction) is the second most dominant and violent group in Andhra Pradesh after the CPI-Maoist. Senior leaders like M.V. Prasad and Raghavulu fell out with Rajanna on the issue of the misuse of funds, floated their own group with the coastal region as its main base. While the Rajanna faction had to confine itself to the Telangana Region, Rajanna chose to have an independent status for his group. On the other hand the break away faction preferred to be affiliated to the CPI-ML (Ramachandran) group at the national level. On August 18, 2005, the CPI-ML Pratighatana and CPI-ML (Ramachandran) merged to form the CPI (Marxist Leninist). Another Janashakti faction, the South Regional Provincial Committee got merged with CPI (ML) of Chandra Pulla Reddy on April 11, 2004, and formed the Communist Party of India (Marxist-Leninist) Janashakti (Chandra Pulla Reddy). Another break away group is the Communist Party of United States of India (CPUSI) also referred to as the Janashakti Veeranna faction. Although there are no ideological differences between the CPI-Maoist and the CPI-ML Janashakti, their operational areas differed. While the CPI-Maoist has been reported to operate in at least 15 states, the Janashakti has its presence in three states. Andhra Pradesh, having a strong presence in the Telangana region, has a marginal presence in the state of Maharashtra and Chhattisgarh.

Maoist Communist Centre (MCC)

The MCC came into existence, in its earlier version, on October 20, 1969, as Dakshin Desh. Due to some tactical differences on the method of party formation, Dakshin Desh did not join the CPI (ML) in 1969 and decided to retain its independent identity (See Figure-4). In 1975, the outfit was renamed as the Maoist Communist Centre (MCC).

Communist Party of India-Maoist (CPI-Maoist)

The Maoist Communist Centre of India (MCC) and the CPI (ML) People's War merged to form a new entity, the Communist Party of

Figure 4: MCC. Faction

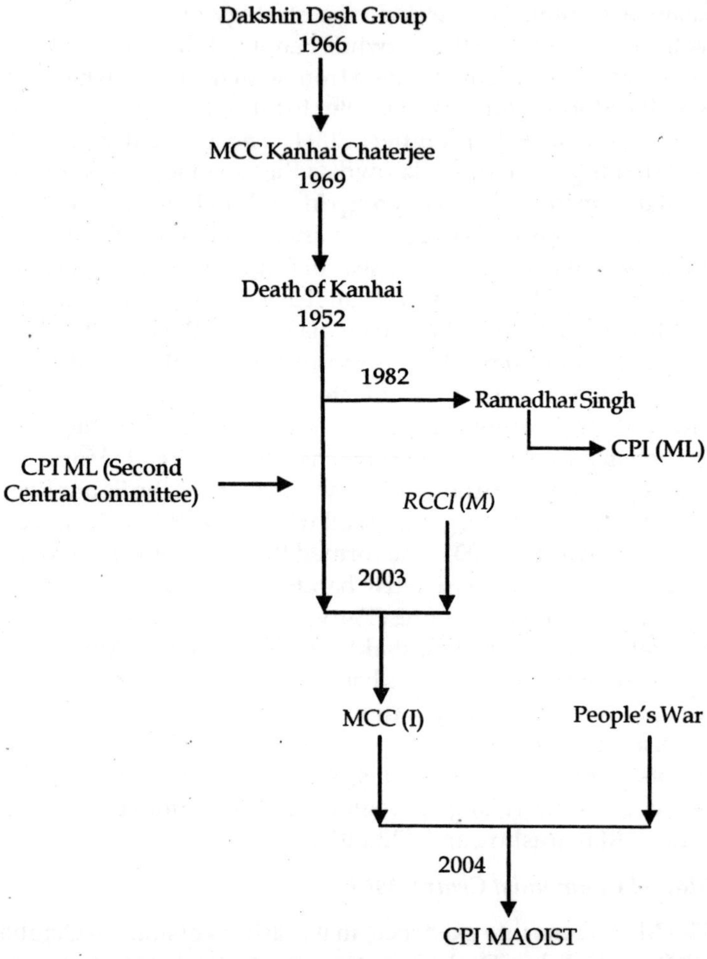

India–Maoist (CPI–Maoist) on September 21, 2004. Officially, the merger was announced on October 14, 2004, by the PWG Andhra Pradesh State Secretary 'Ramakrishna', at a news conference in Hyderabad, on the eve of peace talks between the PWG and the State Government. During four rounds of negotiations between high-level delegations of the two outfits and the respective Central Committees (CC), a final agreement was reached in September 2004. The five documents—1. Marxism–Leninism–Maoism, 2. Party programme,

3. Strategy and tactics, 4. Political Resolution on the international and domestic situation, and 5. The party constitution, were adopted and also decided to be translated into 10 regional languages for wider deliberations throughout the outfits' bases across India.

Cadre and Command Structure

Although no further information with regard to the organizational structure has been declared or ascertained, reports indicate that the structure within new outfit retains all the hierarchies that were present in the erstwhile outfits, including a Central Committee, Regional Bureaus, Zonal or State Committees, District or Division Committees and Squad Area Committees. The two guerilla armies of the PWG and the MCC–the People's Guerilla Army (PGA) and the People's Liberation Guerilla Army (PLGA) respectively–have also merged under the agreement. The new armed force reportedly operated under the name of PLGA since December 2, 2004 (Duggal, 2005). The PWG is estimated to have 3500 armed cadres and around 3000 firearms. This includes a large number of rifles of AK-47 variety, light machine guns, self-loading rifles, carbines-303's, grenades, revolvers, pistols and land mines technologies. The PWG also has a technical squad, which manufactures 12 bore guns and its ammunition. It can also repair all kinds of weapons and assemble grenades.

Areas of Operation

Following the merger, the MCC outfit is active in 156 districts of 13 states that include Andhra Pradesh, Chhattisgarh, Jharkhand, Bihar, Orissa, Uttar Pradesh, Madhya Pradesh, Maharashtra, West Bengal, Karnataka, Tamil Nadu, Uttaranchal and Kerala (See Figure 5). The outfit has also been making attempts to establish and expand its presence in several other states such as Gujarat, Haryana, Punjab, Rajasthan and Himachal Pradesh. The MCC's current areas of influence extends over Bihar and Jharkhand, with some sway in Uttar Pradesh, Chhattisgarh, Orissa, West Bengal, Uttaranchal and in few pockets of Madhya Pradesh. The PWG's areas of dominance include Andhra Pradesh, Orissa, Chhattisgarh, Karnataka, Maharashtra and Tamil Nadu. The merger now makes the CPI–Maoist a pan–Indian revolutionary group, and brings the Maoists closer to their objective of 'liberating' their proposed Compact Revolutionary Zone (CRZ). This area extends from Nepal through

Bihar in the North to Dandakaranya region (forest areas of Central India) and Andhra Pradesh in the south (Sahni, 2004). The intention is to have a continuous stretch of territory under their influence and control, with the ultimate goal of eventually 'liberating' the entire zone. Large parts of this territory have already been brought under the extremist influence with only some link-ups now necessary in the remaining pockets to make the CRZ a reality. Once achieved, the CRZ will virtually drive a wedge through the vital areas of the country. It would help crystallize linkages with other Maoist groups operating in South Asia, including the Communist Party of Nepal – Maoist (CPN-M) and the Communist Party of Bhutan – Maoist (CPB-M). In the view of the police and politicians, 'the problem of Naxalite movement is only the problem of law and order'. Whereas, for the Naxalites 'Naxalite movement is not a problem but the solution to the problems'. According to them the real 'problems' are of democratic rights, deep-rooted poverty, landlessness, hunger, joblessness, rising debts and suicides, growing bankruptcies and its devastation, the state terror and 'black' murderous gangs, and the rising inequalities.

Government's View of the Movement

The Ministry of Home Affairs, Government of India, admits the spread of Naxalite movement to 76 districts in 9 states of the Union, namely, Andhra Pradesh, Bihar, Madhya Pradesh, Maharashtra, Orissa, Chhattisgarh, Jharkhand, Uttar Pradesh and West Bengal. It further agrees that the People's War and the MCCI are trying to increase their influence and operations in some parts in Tamil Nadu, Karnataka and Kerala states. According to the Institute for Conflict Management, New Delhi, the movement has actually spread over 165 districts in 14 states and that the Home Ministry's assessment in this regard is an understatement (Singh, 2007). The movement got a tremendous boost when its two major components, the People's War (PW) and the Maoist Communist Centre of India (MCCI), decided to merge on March 21, 2004; though a formal announcement was made on October 15, 2004 only. The unified party was called the Communist Party of India (Maoist) (*The Hindu*). The merger, apart from augmenting the support base of the movement has given the character of a pan-Indians revolutionary group. The Naxalite's plan to have a Compact Revolutionary Zone (CRZ) stretching from Indo-Nepal border to the Dandakaranya Region is likely to get a fillip with the unification of their ranks (Kamat, 2003).

Figure–5

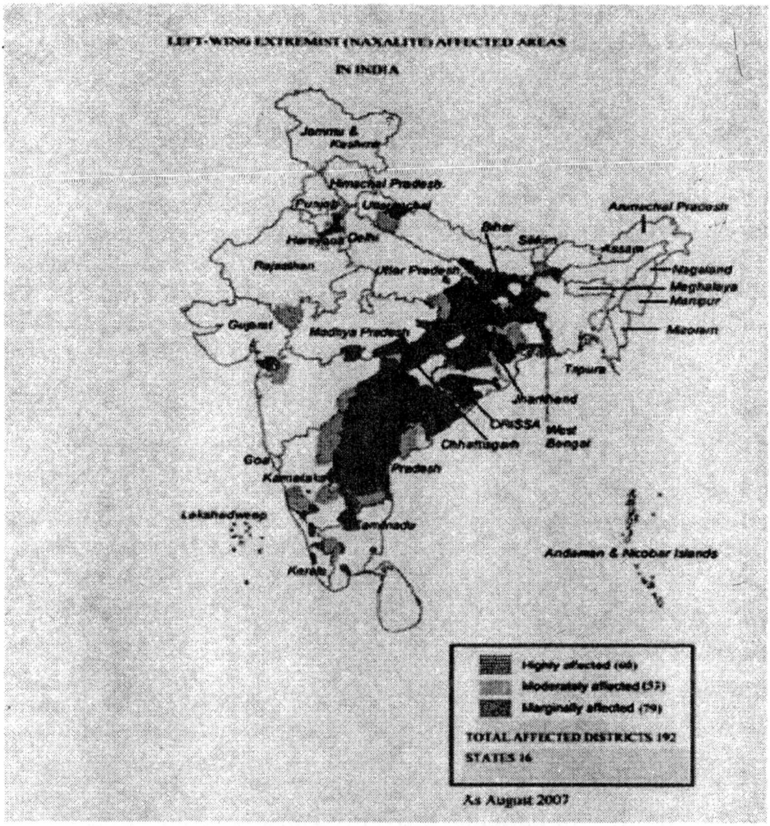

Source: Institute for Conflict Management, New Delhi, India.

State Policy Towards Naxalite Movement

In 1969, Jalagam Vengala Rao, the then Chief Minister treated it as a law and order problem (Mohanty, 1977). In 1983, N.T. Rama Rao, the then Chief Minister representing Telugu Desam prasied them initially, but later adopted a tough line of action against them. Following the kidnap of six IAS Officers in East Godavari district in 1987, the government strengthened the police department with the institution of 'Grey Hounds'* and nearly 1,000 personnel were drawn on deputation from the special armed police and the Andhra

---

* Greyhounds: A police outfit to combat Naxalites.

Pradesh Reserve Police who were specially trained for the purpose. The kidnap and killing of Telugu Desam Mandal President Malhar Rao (1989) in Karimnagar district, Mr. Rama Rao talked of matching Naxalite violence with police violence, and proposed to bomb remote forest and hilly tracts using helicopters and flush out Naxalites from their hideouts. The state also sought the permission of the Union Government to set up an ammunition factory to supply arms at reasonable rates to the people to protect themselves from Naxalites. Issuing of licences for fire arms was liberalized and village self-defence squads and district coordination committees were set up to monitor the implementation of the welfare schemes.

In 1989, the Congress Party returned to power and Dr. M. Chenna Reddy became the Chief Minister of the State. In view of the reports of police excesses and human rights violations and the kidnap of two legislators, Mr. Mandava Venkateswara Rao of TDP and Mr. Krishna Reddy of Congress in two separate incidents Dr. Chenna Reddy adopted a conciliatory policy with the hope that the PWG would stop abductions and attract the Naxalites to join the mainstream. Under trial Naxalite prisoners numbering 150 were released and the Disturbed Areas Act in force in select divisions of Karimnagar, Warangal, Nizamabad and Khammam districts since 1978 was withdrawn. Likewise, the Terrorist and Disruptive Activities (prevention) Act (TADA)* and a special security force were created to counter the problem. During this period when the state adopted a 'soft' , liberal policy, Naxalites held a series of meetings in which leaders of their front organizations like Gaddar, a folk singer against whom non-bailable warrants were pending, took part, (Subrahmanyam,1994: 388). The PWG conducted a number of mammoth rallies, public meetings and achieved higher 'political consciousness' and mobilized 'organized political opinion'.

The Naxalites also organized praja courts (People's Courts) to dispense with instant justice. As recorded by Reddy (1990), 'people's

---

* TADA act was revised in 1987 and 1993. Section 3(i) of TADA said: "Whoever, with intent to overawe the Government as by law established or to strike terror in the people or any section of the people or to alienate any section of the people or adversely affect the harmony amongst different section of the people does any act or thing by using bombs,........or any other person to do or abstain from doing any act commits a terrorist act."

court became the main instrument not only for solving the economic problems of the exploited classes but also deal with legal matters, family disputes, corruption in administration and dowry harassment cases'.

In early 1991, under the Chairmanship of the Union Home Minister, a Joint Coordination Committee with representatives of four states, Andhra Pradesh, Maharashtra, Madhya Pradesh and Orissa was formed to deal with the problem, coordinate police activities and ensure that the local people did not support the Naxalites. In August 1991, the Chief Minister of the four states favoured the setting up an apex body for intelligence gathering and coordination of anti-extremist operations as Hyderabad. A joint action plan was also drawn up in October 1991. However, the Union Home Minister in February 1992 denied the setting up of an apex intelligence body.

Subsequently, the N. Janardhan Reddy Government adopted a hard-line strategy and declared the People's War group and eight of its front organizations as unlawful and banned it for three years on June 5, 1991. The other organizations which were banned were Radical Students Union (RSU), Radical Youth League (RYL), Rythu Coolie Sangham (RC), the Singareni Karmika Samakhya (Dandakaranya), the Girijan Rythu Coolie Sangham, All India Revolutionary Women's League and the Organization for Protection of Girijan Rights. The State Government declared a ban on PWG and its front organizations under the Criminal Law (amendment) Act (1908) applicable to the Andhra area and under the Andhra Pradesh (Telangana area), Public Security Act (1348 Fasil) for "indulging in mindless violence, taking life, destruction of public property and for disturbing general peace by their violent activities."

In December 1994, after N.T. Rama Rao took over as the Chief Minister of the State, the Government declared that it proposed to handle the extremist activity as a socio-economic issue and not merely as a law and order problem. The Government embarked on a different approach to cut arms supply to the hardcore groups and wean away people from the movement through socio-economic measures. Naxalites were invited unconditionally in the hope of abjuring violence and joining the mainstream. They were asked to identify excess lands with the landlords for distribution. The Government directed the police to stop all 'encounters' and released

Kondapalli Seetharamaiah from jail on humanitarian grounds after withdrawing cases against him. When it was time to review the ban on PWG and its front organizations on June 21, 1995, Chief Minister N.T. Rama Rao decided 'to allow it to lapse'. Mr. Chandrababu Naidu who succeeded Rama Rao as Chief Minister decided to maintain status quo. However, the ban was reclaimed on June 23, 1996 on the ground that "development in the Telangana districts was being impeded because of Naxalites."

The State continues to portray the Naxalite movement as a law and order problem and does not wish to acknowledge the fact that the movement is essentially an expression of the peoples' aspirations to a life of dignity and self respect. However, the state leadership shifted its political burden to the police, encouraging them to indulge in encounters, which are no other than custodial and targeted killings, even if they are euphemistically described as an encounters, the extinguishing of human life and right to life by the Government. Dr. Y.S. Rajasekara Reddy who took over as the Chief Minister of the State on May 14, 2004 made an announcement immediately after being sworn in that he would review and if possible, lift the ban on People's War if they created a congenial atmosphere in the sate by putting an end to violence on the government's part. He said that he would strongly advise the police to reciprocate by not resorting to fake encounters and acts of repression (*The Hindu*, May 15, 2004). The United Progressive Alliance (UPA) which came to power at the Centre also stated in its common minimum needs programme (May 27, 2004) that "The UPA is concerned with the growth of extremist violence and other forms of terrorist activity in different states. This is not merely a law and order problem but a far deeper socio-economic issue which will be addressed more meaningfully than has been the case so far. False encounter will be permitted." On June 4, 2004, making a suo motu statement on the post-election law and order situation in the state in the Legislative Assembly, Home Minister Jana Reddy announced the decision to stop giving cash rewards on the heads of Naxalites and the constitution of what he termed as, "a conciliation committee to identify problems of people espoused by Naxalites." The previous government announced a series of monetary rewards on the heads of around 1,100 Naxalite leaders ranging between Rs. 20,000 to Rs. 13 lakh depending upon the position they occupied (*The New Indian Express*, June 5, 2004). On July 21, 2004 the State Government has allowed the ban on the militant

People's War and its six frontal organizations to lapse. The Government has decided not to extend the ban, due to expire on July 22, 2004, as a prelude to 'direct' peace talks with 'representatives of the outfit' (*The Hindu*, July 22, 2004).

Peace Talks

By the middle of May 2002, the CPI (ML) Peoples' War and the Government agreed in principle for the talks. Later, Peoples' War announced a ceasefire and the Government agreed too. It termed it as the creation of a conducive atmosphere for the talks. The CPI (ML) and the Peoples' War nominated two representatives and the Government nominated two Cabinet Ministers to represent it for the preliminary talks on modalities. The talks on modalities commenced on the June 5, 2002 and there were two further sittings on 9 and 20 June, 2002 respectively. However, the occurrence of encounter killings in Karimnagar district on the July 2, 2002 vitiated the atmosphere and jeopardized the talks. In this attack four members of the Peoples' War including a senior leader were killed. On the July 15, 2002, the CPI (ML)-PW declared that the ceasefire was withdrawn and their 'war of resistance' would continue; at the same time, they mentioned that they were prepared for talks if a conducive atmosphere emerged. The Government too, on its part, through its press statements expressed its continuing readiness for talks, along with statements that the Naxalites should give up armed struggle or declare laying down of arms before talks. The process of talks in 2002 thus came to an abrupt end. The issue of Naxalite movement became the central issue in the elections to Andhra Pradesh Assembly which took place in April, 2004. The then Telugu Desam Government clearly stated in the recommendations to the Governor to dissolve the Assembly in November 2004, as it wanted to take the issue of Naxalite movement head – on and extremism was to be made the central issue in the elections. In its election manifesto, the Telugu Desam Party stated that it would take steps to put down Naxalite movement firmly. In contrast, the Congress Party declared in its election manifesto that the policy of 'bullet for bullet' of the State Government did not really help in containing the situation. On the other hand, "the Congress which over the years painstakingly built up democratic institutions in the country believes that the extremist movement in the state should be viewed from a larger socio-economic perspective and tackled holistically by engaging them in a dialogue. The Congress Party therefore is committed to resolving this issue through a process of dialogue and consultation." The elections to the Andhra Pradesh Assembly as well as the General Elections to Parliament took place in April-May 2004. The Congress Party came to power in Andhra Pradesh and the United Progressive Alliance (UPA) led by Congress, assumed office at the national level. Consequent upon the promise made in the election manifesto of the Congress Party, the possibility of talks between the Government and the Naxalites* got reviewed. The long awaited peace talks which finally commenced on October 15, 2004 ended after four days.

End of Peace Talks

After six months of ceasefire and all pervasive peaceful atmospheres, there were a series of statements and actions on the part of the Government and the Naxalites which contributed to a fast deterioration of law and order in the atmosphere. After the first round of talks was over, it became a common practice on the part of the Government to refuse permission for the holding meetings or for unveiling martyrs' memorials by the Naxalites. On December 15, 2004 four constables were hurt in land mine blast by CPI (ML)-People's War in Visakhapatnam district. On January 6, 2005, a Naxalite belonging to CPI (ML) Janashakti was killed in police action in Warangal district. On January 8, 2005 a women functionary of Chitanya Mahila Samakhya was killed in Prakasam district in an alleged police encounter. On the January 15, 2005, six Maoists were killed in alleged encounters in Mahboobnagar and Prakasam districts. The Naxalite parties too killed an alleged informer and a sarpanch. On the January 17, 2005, CPI (Maoist) and CPI (ML) Janashakti Parties made a formal announcement "withdrawing from the talks" as a protest against the combing operations and encounters resulting in the death of as many as eleven persons since January. In their statement, they mentioned that the first round of talks was completed as a mere formality that the Government felt threatened by the surge of support for the Naxalites, government did not extend the ceasefire after December 16, 2004, that the ruling

---

* The main points of the discussions are: 1. land and tenancy reforms, 2. withdrawal of criminal cases against Naxalites and also price on their heads, 3. strict implementation of government rules in tribal areas, 4. withdrawal of cases filed against people who participated in public agitations, 5. review of public security acts, and 6. preparation of land inventory.

classes are incapable of solving peoples basic problems and the "talks" was a conspiracy to tie the hands of the parties and that the only alternative for resolving peoples problems was Peoples War. Hence they withdrew from the talks. The encounters as well as killings by Naxalite parties continued unabated with serious incidents such as in Vempenta in Pamulapadu Mandal of Kurnool district on February 28, 2005 by CPI (Maoist), in Manala in Nizamabad district on the March 7, 2005 by police and Chilakaluripet in Güntur district on the March 11, 2005 by CPI (Maoist). But the sporadic political statement from the government expressed interest in talks.

Recommendations of Commissions and Committees

The practice of "extra judicial killings", popularly known as 'encounters' came into vogue from around 1968 as a method of containing the Naxalite movement (See Appendix-II). The state used to carry out such killings in areas declared as disturbed areas. The A.P. Suppression of Disturbance Act 1947 was aimed at containing the spread of the Communist Movement in the erstwhile Madras Presidency. During the period of Emergency* about 77 persons were killed in the manner which was considered a large number in those days. (Mohanty, 1977). As a part of the general criticism of authoritarian governance during Emergency, the practice of encounters got highlighted, particularly in the context of the opposition of Lok Nayak Jaya Prakash Narayan to the execution of unlawful orders by officials. He appointed an unofficial committee headed by Justice V.M. Tarkunde. Investigations by the Tarkunde Committee led to the appointment of a one person commission of inquiry under the 1956 Act by the Andhra Pradesh Government. In 1978, the Andhra Pradesh Government appointed Justice V. Bhargava to enquire into these killings.

As Bhargava (1989: 71) pointed out:

> "...the phenomenon of fake encounters saw birth, especially in the wake of imposition of internal emergency by Indira Gandhi in June 1975; scores of young men were put to death as Naxalites. Many of the victims were, no doubt radicals but they were arrested in connection with the agrarian

---

* The Central Government of India, by an order Number SO 305(E), dated July 3, 1975, banned all the 10 Naxalbari, Maoist Groups in the country.

disputes and killed in cold blood officially, and however, they were supposed to be armed desperadoes killed by the police in self defiance..."

Further, Justice Prabha Shanker Mishra when he was the Chief Justice of Andhra Pradesh in 1995 closely examined 'encounter deaths' in the Judgment. The Andhra Pradesh High Court in its judgment dated August 14, 1995 in Writ Petition No. 16868 of 1995 (Madhusudhan Raj Yadav case) clearly directed that a case should be registered and investigated in all such instances. High Court Judges Justice M.N. Rao and Justice N.R. Naik in their judgment dated July 1, 1996 observed that the police led encounters and brutalities on the Naxalites be ceased immediately. They further recommended the setting up a `Shanti Sanghams' (a forum for promotion for peace).

Similarly, some non-political intellectuals wielding large influence in the society made a similar appeal from the newly launched organization, "Committee of Concerned Citizens" in 1997. S.R. Sankaran, a retired I.A.S. Officer who held several important positions both in the State and the Central Government commands respect from all sections of the society and well-known veteran editor, Pothuri Venkateswara Rao, apart from a few noted journalists, respected and influential professors and lawyers were members of the organisation. Civil rights activists like K.G. Kannabiran, Prof. Haragopal and Bojja Tarakam made sincere efforts to find a solution to the problem. The committee brought out its first report "In search of Democratic Space" in 1999. On April 17, 2000 the committee released its second report entitled the report of the Committee of Concerned Citizens (1997-2000) containing a detailed account of the efforts of the committee during the three years. The committee published its 'third report' in December 2002 placing the details before the people in the hope that there would be a debate generating public pressure to have a democratic dialogue. The committee however noticed with regret that in spite of all the efforts, the talks of 2004 also reached a dead end with the return of the cycle of violence.

However, Committee of Concerned Citizens strongly criticized the government in the way, "the encounter killings in Andhra Pradesh are not stray occurrences but have become part of a policy action of the state and this inhuman policy of extermination of individuals is being followed in the misguided belief that eliminating individuals will eliminate a movement. This approach will only serve to aggravate the situation". (CCC letter to NHRC December 3, 1999). In view of the intensifying state repression, liquidation of leaders and activities in the name of encounters, and the growing suspicion over Koyyur Encounter*, the APCLC felt it necessary to inquire into the incident by a Joint Fact Finding Team consisting of civil and democratic rights organizations of India. The members of the Joint Fact Finding Team, based on the events of Koyyuru Encounter were of the opinion that three leaders of the People's War were arrested at Bangalore "were later tortured and killed." In order to have credence to their "encounter story they also picked up Laxmirajyam an innocent from Garjanpalli village killed him later and dumped off the body along with their three bodies." There is every reason to say that the Koyyuru Encounter is a fake (A Report on Koyyuru Encounter, 1999). The Task Force on Naxalite movement–headed by the Andhra Congressman M. Shashidhar Reddy set up by the All India Congress Committee (AICC) in October 2004–attributed its growth in recent years to socio-economic factors and not the ideological content of the movement. (*The Hindu,* April 3, 2005).

Review of Some Studies: News Worthiness of Naxalite Movement and its' Related Events

In relation to the coverage of the news about Naxalite movement, newspapers adopt certain news values in the selection of news. Some studies done in this direction mention certain criteria for the selection of news. In the coverage of any terrorism-related events, certain measures are taken into consideration. They are:

1. the extent of disruption of the status quo (intensity);
2. the number of persons affected by the event (extensity);
3. the nearness of the event (proximity);
4. the recency of the event (timeliness);
5. the extent of results to flow from the event (consequence on significance) and
6. the variety of news values in the event (variety).

---

* Nall Adi Reddy alias Shyam, a member of the Central Organisation Committee, CPI (ML) People's War Party, Eerramreddy Santosh Reddy alias Mahesh, the Secretary of A.P. Provincial Committee and Sellam Naresh alias Murali, the Secretary of North Telengana Special Zone Committee, they were killed in an encounter on December 2, 1999 in Koyyur forest, Karimnagar district, Andhra Pradesh.

In journalistic parlance, these intrinsic characteristics of the event are called as news values which have been evolved by western communication scholars, journalists and professional journalists' associations. The Indian newspapers also follow these news values while deciding and selecting news for the day. However, there is a note of dissent on the news values adhered to by the Indian Press. Most conflicts are newsworthy as they are disruptive in nature. Actual conflict is generally news worthy because it is physical and usually leads to injury and damage. Violent in itself, it arouses the emotions of the members of the society and seems to be of enormous importance. Wars, murders, violent protests, and conflicts of a more disruptive nature have tension and suspense as corollary qualities.

Role of Media in Conflict

The media contributes to the democratic process by bringing issues into the open. While the press does serve as a mirror, it is a part of the reciprocal process, being affected by the system and in turn is affecting the society. The press is pushed into reporting events by organized forces in the system and its reports become an integral part of the social process which bears on the nature of future events. Groups in a society may use the press as sources of intelligence, as indications of reaction of the public to events, and as a device for creating awareness and defining problems. The performance of the press or other media becomes a part of the conflict/controversy. There are several aspects to it which are proposed by Tichenor *et.al.*, (1994: 96) based on surveys of general populations, interviews with political elects and newspaper content analysis data.

Information Processing

The newspapers are not mere channels but they make judgments about selections and presentation of news. The nature of newspaper's decision or judgment is a result of the social structure in which the newspaper operates. These decisions constitute a pattern of information control that has far reaching implications for what the society will hear about, think about and talk about.

Information Control

Information control is one aspect of all information activities, including the conduct of social conflict. In the process of information control, it is to be understood that the press lives with the most intense conflicts but does not necessarily turn the conflicts into public issues. They may play these conflicts down or avoid them or they may give the conflicts sustained front page coverage. Another aspect is that information is part of a general process of social control which includes media participation within different social structures. Information is a prime resource in the creation and maintenance of social power, a point which may become increasingly visible as social conflicts progress. Importance of information control is illustrated by the increasing development of specialized communication centres in business, government, education and other agencies and interest groups.

System Reinforcement

Another generalization is that since they are dependent upon other parts of the system, newspapers and other media participate in social conflict in circumscribed ways which are reinforced within the system. Media will tend to reflect the perspectives of organizational power centers, which is apparent not only in small homogeneous communities but is also illuminated in communities or regions where values and outlooks on major issues are highly diverse. Where there is diversity in social power, media tend to reflect the orientations of those segments that are higher on the power scale. This tendency to reflect the outlook of dominant power groups can have consequences in conflict situations.

Knowledge Gap

Being an integral part of a conflict process within a social structure, mass media in performing their particular roles may contribute to either the widening or narrowing of disparities in knowledge within the system. Conflict has the basis in social differentiation, and newspapers and other media may contribute to increasing intensity and broadening of the scope of these conflicts while performing according to their traditional roles. This participation may serve to reinforce the differences in orientation and outlooks between different interest groups and sectors of society. The knowledge gaps may not always increase but may decrease in a given set of conditions. One of these conditions is the existence of increasingly intense levels of social conflict particularly that associated with community issues that are related to basic concerns of different groups among the population.

Agenda Setting

Examining the agenda setting role of mass media for a group of issues that aroused community conflict, Tichenor, *et.al.*, (1994: 106) observed:

> Mass media bring conflicts to public attention and highlight particular aspects of a conflict so that they become focus of public discussions and action. They conclude that the media's agenda setting power lies in their ability to bestow publicity or to deny it in conflictual situations contrary to widespread beliefs, media do not initiate and shape conflicts.

Newspapers receive information and ideas from myriad organized sources, and there is competition from parties in a conflict for media space and time (Bethell, 1977: 33). The role of the media, including that of the press assumes greater significance especially when a group becomes mobilized for action out of the frustration and deprivation it has experienced in the intense competition for socio-economic gain.

Wolfsfeld (1984: 363) points out media publicity is one of the strategies among others through which groups can bring their concerns to the attention of the Government. Although media attention is useful for all protest groups, the groups' characteristics and goals determine the type and extent of publicity likely to be most helpful as well as the diverse obstacles each group will face in gaining media attention. Lee and Maslog (2005) studied the extent to which four Asian Regional Conflicts involving India and Pakistan, Sri Lanka, Indonesia, Philippines in the context of peace journalism being followed by select newspapers in these countries.

Barnes, *et.al.*, (1979) found that direct action techniques – a main stray of the media arena had become increasingly popular forms of political action. Lipsky (1970: 181) emphasizing the importance of the mass media in protest strategy argued that "protest was the only political resource at the disposal of the weak and powerless and therefore action groups depend on the media to activate reference publics in "ways favourable to protest goals."

Later studies (Gitlin, 1980: 3, Bromley and Shupe, 1979; Molotch 1979) also pointed out that protest leaders often find themselves paying a heavy price for such publicity, as they attempt to overcome the internal conflict of carrying out actions that will be covered by the media without alienating supporters or the general public.

Social movement groups use events such a marches, rallies or demonstrations to attract media coverage to reach both the public and elected officials (Rucht 1991).

The costs of entering the media are equivalent to the definition of newsworthiness (Tuchman, 1978) Groups must plan and execute protests to fit media "frames" (Gitlin, 1980: 21), which serve as institutional filters designed to meet the structural and commercial needs of the Press (Bromley and Shupe, 1979). While conflict is the central issue for the media, its prevalence in the society's demands that a groups actions exhibit unusual amounts of drama, violence and novelty. McCombs (1981) observes that small unstructured groups have a great need for media attention; as such publicity offers the real entrance to the public agenda of important issues involving rewards and risks. Leaders find themselves unable to control the messages that they try to transmit to the media filter (Gitlin, 1980, Bromley and Shupe, 1979, Molotch, 1979). In his theoretical framework, Wolfsfeld (1984) raises questions about the role of the mass media in political collective action. Alternative conceptualizations may consider the press merely as an additional resource that groups try to mobilize in their attempts to challenge the authorities.

Bishara (1985: 16) provides Palestinian views of the Palestinians print press in the West Bank and the Gaza Strip. She says that the Palestinian press suggests the twin contradictory objectives of "Israel to maintain its occupation at minimal cost, and that of the Palestinians to rid themselves of the occupation. Arab Press has adopted and amplified the views of the PLO, silencing the moderate views and serving as a catalyst for unrest (Bishara, 1985). War reporting is often sensational, and a mere device to boost circulations and ratings (Allen and Seaton, 1999, Hachten, 1999, Toffler and Toffler 1994).

In recent years, some journalism scholars have urged journalist to discard war reporting in favour of peace journalism to promote a culture of peace. For instance, Norwegian scholar Johan Galtung first proposed peace journalism in the 1970s as self conscious, working concept for journalists covering wars and conflicts (Mc-

Goldrick and Lynch 2000). Lynch 2000, described peace journalism as a "broader, fairer and more accurate way of framing stories, drawing on the insights of conflict analysis and transformation."

In general, the media can have four inputs on any peace process

1. they help in defining the political atmosphere in which the peace process takes place.
2. the media has an active influence on the strategy and behaviour of the stakeholders to the conflict.
3. the media has an important influence on the nature of debate about a peace process.
4. the media can buttress or weaken public legitimacy of the stakeholders involved in the peace process. (Wolfsfeld–1997).

Coverage of Terrorism

In conflict-ridden studies, words have specific meanings, and therefore different definitions emerge depending upon the context. The words 'extremism' and 'terrorism' are generally used synonymously. "Terrorism is the threat or use of violence for political ends (Crozier 1960)." As a military arm terrorism is a weapon of psychological warfare (Mallin, 1974). "Political terrorism can be defined as coercive intimidation and is one of the oldest techniques of psychological warfare (Wilkinson, 1987)." Terrorism is a special mode of violence which may be briefly defined as coercive intimidation. It involves the threat of murder, injury of destruction to terrorize a given target into considering to the terrorists will (Wilkinson, 1994). A comprehensive definition of terrorism is contained in US Army regulations which state that terrorism is "the calculated use of violence or the threat of violence to attain goals, political, religious or ideological in nature. Burnet (1971), Schmid and Graaf (1982), Midgley and Rice (1984) summarized studies of press coverage of terrorism and compiled a bibliography consisting of 500 papers. The 1986 bibliography of studies conducted by the Rand Corporation lists some 90 publications on international terrorism alone. Although international terrorism by and against states received most attention. Bassiouni (1981, 1982: 128) pointed out the terrorist acts in a national context outnumbered international ones in the USA. Disappearances, bombings, kidnappings, and state violence in many countries, often unreported, claim thousands of times more victims than do well publicized acts of international terror. Wurth-Hough (1983: 403) documented the roles of media converge of terrorism in selecting events while analyzing the *New York Times*" coverage of the Irish Republic Army (IRA), the Red Brigades, and the Fuerzes Armadas de Liberation National (FALN) from July 1, 1977 to June 30, 1979. He found no basis for the charges that coverage legitimizes the cause of neither terrorist organization nor its supporters. Knight and Dean (1982: 144) provided a detailed account of how the Canadian Press coverage of the siege and recapturing of the Iranian embassies in London from Arab nationalist 'gunmen' served to assert the efficiency and legitimacy of violence by the British Special Air Services.

Terrorism and Publicity

Terrorism experts, public officials, and even some members of the media have blamed the mass media-especially television–for rewarding terrorists acts with disproportionate coverage that plays into the hands of terrorists. Moreover, since the most gruesome and deadly incidents receive the greatest volume of reporting, media critics have charged that terrorists resort to progressively bloodier violence to satisfy the media's appetite for shocking news (Brigitte, 2000). If terrorism is seen as political theatre performed for audiences (domestic and international publics, particular groups and individuals and of course, political elites), clearly the mass media plays a crucial role. Without massive news coverage the terrorist act would resemble the proverbial tree falling in the forest: if no one learned of an incident. It would be as if it had not occurred. For this reason, media critics have suggested that political violence would radically decline or even disappear, without the media's eagerness to highlight terrorists' acts. Publicity in the form of news coverage is therefore perceived as the lifeblood or as former British Prime Minister Margaret Thatcher put it, the "oxygen" of terrorism. Most terrorist groups or loners have short and long-term goals that transcend their publicity objectives. Freeing imprisoned comrades, exacting revenge, or creating fear and confusion are common short-term goals that can be accomplished with a single violent act. The same group or person may also have far a more ambitious long-term goal-regime change or national independence, for example—that will not occur with one bold act of terror. To achieve these ultimate goals, terrorists need the attention of the mass media to manipulate, threaten, intimidate, or co-opt the general public, specific and brutal acts and thereby heightening the threshold of violence; terrorists are assured of substantial press coverage.

Studies on Naxalite Movement

Many studies have been taken in India on the issue of Naxalite movement. Since Naxalite movement is an off-shoot of communist philosophy, the discussion on Naxalite movement interpolates with communism. Ram (1973) dealt with the splits that took place in the Indian Communist Movement in general. He opined that the Telangana Armed struggle was the first experiment in the application of Maoist strategy in India. It was suppressed for some time on account of some reactionary and revisionist policies but later reappeared in 1967. Johari (1972) discussed about Naxalbari Movement, along with the formation of the CPI (ML) party and its ideology, as also about the differences among revolutionaries. Ram (1971) brought out another study about Radical Marxism in India, in which an attempt was made to analyze the Maoist strategy in India. This in depth study deals with the trends in the implementation of the Maoist strategy of revolutionary struggle and politics in India. He deplores the 'degeneration' of Maoist Movement into 'individual' Terrorism.

Rai and Prasad (1972) in their study opined that Naxalite movement is basically a socio-economic problem and only superficially a law and order problem. Dasgupta (1973) commencing his study with a definition of Naxalite movement and its characteristics, pointed out that the urban targets of the CPI (ML) terror were mainly policemen and members of the CPI (M), in the study differences among CPI (ML) parties were also discussed. Ghosh (1975) viewed that the policy of offensive terror which was behind the campaign of annihilation of the class enemies, described about the origin of the movement, along with the formation of CPI (ML) and differences in the party.

Roy (1975) made an attempt to place in an international communist strategy especially, the Maoist strategy and to trace the evolution of the Chinese line for Indian revolution, leading to the call for a Maoist Revolution in the Mid-1967, as part of the general strategy of the People's War for the Third World countries.

Mohanty (1977) after a critical study dismissed the observations made by others on the Naxalite movement by saying that it was a youth movement of the new left type, like that of the Bengali Bhadralok extremism. However, Mohanty identified four dimensions of the revolutionary movement as environment, ideology, organization and strategy and concluded that the Maoist movement in India was by and large pre-organizational in character and it was confined basically to mass activity without a new work of any organization whatsoever.

Naxalite Movement and Media

Few studies are available that have analysed the role of media in the Naxalite movement. Although these studies have analysed the role of media in Naxalite movement, they are not comprehensive and dealt with stray news items or a review of some film that deals with Naxalite problem in Andhra Pradesh. For instance, Dasgupta (1973: 228) while writing about the newspapers' coverage of Naxalite movement described the press as anti-Communist and journalists depicted the Movement as a law and order problem. For instance, he found "the press reports about secret movements, mysteries, conspiracies, killings and all that existed and sensational and made stimulating reading. The less charitable explanation would be, in view of the anti-Communist tradition of the Indian Press that such reports were given to scare the uncommitted, to consolidate anti-Communist opinion and also to split further the Indian Communist movement." Contrary to this argument, a police officer Aravinda Rao (1996) argued that the press was exaggerating the Naxalite movement as a great movement and "many left wing extremist groups in our country have been churning out volumes of literature, pamphlets, booklets etc." However, Stevenson (1998) observed that "there is a general weakness for the Indian Press as it focuses on events instead of processes. Stevenson wrote:

> A landmine blast or an encounter, police combing operation, Naxalite movement in the forest, and kidnaps become news for journalists. But the socio-economic milieu that contributes to the emergence and sustenance of the Naxalite phenomenon is often ignored by the press due to its obsession with event related reporting.

2

Research Methodology

The present chapter begins with a statement of objectives followed by a description of the procedure adopted for the selection of newspapers for study. Next, the operational definitions of subject categories are given followed by a description of the method of directional analysis used, followed by the conclusions.

Objectives of the Study

The purpose of the present study is to ascertain the differential coverage given to Naxalite Movement by selected newspapers. Four newspapers were selected for this purpose, two each in English and Telugu. Content analysis was used to compare the news content of the sample newspapers and to draw inferences about the coverage given to the phenomenon under study in the sample newspapers.

The specific objectives of the study are:

1. To find out the frequency and the extent of space allocated to different categories of news covering Naxalite related issues in the front page and inside pages of the sample dailies.
2. To find out and make a comparative analysis in terms of frequency and space of the differences in the coverage of various categories of the Naxalite related news in the specific English and Telugu newspapers.
3. To find out the differences in the frequency and space devoted to the Naxalite themes related to local, state and national items, and to find out the direction of treatment given by the sample newspapers to the Naxalite related news.
4. To make a comparative analysis of the frequency of coverage

of Naxalite movement related editorials, letter to the editor, articles, photos and cartoons which appeared in the sample newspapers.

Content Analysis as a Research Method

Content analysis is a method of communication analysis, as well as a method of observation (Kerlinger, 1973). It is a versatile research technique in mass communications, as well as, in social science research, where data from archival records and documents can be analyzed systematically and scientifically to draw valid conclusions.

As a method of observation, content analysis enables the researcher to take communications people have produced and ask questions about each communication to draw inferences (Kerlinger, 1973). Thus the content of communications becomes the basis of inference.

According to Dremers and Nichols (1987: 10), content analysis is one of the three major methods of precisions journalism, the two other methods being survey research and field experiment. They state that content analysis typically uses documents or records as the subjects where as survey research uses people as subjects.

No uniform definition of content analysis is available; Holsti (1969) defined it as "any technique for making inferences by systematically and objectively identifying specified characteristics of messages." According to Berelson (1952) it is "a research technique for the objective, systematic and quantitative description of the manifest content of communications." Chadwick (1984) observed that content analysis is used as a research tool in "systematically coding messages of information into categories, thus allowing for quantitative analysis." Therefore, content analysis is a method which provides a precise means for describing the contents of any sort of communications-be they newspapers, radio programmes, films, everyday conversations, verbalized free associations and so on.

Content Analysis and Communication Research

Communication process has four components the source, the message, the channel, and the receiver. Lasswell (1948) put it as "who says what in which channel to whom and with what effect." As Lasswell described the communication situation in the form of questions, the central concept of 'what' or 'the message' forms the basis for content analysis.

Emergence of the Method

According to Woodrum (1984), American journalists during the late 19th century and sociologists in the subsequent decades widely employed this technique. It was also adopted for the historical and political research as well (Holsti, 1969). However, content analysis gained more currency during World War II when the United States Government sponsored a project under the directorship of Harold D. Lasswell to evaluate enemy propaganda (Lasswell *et.al.*, 1965). The resources made available for research and the scope of problems studied in this project resulted in the development of content analysis as a full fledged scientific method and spread to numerous other disciplines (Woodrum, 1984).

Purpose and Applications

According to Holsti (1969: 601) the purpose of content analysis is to test hypothesis and to make inferences about (1) characteristics of the text; (2) causes or antecedents of the message, and (3) effects of the communication.

Berelson (1952) listed out the many uses of content analysis in communications. Some of them are:

1. to describe the international differences in communication content;
2. to expose propaganda techniques;
3. to discover stylistic features and trace the development of scholarship; and
4. to aid in technical research operations such as to code open ended questions in survey research.

Devi Prasad (2008) lists out several important uses of content analysis. One important application has been to study social change. For example, an index of discrimination against women or minority groups is measured by counting the frequency of negative stereo types in history books, cartoons in newspapers and magazines, radio or television. Similarly public attitudes towards important issues like unemployment, health, inflation, civic amenities and so on where assessed by analyzing the content of editorials or letters to the editor in newspapers (Inkeles *et.al.*, 1952: 1953; Vacin, 1965: Devi Prasad, *et.al.*, 1992).

Content analysis is also used by many researchers in different contexts, particularly to ascertain trends in the communication content of dailies, weeklies, comics and political coverage of elections (Cornwell, 1959; Barcus, 1962; Buckman, 1993).

Several studies were conducted to elicit information on various issues covered in newspapers by analyzing their news content (Batlin, 1954: Alisky, 1958, Bush, 1960; Coulson, *et.al.*, 1995). One significant area is the analysis of newspaper content of the election converge and editorial treatment to mould the opinion of voters (Davis and Rarick, 1964; Gregg, 1965; Haskins, 1965; Devi Prasad, *et.al.*, 1991). For example Devi Prasad *et.al.*, analyzed the editorials and letters-to-the editor published in four dailies in India before the 1991 elections to find out the prominence given to certain election related themes.

It has been found that systematic analysis of advertisements in newspapers and magazines can yield useful insights into national culture as well as media preferences of advertisers (Auter 1993, Busby, *et.al.*, 1993; Wang, 1966). Similarly television, radio and movies (Head, 1952; Lowry, 1989; Entaman, 1994; Olson, 1994). Content analysis is an equally useful technique in social sciences for analyzing social issues. In political science, the method was adopted to analyze the propaganda devices used by the Warring Groups (George, 1959; Lasswell, *et.al.*, 1965; King, 1989).

Content analysis is also used by many researchers in different contexts like War Journalism (Hallin, 1986, 1987, Hallin and Gitlin, 1994, Carruthers 2000), Peace Journalism (Lee 2005), International News (Bansal, 2002), Developmental News (Murthy, 2000).

Advantages and Limitations

Any research technique has its advantages and limitations and the method of content analysis is not an exception to this. Woodrum (1984) listed out these advantages of the method as follows:

1. It is a safe method in the sense that if the researcher found that a portion of the necessary information was missing or incorrectly coded, it is possible to return to the text and

supplement the missing data. This not always possible in experimental or survey research.

2. It is a shoestring methodology which is typically labour intensive and requires minimum capital investment.
3. This research technique focuses directly on the symbolic message patterns of the communication and facilitates the use of quantitative techniques for drawing theoretically relevant inferences from data.
4. It has the advantage of forcing researchers to specify category criteria and assess their success in measuring qualitative phenomena.
5. It is an unobtrusive research technique.

Some Limitations of this research technique are:

1. Symbols are processed and coded according to the attribution given by a coder;
2. The reliability and validity issues in content analysis still remain unresolved (Krippendorff, 1980).
3. Some times it is difficult to locate messages relevant to the research question; and
4. The method cannot be used to test causal relationship between variables (Chadwick, 1984).

The Sample Framework

A purposive sample consisting of four leading daily newspapers (two English and two Telugu) were taken. The papers in English were *The Hindu, The New Indian Express* and in Telugu *Eenadu* and *Vaartha*. The prime consideration in the selection of these newspapers was the prominence as reflected in their circulation and their regional representation. While *The Hindu* and *The New Indian Express* are considered elite dailies in English, the other two are premier Telugu newspapers in Andhra Pradesh. The important considerations went into the selection of the two different language dailies (See Appendix-III for profiles of newspapers).

1. English being the associate official language and the main medium of intellectual exchange among the elite in the country, the English dailies are read by the majority of policy makers, decision-makers and administrators.
2. The language newspapers are read by the masses and reach the majority of the population in the region.

Sampling Procedure

The universe for this study comprises all the editions of the four selected dailies published during the calendar years i.e., January 1, 1999 to December 31, 2006.

This study was based on the complete census during the eight years time span—not a random sample. From a preliminary analysis it was concluded that a small sample of issues would result in unfair representation of Naxalite movement related news coverage. Through out the year, news of Naxalite movement is distributed in various proportions. If a random sample were taken, the risk of missing important instances of Naxalite movement coverage would be high. Therefore, hundreds of newspaper issues had been sampled.

The leading English Daily *The Hindu* and the leading regional language (Telugu) daily *Eenadu* were taken as a 'base' daily newspapers.

Two steps were adopted to select the editions (dates) to constitute the study.

First step: The researcher identified 100 major incidents for study period from January 1, 1999 to December 31, 2006. (The list of events is given in Appendix IV).

Second step: In the second step, the researcher examined the consequences of major incidents. Actions and reactions, follow up news coverage were considered for analysis.

There were 320 editions per daily and a total of 1280 editions for four sample dailies came up for analysis, and found 7071 news stories (all units).

Units of Analysis

The units of analysis for this study consisted of the news items, editorials, articles, letters-to-the editor, photos and cartoons published in the front page and inside pages of four selected dailies.

Operational Definitions of Units of Analysis

Following are the operational definitions of units of analysis used in this study:

1. A news item is any item dealing with timely event with current dateline. It is defined as an account of events reported

by the paper's own correspondents or reporters and wire service stories. Human interest stories are included in this item (Parthasarathy, 1984; 107-108).

2. An editorial is an article giving a newspaper editors' opinion on a topical issue or an editorial is an opinion piece which projects the viewpoint of the newspaper on a particular policy, programmes or event. It gives digest of facts, evaluates them and arrives at a logical conclusion step by step (Mehta, 1979: 133).
3. A letter-to-the editor is an opinion piece expressed by the reader on an issue or an event. It is an indicator of public opinion when compared and contrasted with a variety of other measures such as news item, features, etc. (Grey and Brown, 1970, 450-56).
4. An article is a nonfiction essay or work on a single subject, usually, written for a periodical, such as a newspaper or magazine; can be as short as a few thousand words but may some times be of book size, especially when run serially in the periodical.
5. Photographs are commonly used in news reports to illustrate a point or points made in the report or to make the layout more aesthetically pleasing (Wanta, 1988).
6. Cartoon is a humorous drawing in a newspaper, magazine, etc., especially as a topical comment, often dealing in a satirical way with something of interest in the news; cartoons have become an inseparable part of journalism. They hold a mirror to the day-to-day happenings in politics and administration. Some times cartoons give moral lessons.

Thus, all the units of analyses as per the above criteria, published in the front page and inside pages of the dailies during the sample period (January 1, 1999 to December 31 2006) were considered for coding into the subject categories developed for the purpose. The details of the subject categories of the study are as follows:

Subject Categories

Keeping in view of the objectives of the study, 10 main subject categories have been identified. The following are the 10 main subject categories with their sub-categories: 1. Naxalite activities, 2. Encounter deaths, 3. Police activities, 4. Agony of sufferers, 5. Government views, 6. Political party views, 7. Peoples reaction,

8. Human rights/courts, 9. Human rights organizations, and 10. Peace talks.

Further, the coverage of the 10 subject categories was analyzed basing on the geographical dimension. Thus the news items were divided on the basis of geographical dimensions into three regions such as local, state and national. All the main subject categories were in turn divided into sub-categories.

Category 1: ***Naxalite Activities***

(a) Ambush
(b) Raids
(c) Destruction
(d) Kidnaps
(e) Attacks on informers
(f) Attacks on coverts
(g) Communication

Category 2: ***Encounter Deaths***

(a) Naxalite
(b) Police personnel
(c) Both

Category 3: ***Police Activities***

(a) Counter measures
(b) Welfare measures
(c) Communication

Category 4: ***Agony of Sufferers***

(a) Naxalite families
(b) Police families
(c) Targeted families
(d) Innocent victims

Category 5: ***Government Views***

(a) Central government
(b) State government (Andhra Pradesh)
(c) Other state governments

Category 6: ***Political Parties' Views***

(a) Congress

(*b*) Bharatiya Janata Party
(*c*) Communists
(*d*) Telugu Desam Party
(*e*) Others

Category 7: ***People's Reaction Against***

(*a*) Naxalites
(*b*) Police

Category 8: ***Human Rights/Courts***

Category 9: ***Human Rights Related Organizations***

(*a*) APCLC (Andhra Pradesh Civil Liberties Committee)
(*b*) PUCL (Peoples Union for Civil Liberties)
(*c*) HRF (Human Rights Forum)
(*d*) CCC (Committee of Concerned Citizens)

Category 10: ***Peace Talks***

Units of Analysis Covering the Sub Themes

Mentioned below were coded accordingly:

1. ***Naxalite Activities***

   (*a*) *Ambush:* News relating to deliberate ambush with land, clay more and directional mines.
   (*b*) *Raids:* News relating to raids on police stations for ammunition.
   (*c*) *Destruction:* News about government and private property destructions.
   (*d*) *Kidnaps:* Politicians, police, state government officials, informers, covert kidnaps.
   (*e*) *Attacks on informers:* Attacks on police informers.
   (*f*) *Attacks on coverts*
   (*g*) *Communication:* Plenaries, sessions, press meets, interviews, press release, courier letters, regrets, news stories, from reliable source and reportage public courts, punishments, wage agreements, settlements, collections, etc.

2. ***Encounter Deaths***

   (*a*) *Naxalites:* Naxalite encounter deaths only.
   (*b*) *Police*: Police deaths only.

(c) *Both:* Naxalites and police deaths in encounter.

3. ***Police Activities***

(a) *Counter measures:* Deliberate ambush, combing operations, quick and surprise attacks, red alert.
(b) *Welfare measures:* Creating awareness among tribals and to discourage them against Naxalite movement through meetings, exhibitions and melas.
(c) *Communication:* Press meets, announcements, statements by police officials, arrests, surrenders, and arms dump recoveries, press reports from reliable source.

4. ***Agony of Sufferers***

(a) Naxalite families
(b) Police families
(c) Targeted families
(d) Innocent victims.

5. ***Government Views***

(a) *Central Government*: President of the Nation, Prime Minister, Central Cabinet and Central Government Higher Officials (Home Secretary, etc.).
(b) *State Government (Andhra Pradesh)*: Governor, Chief Minister, Home Ministers, State Officials (excluding police officials).
(c) *Other State Governments:* Affected by Naxalites
Example: Orissa, Karnataka, Tamil Nadu, Madhya Pradesh, Bihar, Chhattisgarh, Jharkhand, Maharashtra, West Bengal, etc.

6. ***Political Parties' Views***

(a) *Congress:* National and State Parties/Presidents and Committee Leaders, Party MPs and MLAs (excluding ministers).
(b) *BJP:* National and State Party leaders, MPs and MLAs.
(c) *Communists:* CPI, CPI (M) National and State Leaders MPs and MLAs.
(d) *TDP:* TDP Party Leaders (excluding Ministers), MPs and MLAs.
(e) *Others:* TRS, AIADMK Party Leaders and others.

7. ***People's Reactions Against***

   (a) Naxalites
   (b) Police.

8. ***Human Rights/Courts***

   National Human Rights Commission (NHRC), Amnesty International Reports, Fact Findings, Lower and Higher Court judgments and directions.

9. ***Human Rights Organizations***

   (a) APCLC (Andhra Pradesh Civil Liberties Committee)
   (b) PUCL (Peoples Union for Civil Liberties)
   (c) HRF (Human Rights Forum)
   (d) CCC (Committee of Concerned Citizens).

10. ***Peace Talks***

    State Government discussions with Naxalites.

Geographical Categories

All news items were analyzed in terms of geographical region–local, state and national. Thus, the geographical regions were defined as follows:

(i) The units of analysis under local category dealt with events which occurred in Visakhapatnam district.

For Example: Visakhapatnam date line news story.

Naxal attack on armed out post
Seven policemen among eight killed

(Staff Reporter)

Visakhapatnam, February 19: Seven Policemen and one Naxalite were killed in an attack on the armed outpost at Darakonda village in Gudem Kotha Veedhi Mandal of Visakhapatnam district on Friday night. (*The Hindu*, February 20, 2000, p. 1)

(ii) State Category included units of analysis that contained events or happenings concerning other districts of Andhra Pradesh state. However, this category excludes local category as defined above.

For Example: *Three top Naxalite leaders killed*

(Special Correspondent)

Manthani, December 2: The outlawed PWG received a major set back when three of the top leaders were killed in a fierce encounter with police at Koyyuru forest of Tadicherla mandal of Andhra Pradesh on Thursday. An unidentified Naxalite was also killed in the encounter.

The slain top leaders were identified as the PWG Central Committee member. Mr. Nalla Adi Reddy, Santosh Reddy alias Mahesh and the North Telangana special zone committee Secretary Seelam Naresh alias Jagan alias Murali...
(*The Hindu*, December 3, 1999, p. 11)

(iii) National Category comprises those units of analyses containing events of relevance for national level excluding the state and local category as defined above. News that happened around the country excluding Andhra Pradesh was also treated as national.

For Example: *5 cops killed in Naxal attack in Orissa*

(Express News Service)

Malkan Giri, August 10: In the worst ever encounter between police and members of the out lowed PWG since the outbreak of Naxalite Movement in South Orissa one SI a Zemadar of Orissa State Armed Police (OSAP) and three OSAP Jawans were killed in Kalimela and Motu around Thursday night. Two Naxalites were also killed in the encounter.

The Naxalites belonging to the Kalimela dalam also blow up the Kalimela Police Station building by bombing and snatched huge arms and ammunition from Kalimela and Motu Police Stations.
(*The New Indian Express*, August 11, 2001, p. 1)

Data Coding Sheet

A code sheet was prepared incorporating the subject categories and geographical categories. The code sheet was pilot tested by the researcher on five editions of the each of the sample newspaper (i.e., on a total of 20 editions) along with a second trained coder who was a research scholar in journalism. Necessary changes were made to the subject categories based on the pretest and the code sheet was finalized (Appendix V).

Procedures of Measurement

The units of analysis, coded into various subject categories, were measured both in terms of their frequencies and space. While all the units of analysis were counted in terms of frequencies, as regards the measurement of space, only the news items were considered for the purpose and recorded in the code sheet in terms of space. The frequencies of the news items photos which appeared on the front page and inside pages were recorded separately. However, as regards the editorials, letters-to-the editor, articles, cartoons, the frequencies were recorded in separate columns of the code sheet.

Space Measurement

Most of the papers are designed to present the contents in eight columns but some times have made their page make-ups in a mixed column style. One of the papers (*Vaartha*) prepared the front page in six columns and the other pages in eight columns. Many items are displayed with the text matter in one and half columns, half a column, two third of a column. For those items the measurements have undergone a mathematical calculation and have been converted to fit in eight column width page to maintain a common unit.

As regards space, all news items were measured in cubic centimeters with a standard wooden scale. The space of all news items was separately recorded both for the front page and inside pages of each newspaper. When a news item continued from the front page to inside page (jump stories), it was treated as front page news item and accordingly the recording was made, when a photograph accompanied a news item, the space of photograph was also treated as part of the news item.

Correction Factor

The four sample newspapers have varied column widths. For instance *Vaartha* has 6 columns where as the other three newspapers have 8 columns each. In order to standardize the total space measured for purposes of comparison among the dailies and for statistical applications, a correction factors 'k' was developed by suggested by Khan and Kumar (1993) and Murthy (2001). The procedure adopted was as follows:

First of all, the news items were measured with standard unit of one centimeter regardless of the type size and width of the (single) column when the total space devoted for all the subject categories for 320 issues of each newspaper was available, it was multiplied by the correction factor calculated for each newspaper for uniformity is comparison (Table-1) The standard unit used in this study was one column centimeter of body type containing four agate lines with the column of 25 ems (12 ems = 1 inch) (Details of calculation of correction factor are given in Appendix VI).

Table-1
The Correction Factor (k) for the Measurement of Space of News Items of Four Newspapers

Name of the Newspaper	*Correction Factor (k)*
The Hindu	0.63
The New Indian Express	0.56
Eenadu	0.54
Vaartha	0.52

Inter-coder Reliabilities

Inter-coder reliabilities were calculated for all the units of analysis under each subject category in order to obtain the level of consistency in coding. Thus, all the 6 units of analysis such as news items, editorials, articles, letters-to-the editor, photos, cartoons were combined together for the purpose of inter coder reliabilities. A trained coder who was a doctoral student in journalism and who was proficient both in English and Telugu languages was employed for the purpose of coding. As part of pilot study five editions of each newspaper were taken for coding. After the first coder (i.e., researcher) coded the five editions of each newspaper, the second coder did the coding of the same editions, when the totals of each subject category of each newspaper were available with the two coders the formula was applied to calculate reliability.

It was found out that the coder reliabilities in each subject category ranged from 90 per cent to 100 per cent (See Table 2).

Table-2
Inter-coder Reliabilities for the Subject Categories by Newspaper

Category	*Dailies*			
	The Hindu	*The New Indian Express*	*Eenadu*	*Vaartha*
Naxalite activities	1.00	1.00	1.00	1.00
Encounter deaths	1.00	1.00	1.00	1.00
Police activities	0.90	1.00	0.95	1.00
Agony of sufferers	0.92	-	0.96	0.92
Government views	0.97	0.96	0.97	0.97
Political parties views	1.00	1.00	1.00	1.00
People's reactions	-	-	1.00	-
Human rights/courts	1.00	1.00	-	-
Human rights organizations	-	1.00	-	1.00
Peace talks	-	-	1.00	1.00

C to calculate reliability, the following formula suggested by Holsti (1969) was adopted.

$$R = \frac{2(C_1, C_2)}{C_1 + C_2}$$

Where C_1, C_2 is the number of category assignments both coders agree on, and $C_1 + C_2$ is the total of category assignments arrived at by both coders (see North *et.al.*, 1963).

Directional Analysis

The purpose of using the directional analysis is to find out how the newspapers have accorded treatment to Naxalite movement related news themes in their coverage of the themes. Here, only the news items coded under Naxalite activities, encounters and police activities relates to subject categories were analyzed to find out the treatment given by the four newspapers on a 3 point scale: favourable, unfavourable and neutral. The method of coefficient of imbalance was used to establish the favourable, the unfavourable and the neutral treatment given to Naxalite movement themes in the news items.

The coefficient of imbalance was developed by Janis and Fadner (1965) as a method of measuring the degree of imbalance i.e., the extent to which favourable, unfavourable or neutral treatment is accorded to a topic or message or theme in a given news item. The method was adopted by Devi Prasad (1993) to find out the degree of imbalance in the coverage of election related issues. In the same way Murthy (2000) used it to find out the degree of imbalance given to developmental news items by four selected newspapers.

Symbol is used to identify those terms (words or phrases) referring to the news actors and the Naxalite activities. In the present study, three types of symbols were used. Favourable (positive), unfavourable (negative) and neutral (denotative) symbols indicating approval or favourable disposition towards the news actors, events or situations (e.g.: popular, top, victims, begged, daring attempt, pathetic, tragic etc.).

> ***Example 1:*** *PWG plans to acquire rocket launchers*
>
> Nizamabad: The banned people's War group is making sustained efforts to revive its movements with plans to acquire more sophisticated assault weapons in the form of grenade rifles and rockets launchers, besides using remote control devices with deadly precision to cause devastation against the police force.
> (*The New Indian Express*, December 2, 1999)
>
> ***Example 2:*** *CPI (ML), MCCI Merge, form new party*
>
> Hyderabad: October 14: The CPI (ML) People's War and the Maoist Communist Centre of India (MCCI) have merged to form a new 'unified' Communist Party of India (Maoist), the PW state secretary Ramakrishna announced at a news conference here today.
> (*The Hindu*, October 15, 2004)

Negative symbols carried features of hostility or unfavourable disposition toward people or event involved with the movement as reported in the news.

> E.g. Vicious, cruel, brutal, barbaric, inhuman, extremist, terrorist, massacre, rampage, prey, cold blood, hacked to death, routine cooked story, etc.

Example 1: *Naxals kill Madhava Reddy in landmine blast*

In a well planned operation, extremists target only minister's car, tossing it 20ft. into the air. This is the first time a minister falls prey to the PWG.

Madhava Reddy was returning from civic poll campaign in his home district of Nalgonda, when the incident took place near a road over-bridge around 11 AM. The driver and the Chief Security Officer of the rank of CI, who was accompanying Reddy in his car, were also killed instantaneously. (*The New Indian Express* March 5, 2000)

Example 2: *Seven Women Naxals killed in encounter*

Karimnagar November 1:

For the first time in the history of Naxalite encounters in Andhra Pradesh, seven women functionaries of the out lawed People's War Group (PWG) were killed in an alleged exchange of fire with the police today in a thick forest bordering Karimnagar-Warangal districts.

There were incidents in the past when some women Naxalites were killed along with their male colleagues in encounters with the police. But this is first time that all the victims were women and as many as seven were killed in a single incident. According to the police, the incident took place in the forests bordering Malhar Mandal in Karimnagar and Bhopalpally mandal in Warangal district. 12 women are stated to have escaped. The police recovered seven weapons 13 kit bags, extremist literature, banners and some cooking articles from the encounter site.

(*The New Indian Express*, November 2, 2000)

Neutral symbols showed no preferential judgmental disposition in the news frame.

Example 1: *Naxalites return to Nallamala forest*

State Government lauded for safe passage.

The 50 strong brigade of CPI (Maoist) and CPI (ML) Janashakti Naxalites retreated into the thick Nallamala forest ranges, here on Wednesday evening after a 10 day long sojourn in the out side world to hold peace talks with the State Government.
(*The Hindu* October 21, 2004)

Example 2: *Killing informers' on rise*

Beside renewed encounter violence between Naxalites and police internecine killings of civilians branded police informers as a on the rise ever since the out lawed PW pulled out from the talks process on July 19. While 12 Naxalites were killed in separate encounters, the PW killed 4 policemen in a mine blast and five civilian branding them as police informers.
(*The New Indian Express,* August 2, 2002)

After coding all the Naxalite movement related stories as favourable, unfavourable or neutral, the coefficient of imbalance was calculated using the following formulae suggested by Janis (1965).

$$cf = \frac{f^2 - fu}{rt} \quad f > u \qquad\qquad cu = \frac{fu - u^2}{rt} \quad f < u$$

Where

f = favourable units of content
u = unfavourable units of content
t = number of units of total content
r = total units of relevant content

Data Analysis

The units of analysis thus coded into code sheets were tabulated by using SPSS for analysis. Once the data were analyzed, tables and cross tables were prepared to test the relationships among variables. Appropriate statistical methods such as mean, standard deviation, correlation and analysis of variance were used to find out the association and significance of relationships among variables. Graphs and flow charts were also developed wherever necessary.

3

Units of Analyses: A Profile

The objective of the present chapter is to provide a profile of unit of analyses covered under different subject categories in terms of frequency, space, region-wise allocation and location of news respectively. For this purpose, two popular English National dailies, viz., *The Hindu* and *The New Indian Express* and similarly two popular Telugu dailies, viz., *Eenadu* and *Vaartha* published during the calendar years, i.e., January 1, 1999 to December 31, 2006 were considered. A total number of 320 issues of each newspaper were chosen for the analysis.

The units of analysis consist of news items, photos, cartoons, editorials; edit articles and letters-to-the editor.

Characteristics

Units of Analyses

In all, a total of 4387 news items, 2330 photos, 55 pocket cartoons, 10 editorial cartoons, 74 editorials, 31 edit articles and 184 letters-to-the editor came up for analysis in these four newspapers, viz., *The Hindu, The New Indian Express, Eenadu* and *Vaartha* (Table 3).

News

During the study period, it was found that *Eenadu* had published the highest number of the news items, followed by *Vaartha, The Hindu* and *The New Indian Express* (Table 4).

Table–3
Total Number of Units of Analyses Analyzed in Select Dailies

Units of Analysis	*Frequency (fr)*	*Per cent (%)*
News	4387	62.0
Photo	2330	32.9
Pocket cartoon	55	0.7
Editorial	74	1.0
Edit article	31	0.4
Letters-to-the editor	184	2.6
Editorial cartoon	10	0.1
Total	7071	100.0

N = 320

Table–4
Percentage Distribution of Units of Analysis by Frequencies in the Sample Dailies

	Unit of Analysis						
Newspaper	*News*	*Photo*	*Pocket Cartoon*	*Editorial*	*Article*	*Letters-to-the Editor*	*Editorial Cartoon*
The Hindu	19.6	10.0	1.8	10.8	-	40.8	-
The New Indian Express	17.1	8.8	-	18.9	6.5	8.1	10.0
Eenadu	31.8	42.9	38.2	21.6	29.0	19.6	50.0
Vaartha	31.5	38.3	60.0	48.6	64.5	31.5	40.0
	100 (4387)	100 (2330)	100 (55)	100 (74)	100 (31)	100 (184)	100 (10)

N = 320 editions for each daily

Regional Focus

Data in Table 5 show the percentage of frequency of news items and the extent of space allotted to news of different regions such as local, state and national by the sample newspapers.

Figure 6
Percentage Distribution of Units Analyses by Frequencies in the Four Dailies

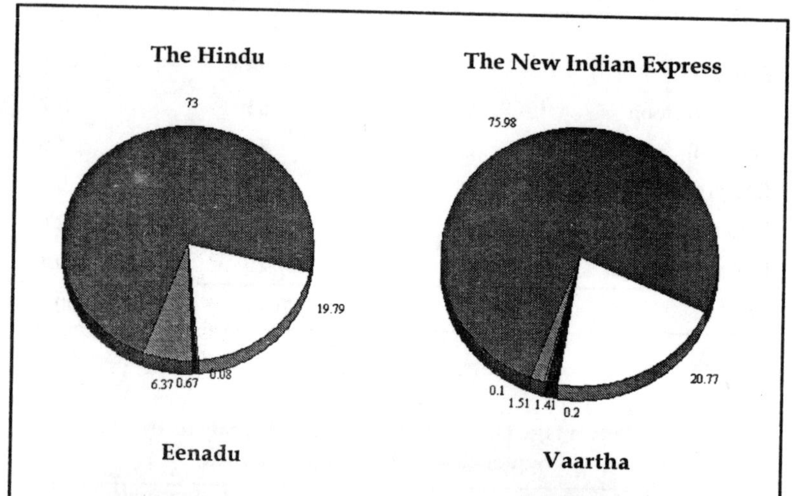

It is evident from Table 5 that the English daily *The Hindu*, the two Telugu dailies *Eenadu* and *Vaartha* allocated more than 85 per cent of the space to state news. Regarding the coverage of local news, *The New Indian Express* covered the highest percentage of news by assigning 14.7 per cent followed by *Eenadu* 7.0 per cent, *The Hindu* 6.7 per cent, *Vaartha* 5.2 per cent while the national news shared the remaining percentage. But, in the coverage of national news, *Vaartha*

dominated all the other three dailies both in terms of frequency and space. It devoted 8.4 per cent of news items and 6.6 per cent of news hole to national news.

Table-5
Percentage Distribution of Frequencies of all News Items and Space by Regional Focus in the Sample Dailies

	Dailies							
Regions	*The Hindu*		*The New Indian Express*		*Eenadu*		*Vaartha*	
	fr	*Space*	*fr*	*Space*	*fr*	*Space*	*fr*	*Space*
Local	6.7	7.6	14.7	14.0	7.0	7.0	5.2	4.8
State	88.4	87.8	77.3	80.0	85.2	87.5	86.4	88.6
National	4.9	4.6	8.0	6.0	7.8	5.5	8.4	6.6
N =	100 (860)	100 (19647.8)	100 (750)	100 (13484.24)	100 (1394)	100 (33132.78)	100 (1383)	100 (35226.36)

Location of News

Table 6 indicates the percentage of distribution of news on the front page and inside pages by the sample dailies. Among the four newspapers under study, *Vaartha* published the highest number of news items (31.7) on the front page, followed by *Eenadu* (30.1), *The New Indian Express* (37.6), and *The Hindu* (29.7). In terms of allocation of space to the various news on the front page, *The New Indian Express* allocated the highest percentage, i.e., 47.5 per cent among the four dailies, while *Eenadu* assigned 45.3 per cent of the total news. *Vaartha* devoted 41.9 per cent of the total print area of news items to the front page, whereas *The Hindu* allocated 31.8 per cent of space to the news on the front page. In the inside pages, *The Hindu* (70.3%) published the highest number of news items as compared to the other dailies while *Eenadu* (69.9%) occupied the second place. As regards the allocation of space to the news, *The Hindu* devoted 68.2 per cent of the total area, followed by *Vaartha* (58.1%) and *Eenadu* (54.7%). Comparatively, *The New Indian Express* devoted less space, i.e., 52.5 per cent to the news items in the inside pages among the four dailies.

Analysis of Subject Categories

Table 7 shows data about the coverage of news under ten different subject categories. As can be seen, in all the four newspapers, the

Table–6
Percentage Distribution of News Items Between Front Page and Inside Pages in the Sample Dailies

Locations	*Dailies*							
	The Hindu		*The New Indian Express*		*Eenadu*		*Vaartha*	
	fr	*Space*	*fr*	*Space*	*fr*	*Space*	*fr*	*Space*
Front Page	29.7	31.8	37.6	47.5	30.1	45.3	31.7	41.9
Inside Pages	70.3	68.2	62.4	52.5	69.9	54.7	68.3	58.1
N =	100 (860)	100 (19305.09)	100 (750)	100 (13484.24)	100 (1394)	100 (33138.72)	100 (1383)	100 (35234.68)

Naxalite activities, ranked first in terms of frequency of coverage, followed by police activities, government views and so on. Thus, the four newspapers allocated more than 70 per cent to these three categories put together while the rest of the seven categories shared the remaining percentage of the news.

Table–7
Distribution of Frequencies and Space*
by Subject Categories in the Sample Dailies

Category	*Dailies*							
	The Hindu		*The New Indian Express*		*Eenadu*		*Vaartha*	
	fr	*sp*	*fr*	*sp*	*fr*	*sp*	*fr*	*sp*
Naxalite activities	310	7508.34	267	4953.76	477	13601.52	474	14392.56
Encounter deaths	103	1987.02	95	1552.88	115	3042.36	134	3565.12
Police activities	212	4042.08	180	2770.88	350	6913.08	329	7018.44
Agony of sufferers	14	447.93	21	478.24	52	1178.82	45	1133.08
Government views	116	3054.87	115	2424.24	215	5158.62	223	5688.8

Contd...

Category	Dailies							
	The Hindu		The New Indian Express		Eenadu		Vaartha	
	fr	sp	fr	sp	fr	sp	fr	sp
Political parties' views	49	1002.96	28	418.88	100	1493.1	94	1528.28
People's reaction	8	124.11	6	126	12	275.94	17	322.4
Human rights/ courts	8	211.05	2	77.84	11	137.16	5	101.4
Human rights organizations	31	532.35	22	278.32	37	474.66	42	728
Peace talks	9	394.38	14	403.2	25	863.46	20	756.6
N =	860	19305.09	750	13484.24	1394	33138.72	1383	35234.68

*space in column centimeters

It is evident that all the dailies were alike by giving the first 5 ranks of importance to news item category. While news pertaining to the category agony of sufferers ranked seventh in English dailies, and sixth in Telugu dailies. The Human rights/courts and the people's reaction categories received the least coverage, in terms of frequency of news items (Table 8).

Table–8
Percentage Distribution of Frequencies of News Items by Subject Categories in the Sample Dailies

Category	Dailies							
	The Hindu		The New Indian Express		Eenadu		Vaartha	
	fr	Rank Order	fr	Rank Order	fr	Rank Order	fr	Rank Order
Naxalite activities	36.0	1	35.6	1	34.2	1	34.3	1
Encounter deaths	12.0	4	12.7	4	8.2	4	9.7	4

Contd...

Category	Dailies							
	The Hindu		The New Indian Express		Eenadu		Vaartha	
	fr	Rank Order	fr	Rank Order	fr	Rank Order	fr	Rank Order
Police activities	24.7	2	24.0	2	25.1	2	23.8	2
Agony of sufferers	1.6	7	2.8	7	3.7	6	3.2	6
Government views	13.5	3	15.3	3	15.4	3	16.1	3
Political parties' views	5.7	5	3.7	5	7.2	5	6.8	5
People's reaction	0.9	9	0.8	9	0.9	9	1.2	9
Human rights/ courts	0.9	9	0.3	10	0.8	10	0.4	10
Human rights organizations	3.6	6	2.9	6	2.7	7	3.0	7
Peace talks	1.0	8	1.9	8	1.8	8	1.5	8
N =	(860)		(750)		(1394)		(1383)	

It is observed that the English dailies *The Hindu* and *The New Indian Express* closely correlated ($r = 0.99$ $p < 0.01$) in terms of frequency of news items devoted to different themes whereas *Eenadu* and *Vaartha* showed close correlation among their news coverage (Table 9).

Table–9
Correlation Coefficients of Frequencies of News Items by Subject Categories among Four Sample Dailies

	Dailies		
	The Hindu	The New Indian Express	Eenadu
The Hindu			
The New Indian Express	0.99		
Eenadu	0.98	0.98	
Vaartha	0.99	0.99	0.99

P < 0.01

Figure–7
Percentage Distribution of Frequencies of News Items by Subject Categories in the Sample Dailies

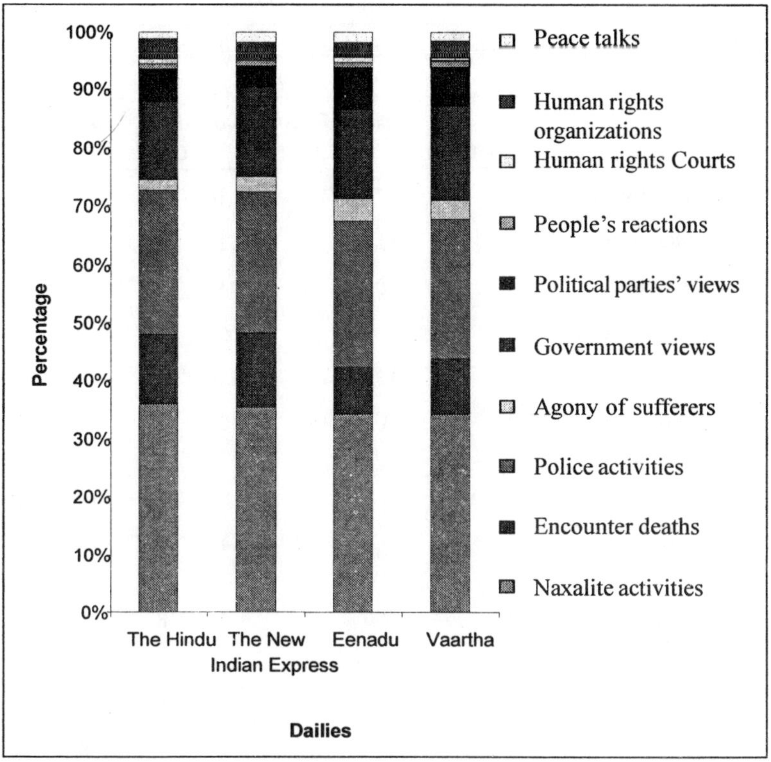

Allocation of Space to Subject Categories

Allocation of space to different themes in the sample newspapers under study is shown in Table 10. As expected, the category Naxalite activities got first priority in all the newspapers in terms of space covered. The other three categories, viz., police activities, Government views and 'encounter' deaths received second, third and fourth places across these four dailies.

Interestingly, however, the four themes put together received more than 85 per cent of the total news hole in all the four newspapers. *Vaartha* gave 87 per cent to these four categories put together and *Eenadu* allocated 86.5 per cent while the two English dailies: *The New Indian Express* devoted 86.7 per cent and *The Hindu* 85.9 per cent.

Table-10
Percentage Distribution of Space by Subject Categories in the Sample Dailies

Category	*Dailies*							
	The Hindu		*The New Indian Express*		*Eenadu*		*Vaartha*	
	Space	*Rank Order*	*Space*	*Rank Order*	*Space*	*Rank Order*	*Space*	*Rank Order*
Naxalite activities	38.9	1	37.0	1	41.0	1	41.0	1
Encounter deaths	10.3	4	11.5	4	9.2	4	10.1	4
Police activities	21.0	2	20.5	2	20.9	2	20.0	2
Agony of sufferers	2.3	7	3.5	5	3.6	6	3.2	6
Government views	15.8	3	18.0	3	15.6	3	16.1	3
Political parties' views	5.2	5	3.1	6	4.5	5	4.3	5
People's reaction	0.6	10	0.9	9	0.8	9	0.9	9
Human rights/ courts	1.1	9	0.5	10	0.4	10	0.3	10
Human rights organizations	2.8	6	2.0	8	1.4	8	2.0	8
Peace talks	2.0	8	3.0	7	2.6	7	2.1	7
N =	100 (19305.09)		100 (13484.24)		100 (33138.72)		100 (35234.68)	

As regards the allocation of space to the political parties' views, *The Hindu* dominated the other three newspapers by giving 5.2 per cent to the theme. The other three newspapers *The New Indian Express, Eenadu* and *Vaartha* allocated 3.1 per cent, 4.5 per cent and 4.3 per cent respectively. However, in terms of space the political parties views category received in fifth rank in *The Hindu, Eenadu* and *Vaartha,* while in *The New Indian Express* it ranked sixth.

As seen from Table 11, even in terms of space the two nationals, *The Hindu* and *The New Indian Express* and the two Telugu newspapers *Eenadu* and *Vaartha* showed high correlation.

Table–11
Correlation Coefficients of Space by Subject Categories among Four Sample Dailies

	Dailies		
	The Hindu	*The New Indian Express*	*Eenadu*
The Hindu			
The New Indian Express	0.99		
Eenadu	0.99	0.99	
Vaartha	0.99	0.99	0.99

People's Reaction against the Naxalites/Police

People's reactions in all the four newspapers found to have a highly dismal coverage in terms of news items and space. *The Hindu, The New Indian Express* and *Eenadu* reported only 0.93 per cent, 0.80 per cent and 0.86 per cent of news items respectively throughout the study period. The other Telugu newspaper *Vaartha* did give slightly more coverage (1.2%) to these themes.

Peace Talks

With regard to the category–'peace talks', the coverage was considerable. Overall, *The Hindu* reported only 1.0 per cent news items out of a total of 860 news items while *The New Indian Express* devoted 1.87 per cent news items out of 750 news items (see Table 8). The two Telugu dailies–*Eenadu* and *Vaartha* allocated 1.8 per cent and 1.5 per cent news items out of a total 1394 and 1383 news items respectively. However, *The New Indian Express* reported more percentage items (1.9%) on 'peace talks' among the four newspapers. But in terms of allocation of space, *The New Indian Express* devoted more space to this theme.

Human Rights/Courts and Human Rights Organizations

Coming to the coverage of Human rights/courts theme, *The Hindu* dominated the other three newspapers by giving 0.9 per cent to the theme. The other three newspapers *The New Indian Express, Eenadu, Vaartha* allocated 0.3 per cent, 0.8 per cent and 0.4 per cent respectively. However, in terms of frequency and space, 'Human rights/courts' theme received ninth rank in *The Hindu*; it is tenth rank in *The New Indian Express, Eenadu* and *Vaartha*. Regarding the news items on Human rights organizations, the two English dailies, *The Hindu* and *The New Indian Express* had given sixth rank in terms of frequency of news items, while in the two Telugu newspapers *Eenadu* and *Vaartha* it is seventh rank. The subject category Human rights organization received 42 news items in *Vaartha*, 37 news items in *Eenadu*, 31 news items in *The Hindu* and 22 news items in *The New Indian Express*.

Photographs

The impact of the story in the news is more often determined by the photograph than the story itself. Because a photograph often affects a reader emotionally, more than words alone, pictorial evidence often have the weight age on the established facts. For this reason, readers often get their first impression about a news story by looking at the photograph on the page. Thus, in the present study, the contents of photographs were analyzed to ascertain, how the newspapers had covered the Naxalite issues.

Out of a total of 2330 photos, the highest number of photographs appeared in *Eenadu* (1000) while *Vaartha* (892), *The Hindu* (233) and *The New Indian Express* (205) came in the descending order.

Table–12
Distribution of Frequencies of Photos in the Sample Dailies

Location	*Dailies*								
	The Hindu		*The New Indian Express*		*Eenadu*		*Vaartha*		*Total*
	fr	%	*fr*	%	*fr*	%	*fr*	%	
Front Page	50	21.5	85	41.0	478	48.0	370	41.5	983
Inside Page	183	78.5	120	59.0	522	52.0	522	58.5	1347
Total	233	100	205	100	1000	100	892	100	2330

Among the four newspapers under study, *Eenadu* published the highest number of photographs (478) on the front page, followed by *Vaartha* (370), *The New Indian Express* (84) and *The Hindu* (50) in that order.

In the inside pages, the two Telugu newspapers *Eenadu* and *Vaartha* published the highest number (522 each) of photographs as compared to the other dailies, *The Hindu* (183) and *The New Indian*

Express (121). Further analysis shows that the four newspapers devoted more number of photographs to cover 'Naxalite activities' theme 1036 (44%) followed by 'Encounter deaths' 446 (19.1%), 'police activities' 356 (15.2%) and 'Government views' 226 (9.6%).

Front Page

Table 13 presents data about the coverage given by photographs on the front page about the different themes under study.

Interestingly, half of the photographs in all the dailies were occupied with the theme-Naxalite activities. As regards the theme 'encounter deaths', among the two Telugu dailies, *Vaartha* published 99 (26.8%) photographs to this theme, while *Eenadu* 96 (20%), of the two English newspapers. *The New Indian Express* published 12 (14.1%) photographs and *The Hindu* 11 (22%). Government views theme was given the highest percentage (17.6%) by *The New Indian Express*, another English daily *The Hindu* gave less coverage (16%) to the theme.

Table–13
Percentage Distribution of Frequencies of Photos by Subject Categories in the Front Page

Category	*Dailies*								
	The Hindu		*The New Indian Express*		*Eenadu*		*Vaartha*		*Total*
	fr	*%*	*fr*	*%*	*fr*	*%*	*fr*	*%*	
Naxalite activities	23	46.0	36	42.4	269	56.3	171	46.2	499
Encounter deaths	11	22.0	12	14.1	96	20.1	99	26.8	218
Police activities	5	10.0	14	16.5	51	10.7	28	7.6	98
Agony of sufferers	1	2.0	1	1.2	3	0.6	15	4.0	20
Government views	8	16.0	15	17.6	44	9.2	40	10.8	107
Political parties' views	-	-	1	1.2	2	0.4	7	1.9	10
People's reactions	-	-	-	-	3	0.6	1	0.2	4
Human rights/courts	-	-	2	2.3	-	-	1	0.2	3
Human rights organization	1	2.0	1	1.2	5	1.0	4	1.0	11
Peace talks	1	2.0	3	3.5	5	1.0	4	1.0	13
N =	50	100	85	100	478	100	370	100	983

Similarly, *The New Indian Express* published 14 (16.5%) photographs on the theme 'police activities', while *The Hindu* devoted 5 (10%) photographs to the same theme. Among the two Telugu dailies, *Eenadu* 51 (10.7%) and *Vaartha* 28 (7.6%) photographs, published on the theme.

Table–14
Percentage Distribution of Frequencies of Photos by Subject Categories in Inside Pages

Category	*Dailies*								
	The Hindu		*The New Indian Express*		*Eenadu*		*Vaartha*		*Total*
	fr	*%*	*fr*	*%*	*fr*	*%*	*fr*	*%*	
Naxalite activities	65	35.5	52	45.0	213	40.8	205	39.3	537
Encounter deaths	3	1.6	7	5.8	111	21.3	107	20.5	228
Police activities	51	21.9	20	16.7	88	16.9	99	19.0	258
Agony of sufferers	7	3.8	7	5.8	30	5.8	36	6.9	80
Government views	25	13.7	26	21.7	33	6.3	35	6.7	119
Political parties' views	15	8.2	1	0.8	8	1.5	17	3.3	41
People's reactions	-	-	-	-	5	0.9	5	0.9	10
Human rights/ courts	1	0.5	-	-	-	-	-	-	1
Human rights organization	12	6.6	1	0.8	4	0.7	8	1.5	25
Peace talks	4	2.2	4	3.3	30	5.8	10	1.9	48
N =	183	100	120	100	522	100	522	100	1347

Inside Pages

Table 14 provides data about the distribution of percentage of photographs, published on the inside pages. The category 'Naxalite activities' related photographs received significant percentage in all the four newspapers which is as follows: *The New Indian Express* 52 (45%), *Eenadu* 213 (40.8%), *Vaartha* 205 (39.3%) and *The Hindu* 65 (35.5%). The two Telugu newspapers gave second place to 'Encounter deaths' related photographs. But, *The Hindu* gave second place to 'police activities' 51 (21.9%) and third place to 'Government views' 25 (13.7%). The *The New Indian Express* gave second place to 'Government views' 26 (21.7%) and third place to 'police activities' 20 (16.7%). But these two English dailies gave less coverage to the photographs of 'Encounter deaths'.

In terms of coverage given to the sub-themes under the 'Naxalite activities' category is shown in Table 15 *Eenadu* published the highest number of photographs on the front page, on the themes ambush (102), raids (73), destruction (22), while *Vaartha* gave prominence to the theme 'attacks on coverts' (13). Among the four dailies, the two Telugu newspapers gave prominence to the sub-theme 'communication under Naxalite activities', whereas the less prominence was given by the English dailies in terms of coverage of photographs. Coming to the photographic coverage of 'encounter deaths', *The Hindu* and *The New Indian Express* published less number of photographs to this theme. Interestingly, all the four newspapers did not record even a single photograph on the theme 'police deaths in encounters'. In terms of coverage given to the sub-themes under the 'police activities' category, *The Hindu* published more photographs as compared to *The New Indian Express*.

Eenadu published more number of photographs (35) on the theme 'peace talks'.

Table–15
Distribution of Frequency of Photographs by Themes under Subject Categories in the Sample Dailies

Category	*Theme*	*Dailies*							
		The Hindu		*The New Indian Express*		*Eenadu*		*Vaartha*	
		Front Page	*Inside Pages*	*Front Page*	*Inside Pages*	*Front Page*	*Inside Pages*	*Front Page*	*Inside Page*
1. Naxalite activities	Ambush	5	4	10	21	102	19	41	15
	Raids	6	9	13	16	73	31	54	37
	Destruction	2	14	4	4	22	26	8	12
	Kidnaps	2	-	2	-	5	-	4	-
	Attacks on informers	-	2	-	-	3	4	1	3
	Attacks on coverts	-	-	1	-	11	3	13	4

Contd...

Category	Theme	The Hindu		The New Indian Express		Eenadu		Vaartha	
		Front Page	Inside Pages	Front Page	Inside Pages	Front Page	Inside Pages	Front Page	Inside Page
	Communication	8	36	6	13	53	130	50	134
2. Encounter deaths	Naxalites	10	3	11	7	90	104	86	66
	Police	-	-	-	-	-	-	-	-
	Both	1	-	1	-	6	7	13	41
3. Police activities	Counter measures	-	-	1	3	10	5	6	13
	Welfare measures	-	1	-	-	-	1	-	2
	Communication	5	50	13	17	41	82	22	84
4. Agony of sufferers	Naxalite families	1	2	-	-	1	4	8	3
	Police families	-	4	1	1	-	15	1	14
	Targeted families	-	1	-	4	2	7	2	7
	Innocent victims	-	-	-	2	-	4	4	12
5. Govt. views	Central	1	5	2	-	7	1	7	2
	State	7	20	13	25	36	31	33	33
	Other states	-	-	-	1	1	1	-	-
6. Political parties' views	Congress	-	4	-	-	-	-	1	5
	BJP	-	1	1	-	1	2	2	2
	Communists	-	-	-	-	-	1	-	-
	TDP	-	10	-	1	-	5	2	8
	TRS	-	-	-	-	1	0	2	2
7. People's reaction against	Naxalites	-	-	-	-	-	5	1	3
	Police	-	-	-	-	3	-	-	2
8. Human rights/ courts	Human rights/ courts	-	1	2	-	-	-	1	-

Contd...

Category	Theme	The Hindu Front Page	The Hindu Inside Pages	The New Indian Express Front Page	The New Indian Express Inside Pages	Eenadu Front Page	Eenadu Inside Pages	Vaartha Front Page	Vaartha Inside Page
9. Human rights organi-zations	Human rights organi-zations	1	12	1	1	5	4	4	8
10. Peace talks	Peace talks	1	4	3	4	5	30	4	10
Total		50	183	85	120	478	522	370	522
Grand Total		233		205		1000		892	

Cartoons

In recent years, cartoons in the Indian news media have become an important form of political communication. As a means of social and political satire, a cartoon, through simple graphic metaphor and comically distorted drawing, addresses the subjects. The cartoons describe state behaviour in a wide variety of situations. Generally cartoons are of two types, i.e., 1 Pocket cartoon and (2) editorial cartoon. In captioned cartoons, the actor is the character who is speaking the line and the agent is the character about whom the actor is speaking. In the actor is the "giver" and the agent is "receiver."

Table–16
Distribution of Frequencies of Cartoons in the Sample Dailies

Unit of Analysis Cartoons	*The Hindu*	*The New Indian Express*	*Eenadu*	*Vaartha*	*Total*
Pocket cartoons	1	-	21	33	55
Editorial cartoons	-	1	5	4	10

From the Table 16, a total of 65 cartoons that appeared in the four newspapers during the study period can be divided into Pocket cartoons (55) and Editorial cartoons (10). The highest number of cartoons are from *Vaartha* (37) followed by *Eenadu* (26). The two English dailies *The Hindu* published only one pocket cartoon to the theme Kidnapping. Similarly, *The New Indian Express* published only one Editorial cartoon on 'the State Government views'. The themes 'Naxalites related communication', 'police counter measures' and 'State Government views' received 6 pocket cartoons each in *Vaartha*. The other themes 'police communication' and 'Naxalites deaths in encounters' received 5 and 4 pocket cartoons respectively. Another Telugu daily *Eenadu* gave prominence to 'State Government views' (5) (See Table 17).

Table–17
Frequency of Cartoons by Subject Categories in the Sample Dailies

Theme	*Dailies*								
	The Hindu		*The New Indian Express*		*Eenadu*		*Vaartha*		*Total*
	Pocket Cartoon	*Editorial Cartoon*	*Pocket Cartoon*	*Editorial Cartoon*	*Pocket Cartoon*	*Editorial Cartoon*	*Pocket Cartoon*	*Editorial Cartoon*	
Ambush	-	-	-	-	2	1	3	-	5
Raids	-	-	-	-	2	-	1	-	3
Destruction	-	-	-	-	1	-	1	-	2
Kidnaps	1	-	-	-	-	-	-	-	1
Communication	-	-	-	-	3	2	6	-	11
Encounter deaths (Naxalites)	-	-	-	-	1	1	4	-	6
Encounter deaths (Both)	-	-	-	-	-	-	1	-	1
Police counter measures	-	-	-	-	2	-	6	1	9
Police communication	-	-	-	-	1	1	5	1	8
Central government views	-	-	-	-	2	-	-	-	2

Contd...

Theme	Dailies								
	The Hindu		The New Indian Express		Eenadu		Vaartha		Total
	Pocket Cartoon	Editorial Cartoon	Pocket Cartoon	Editorial Cartoon	Pocket Cartoon	Editorial Cartoon	Pocket Cartoon	Editorial Cartoon	
State government views	-	-	-	1	5	-	6	2	14
People's reaction against to Naxalites	-	-	-	-	1	-	-	-	1
Peace talks	-	-	-	-	1	-	-	-	1
N =	1	-	-	1	25	5	33	4	65

Editorials

Editorials are the opinion pieces expressed by newspapers on current topics. In fact, editorials give an opportunity to newspapers to articulate their opinion and the freedom to debate on public issues. Very often, editorials present an argument or a rational reasoning to educate the public as well as the Government, in deciding the policy matters. Thus, in the present study, the contents of editorials are analyzed to ascertain how the newspapers under study have covered the Naxalite movement issues.

In the total editorials of 74, *Vaartha* leads with 36, followed by *Eenadu* (16), *The New Indian Express* (14) and *The Hindu* (8). Table 18 presents data about the coverage given by the editorials about the different themes under the study.

It can be seen from the Table 18 that of a total of 1723 editorials appeared in the four newspapers during the study period, the highest number of editorials are from *The New Indian Express* (556), followed by *The Hindu* (549), *Eenadu* (327) and *Vaartha* (291).

Further analysis shows that the four newspapers devoted very few editorials to Naxalite issues. *Vaartha* published 36 (14.1%) editorials on the theme, followed by *Eenadu* 16 (5.1%), *The New Indian Express* 14 (2.5%) and *The Hindu* 8 (1.4%) editorials on the theme.

Table-18
Percentage and Distribution of Editorials in the Sample Dailies

Unit of Analysis	Dailies			
	The Hindu	The New Indian Express	Eenadu	Vaartha
Other editorials (fr)	541	542	311	255
Naxalite movement related editorials (fr)	8	14	16	36
%	1.4	2.5	5.1	14.1
N = 1723	549	556	327	291

As regards the 'State Government views', *Vaartha* published 10 editorials, while *Eenadu* devoted 2 editorials to the same theme. The two English dailies completely ignored the theme (See Table 19).

Table-19
Frequency of Editorials by Subject Categories in the Sample Dailies

Theme	Dailies			
	The Hindu	The New Indian Express	Eenadu	Vaartha
Ambush	2	1	4	3
Raids	1	3	1	4
Destruction	1	1	1	2
Attacks and coverts	-	-	-	2
Communication	-	1	5	5
Encounter deaths (Naxalites)	-	-	-	2
Police counter measures	-	-	-	1
Police communication	-	1	-	1
Central government views	3	3	2	-
State government views	-	-	2	10
Other state government views	-	2	-	-
Political parties' views	-	-	-	1
Peace talks	1	2	1	5
N =	8	14	16	36

In relation to the 'Central Government views', *The Hindu* and *The New Indian Express* presented an equal number of editorials (3), while *Eenadu* dedicated 2 editorials and *Vaartha* did not write even a single editorial on the theme. *Vaartha* devoted 5 editorials on peace talks while *Eenadu* wrote one editorial on the theme. Similarly the two Telugu newspapers-*Eenadu* and *Vaartha* devoted 5 editorials each on the theme 'communication'.

Notably, the 'encounter deaths' obtained 2 editorials in *Vaartha,* on the other hand, *Eenadu* and the two English dailies did not spare even a single editorial to the same theme.

The two English dailies-*The Hindu* and *The New Indian Express* spared 2 and 1 editorials respectively to the theme 'Ambush' while the Telugu dailies, *Eenadu* and *Vaartha* wrote 4 to 3 editorials on the theme.

Edit Articles

The edit articles that appeared in the editorial page of the newspapers contain background material to provide a context to the theme and its analysis. They are not only informative but also educate the readers regarding the implications of the Government's stance and that of the Naxalites. Thus, in the present study, the contents of edit articles are analyzed to ascertain how the newspapers have covered the Naxalite issues.

Table–20
Percentage Distribution of Edit Articles in the Sample Dailies

	Dailies			
Unit of Analysis Edit Articles	*The Hindu*	*The New Indian Express*	*Eenadu*	*Vaartha*
Other articles (fr)	532	542	308	272
Naxalite related articles (fr)	-	2	9	20
%	-	0.3	2.9	7.3
N =	532	544	317	292

Table 20 presents data about the coverage given by edit articles about the different themes under the study. It can be seen from the table that of a total of 1685 edit articles appeared in the four newspapers during the study period, the highest number of edit articles are from *The New Indian Express* (544), followed by *The Hindu* (532), *Eenadu* (317) and *Vaartha* (292). Further analysis shows that the four newspapers devoted very few edit articles to cover Naxalite issues. *The Hindu* did not spare any edit article on the Naxalite issue during the study period. The Telugu newspaper *Vaartha*, wrote more number of edit article (20) on Naxalite theme. Another Telugu daily *Eenadu* also wrote 9 edit articles on the same theme, followed by *The New Indian Express* which published only 2 edit articles on the theme. *Vaartha* published 6 edit articles on 'State Government views', while *Eenadu* published only one on the same theme. *Vaartha* gave in its edit articles second place to the category peace talks (5), while *Eenadu* (4) gave first rank to the same theme. (See Table 21)

Table–21
Frequency of Edit Articles by Subject Categories in the Sample Dailies

Theme	*Dailies*			
	The Hindu	*The New Indian Express*	*Eenadu*	*Vaartha*
Ambush	-	-	2	1
Raids	-	-	-	-
Destruction	-	-	1	-
Attacks and coverts	-	-	-	-
Communication	-	-	-	4
Encounter deaths (Naxalites)	-	-	-	1
Police counter measures	-	-	-	-
Police communication	-	-	-	3
Central government views	-	-	1	-
State government views	-	-	1	6
Other state government views	-	1	-	-
Political parties' views	-	-	-	-
Peace talks	-	1	4	5
N =	-	2	9	20

Eenadu published 2 edit articles on the theme 'Ambush', when *Vaartha* published one edit article on the theme. Among the two Telugu dailies, *Eenadu* published only one edit article on the theme 'Destruction'. Interestingly *Vaartha* published 4 and 1 edit articles to the themes 'Naxalites involved communication' and 'Naxalites encounter deaths', but the other three sample dailies did not spare any edit article to the theme. Notably, the theme, 'other State Government views' obtained one edit article in *The New Indian Express,* and the other theme 'Central Government views' obtained one edit article in the Telugu daily *Eenadu.*

Letters-to-the Editor

The non-news unit 'Letters–to-the Editor' is equally important like a news item and an editorial in a newspaper. Quite often, the letters in a newspaper are indicators of public opinion as most of the readers try to express their opinions through 'the letters-to-the editor'. Thus, the present study has made an attempt to analyze the readers' response to various issues and happenings in the column.

Table–22
Percentage Distribution of Letters-to-the Editor in the Sample Dailies

	Dailies			
Unit of Analysis Letters-to-the Editor	*The Hindu*	*The New Indian Express*	*Eenadu*	*Vaartha*
Other (fr)	3358	1318	1220	1260
Naxalite related (fr)	75	15	36	58
%	2.2	1.1	2.9	4.6
N =	3433	1333	1256	1318

As can be seen from Table 22, the highest number of letters appeared in *The Hindu* (3433) followed by *The New Indian Express* (1333), *Vaartha* (1318) and *Eenadu* (1256).

Table 23 presents data about the appearance of letters under the different themes are shown. But, more number of letters appeared on Naxalite issues in *The Hindu* as compared to other dailies, as *The Hindu* published 75 (2.2%) of letters on the Naxalite movement, *Vaartha* devoted 58 (4.6%), followed by *Eenadu* 36 (2.9%) and *The New Indian Express* 15 (1.1.%).

Similarly out of a total of 184 letters, the highest number of letters appeared on the theme 'ambush'. Among the four dailies, while *The Hindu* gave 25 letters, *The New Indian Express* spared only 2 letters, of the two Telugu dailies *Eenadu* published 11 letters, *Vaartha* allocated 3 letters to the same theme.

The theme 'peace talks' received second place in *The Hindu* (28). *Vaartha* published 7 letters and the other Telugu daily *Eenadu* devoted only a single letter to the same theme. *The New Indian Express* published 2 letters on the 'peace talks'.

Vaartha devoted 17 letters on 'the State Government views', followed by *Eenadu* (5), *The Hindu* (4) and *The New Indian Express* (3) letters. Similarly out of a total of 19 letters published by *Eenadu*, 13 letters are on the theme 'Naxalites involved destruction' (See Table 23).

Table–23
Frequency of Letters-to-the Editor by Subject Categories by Themes in the Sample Dailies

Category	*Theme*	*Dailies*				
		The Hindu	*The New Indian Express*	*Eenadu*	*Vaartha*	*Total*
1. Naxalite activities	Ambush	25	2	11	3	41
	Raids	4	4	1	2	11
	Destruction	4	1	13	5	19
	Kidnaps	-	-	-	-	-
	Attacks on informers	-	-	-	-	-
	Attacks on coverts	-	-	-	-	-
	Communication	1	2	1	6	10
2. Encounter deaths	Naxalites	1	-	-	3	4
	Police	-	-	-	-	-
	Both	-	-	-	-	-
3. Police activities	Counter measures	-	1	-	4	5
	Welfare measures	-	-	-	-	-
	Communication	-	-	1	4	5

Contd...

Category	Theme	*Dailies*				
		The Hindu	*The New Indian Express*	*Eenadu*	*Vaartha*	*Total*
4. Agony of sufferers	Naxalite families	-	-	-	1	1
	Police families	-	-	-	-	-
	Targeted families	-	-	-	-	-
	Innocent victims	-	-	-	-	-
5. Government views	Central	7	-	1	-	8
	State	4	3	5	17	29
	Other states	-	-	-	1	1
6. Political parties' views	Congress	-	-	-	-	-
	BJP	-	-	-	-	-
	Communists	-	-	-	-	-
	TDP	-	-	-	2	2
	TRS	-	-	-	1	1
7. Peoples Reaction against	Naxalites	-	-	-	-	-
	Police	-	-	1	-	1
8. Human rights/ courts	Human rights/ courts	-	-	-	1	1
9. Human rights organizations	Human rights organizations	-	-	1	1	2
10. Peace talks	Peace talks	28	2	1	7	38
Total		75	15	36	58	184

4

Naxalite Movement: News Coverage in the Front and Inside Pages

This chapter presents the news coverage given to different themes of Naxalite movement during the sample period of eight years (1999-2006) in the select dailies. The chapter presents data relating to the coverage given under different themes in terms of geographical categories.

Front Page

Invariably, the front page in a newspaper is the most significant news page. The display of important news stories on the front page gives prominence to different newspapers. In this process, the newspapers attempt to capture the attention of the readers in their day-to-day activity. Thus, the display of news stories on the front page has acquired significance for analysis. With this in view, an attempt has been made in the present study to find out the differential coverage given to the themes on the front page by the sample dailies.

Frequency of Coverage

Table 24 indicates the percentage of frequencies of different themes on the front page. As can be seen, the four newspapers, *The Hindu, The New Indian Express, Eenadu* and *Vaartha* gave the first priority to the news related to Naxalite activities. Among the four newspapers, *The Hindu* gave the highest number of news items (42.8% followed by *Eenadu* (41.5%), *The New Indian Express* (39.7%) and *Vaartha* (35.6%).

The Hindu gave more coverage on the front page to the encounter deaths, whereas the other two regional dailies and *The New Indian*

Table-24
Distribution of Frequency and Space by Subject Categories on Front Page in Sample Dailies

Category	*Dailies*							
	The Hindu		*The New Indian Express*		*Eenadu*		*Vaartha*	
	fr	*sp*	*fr*	*sp*	*fr*	*sp*	*fr*	*sp*
Naxalite activities	107	2652.93	112	2614.08	174	7098.3	156	6007.56
Encounter deaths	60	1411.83	57	1083.04	72	2356.56	74	2515.76
Police activities	28	621.18	39	774.48	64	1939.68	72	2038.4
Agony of sufferers	2	44.1	4	99.68	10	172.8	10	385.32
Government views	38	987.84	58	1401.68	73	2386.8	92	2691
Political parties' views	3	57.33	1	40.32	8	326.16	12	426.92
Peoples reaction	-	-	-	-	1	54.54	2	44.2
Human rights/ courts	3	77.49	2	77.84	3	42.66	3	88.4
Human rights organizations	4	108.99	2	75.6	5	162.54	10	253.24
Peace talks	5	175.14	7	238.56	9	463.32	7	308.36
N =	250	6136.83	282	6405.28	419	15003.36	438	14759.16

Express gave priority to government views over encounter deaths. On the other hand the theme 'police activities' received fourth rank consistently in all the four dailies. *Vaartha* (16.4%) and *Eenadu* (15.3%) allocated more percentage than the two English dailies *The New Indian Express* (13.8%) and *The Hindu* (11.2%) (See Table 25).

Table–25
Percentage Distribution of Frequency of News Items by Subject Categories on Front Page in the Sample Dailies

Category	*Dailies*							
	The Hindu		*The New Indian Express*		*Eenadu*		*Vaartha*	
	%	*Rank Order*	*%*	*Rank Order*	*%*	*Rank Order*	*%*	*Rank Order*
Naxalite activities	42.8	1	39.7	1	41.5	1	35.6	1
Encounter deaths	24.0	2	20.2	3	17.2	3	16.9	3
Police activities	11.2	4	13.8	4	15.3	4	16.4	4
Agony of sufferers	0.8	9	1.4	6	2.4	5	2.3	6
Government views	15.2	3	20.6	2	17.4	2	21.0	2
Political parties' views	1.2	8	0.4	8	1.9	7	2.7	5
Peoples reaction	-		-		0.2	10	0.5	9
Human rights/ courts	1.2	7	0.7	7	0.7	9	0.7	8
Human rights organizations	1.6	6	0.7	7	1.2	8	2.3	6
Peace talks	2.0	5	2.5	5	2.1	6	1.6	7
N =	100.0 (250)		100.0 (288)		100.0 (419)		100.0 (438)	

Note: Figures in parentheses are totals.

The theme, 'agony of sufferers' received insignificant coverage in terms of frequency in all the four newspapers. While *The Hindu* gave 0.8 per cent to the theme, *The New Indian Express* allocated slightly more percentage (1.4%) to the same. The two Telugu newspapers–*Eenadu* and *Vaartha* dedicated 2.4 per cent and 2.3 per cent respectively to the theme. Interestingly, *The New Indian Express* and *Vaartha* ranked 'agony of sufferers' theme sixth place, while *Eenadu* and *The Hindu* gave it the fifth and ninth rank respectively.

Space

Table 26 shows the percentage allocation of space to different themes on the front page, like the frequency of news items. The theme Naxalite activities ranked first in all the four newspapers and the space allocation to it is as follows: *Eenadu* (47.3%), *The Hindu* (42.2%), *The New Indian Express* (40.8), *Vaartha* (40.7%) in that order. Interestingly, the three newspapers *The Hindu, The New Indian Express* and *Eenadu* put the peace talks theme in the fifth place while *Vaartha* gave it seventh rank. Similarly, the theme 'Human rights organizations' received eighth rank in the three newspapers and in *The Hindu*, it ranked sixth place in terms of Space. *Eenadu* and *Vaartha* dedicated 0.4 per cent and 0.3 per cent of the space respectively to the category 'people's reaction' on the front page but the other two English dailies did not feature even a single news item on this theme.

Table–26
Percentage Distribution of Space by Subject Categories on Front Page in the Sample Dailies

Category	*Dailies*							
	The Hindu		*The New Indian Express*		*Eenadu*		*Vaartha*	
	sp	*Rank Order*	*sp*	*Rank Order*	*sp*	*Rank Order*	*sp*	*Rank Order*
Naxalite activities	42.2	1	40.8	1	47.3	1	40.7	1
Encounter deaths	23.0	2	16.9	3	15.7	3	17.0	3
Police activities	10.1	4	12.1	4	12.9	4	13.8	4
Agony of sufferers	0.7	9	1.6	6	1.1	7	2.6	6
Government views	16.1	3	21.9	2	15.9	2	18.2	2
Political parties' views	0.9	8	0.6	9	2.2	6	2.9	5

Contd...

Category	Dailies							
	The Hindu		*The New Indian Express*		*Eenadu*		*Vaartha*	
	sp	*Rank Order*	*sp*	*Rank Order*	*sp*	*Rank Order*	*sp*	*Rank Order*
People's reaction	-		-		0.4	9	0.3	10
Human rights/ courts	1.3	7	1.2	7	0.3	10	0.6	9
Human rights organizations	1.8	6	1.2	8	1.1	8	1.7	8
Peace talks	2.9	5	3.7	5	3.1	5	2.1	7
N =	100.0 (6136.83)		100.0 (6405.28)		100.0 (1503.36)		100.0 (14759.16)	

Note: Figures in parentheses are totals.

Inside Pages

Frequency

Table 27 and 28 shows the nature of coverage of themes on the inside pages in terms of frequencies. The category Naxalite activities, ranked first in all the newspapers in terms of frequency. The two other categories-police activities and government views received second and third places across the four dailies. Further these three categories received more than 70 per cent of frequency of news items in all the four dailies. Another category Human rights/courts received more news items in *Eenadu* (8) followed by *The Hindu* (5), *Vaartha* (2), while *The New Indian Express* did not publish not even a single news item in the inside pages. As regards the category of 'encounter deaths' it is in fourth rank in *The New Indian Express* (8.1%) and on the other hand it took fifth place in the three dailies, viz., *The Hindu* (7.5%), *Eenadu* (9.4%) and *Vaartha* (8.7%). Political parties views category got fourth place in three newspapers, viz., *The Hindu, Eenadu* and *Vaartha,* while *The New Indian Express* ranked the theme to fifth place.

Table–27
Distribution of Frequency and Space by Subject Categories on Inside Pages in Sample Dailies

Category	*Dailies*									
	The Hindu		*The New Indian Express*		*Eenadu*		*Vaartha*		*Total*	
	fr	*sp*	*fr*	*sp*	*fr*	*sp*	*fr*	*sp*	*fr*	*sp*
Naxalite activities	203	4855.41	155	2339.68	303	6503.22	318	8385.00	979	22083.31
Encounter deaths	43	575.19	38	469.84	43	685.8	60	1049.36	184	2780.19
Police activities	184	3420.9	141	1996.4	286	4973.4	257	4980.04	868	15370.74
Agony of sufferers	12	403.83	17	378.56	42	1006.02	35	747.76	106	2536.17
Government views	78	2067.03	57	1022.56	142	2771.82	131	2997.8	408	8859.21
Political parties' views	46	945.63	27	378.56	92	1166.94	82	1101.36	247	3592.49
People's reaction	8	124.11	6	126	11	221.4	15	278.2	40	749.71
Human rights/courts	5	133.56	-	-	8	94.5	2	13	15	241.06
Human rights organizations	27	423.36	20	202.72	32	312.12	32	474.76	111	1412.96
Peace talks	4	219.24	7	164.64	16	400.14	13	448.24	40	1232.26
N =	610	13168.26	468	7078.96	975	18135.36	945	20475.52	2998	58858.10

Table-28
Percentage Distribution of Frequency of News Items by Subject Categories in the Inside Pages of the Sample Dailies

Category	*Dailies*							
	The Hindu		*The New Indian Express*		*Eenadu*		*Vaartha*	
	%	*Rank Order*	*%*	*Rank Order*	*%*	*Rank Order*	*%*	*Rank Order*
Naxalite activities	33.3	1	33.1	1	31.1	1	33.6	1
Encounter deaths	7.1	5	8.1	4	4.4	5	6.3	5
Police activities	30.2	2	30.1	2	29.3	2	27.2	2
Agony of sufferers	1.9	7	3.6	7	4.3	6	3.7	6
Government views	12.8	3	12.2	3	14.6	3	13.9	3
Political parties' views	7.5	4	5.8	5	9.4	4	8.7	4
People's reaction	1.3	8	1.3	9	1.1	9	1.6	8
Human rights/ courts	0.8	9	-		0.8	10	0.2	10
Human rights organizations	4.4	6	4.3	6	3.3	7	3.4	7
Peace talks	0.7	10	1.5	8	1.6	8	1.4	9
N =	100 (610)		100 (468)		100 (975)		100 (945)	

Space

Table 29 focuses on the extent of space allocated to different themes in the inside pages. The themes, 'Naxalite activities', 'police activities' and 'Government views' received first three places respectively in all the four newspapers with different proportions of space.

Table–29
Percentage Distribution of Space by Subject Categories on Inside Pages in the Sample Dailies

Category	*Dailies*							
	The Hindu		*The New Indian Express*		*Eenadu*		*Vaartha*	
	sp	*Rank Order*	*sp*	*Rank Order*	*sp*	*Rank Order*	*sp*	*Rank Order*
Naxalite activities	36.9	1	33.0	1	35.9	1	41.0	1
Encounter deaths	4.4	5	6.6	4	3.8	6	5.1	5
Police activities	26.0	2	28.2	2	27.4	2	24.3	2
Agony of sufferers	3.1	7	5.3	5	5.6	5	3.7	6
Government views	15.7	3	14.4	3	15.3	3	14.6	3
Political parties' views	7.2	4	5.3	5	6.4	4	5.4	4
People's reaction	0.9	10	1.8	8	1.2	9	1.4	9
Human rights/ courts	1.0	9	-		0.5	10	0.1	10
Human rights organizations	3.2	6	2.9	6	1.7	8	2.3	7
Peace talks	1.6	8	2.3	7	2.2	7	2.2	8
N =	(13168.26)		(7078.96)		(18135.36)		(20475.52)	

The two Telugu newspapers *Eenadu* and *Vaartha* and English daily *The Hindu* assigned fourth rank to the theme 'political parties views' whereas the English daily *The New Indian Express* assigned fifth rank to the theme. While the category, 'encounter deaths' figured in fourth place for *The New Indian Express,* it is in fifth rank in *The Hindu* and *Vaartha* and in *Eenadu* it ranked sixth place. Coming to the 'Human Rights/courts' theme in terms of space, its coverage of the theme is highly dismal as it can be seen that, *Eenadu* and *Vaartha* reported only 0.5 per cent and 0.1 per cent respectively. The other English daily *The Hindu* did give slightly more coverage (1.0%) to the theme and *The New Indian Express* did not feature it at all.

Geographical Category

The present study analyzed the news coverage, in relation to the geographical area, such as local, state and national. The purpose of this analysis is to know the significance assigned by the sample dailies to these ten themes by region.

Local

Table 30 reveals the trend of the news coverage, on local issues in terms of frequency and space. As it can be seen from Table 30, *The New Indian Express* topped by publishing 110 local news items, followed by *Eenadu* (98), *Vaartha* (72) and *The Hindu* (58).

Table–30
Distribution of Frequency of Local News Items and Space by Subject Categories

Category	*Dailies*							
	The Hindu		*The New Indian Express*		*Eenadu*		*Vaartha*	
	fr	*Space*	*fr*	*Space*	*fr*	*Space*	*fr*	*Space*
Naxalite activities	24	648.9	41	778.96	45	1385.64	27	698.88
Encounter deaths	1	7.56	3	36.96	5	65.34	4	143
Police activities	24	474.39	44	657.44	30	451.44	28	577.2
Agony of sufferers	2	88.83	8	177.52	9	196.02	9	225.68
Government views	2	74.34	4	113.68	2	41.04	-	-
Political parties' views	1	9.45	3	36.4	3	44.28	3	33.8
People's reaction	1	26.46	1	20.72	2	29.16	-	-

Contd...

Category	Dailies							
	The Hindu		The New Indian Express		Eenadu		Vaartha	
	fr	Space	fr	Space	fr	Space	fr	Space
Human rights/ courts	-	-	-	-	-	-	-	-
Human rights organizations	2	19.53	5	41.44	1	11.88	1	6.24
Peace talks	1	63	1	26.88	1	82.08	-	-
N =	58	1412.46	110	1890	98	2306.88	72	1684.8

The Hindu and *Eenadu* gave top priority to the theme 'Naxalite activities' in the coverage of local news on the other hand *The New Indian Express* and *Vaartha* gave top priority to police activities and *The Hindu* gave some importance to the peace talks, in the local news, which is least covered by the other 3 dailies (Table 31). Government views are least represented in the local news by *Eenadu* and *Vaartha* (Table 32).

Table-31
Percentage Distribution of Frequency of Local News Items by Subject Categories

Category	Dailies							
	The Hindu		The New Indian Express		Eenadu		Vaartha	
	%	Rank Order	%	Rank Order	%	Rank Order	%	Rank Order
Naxalite activities	41.4	1	37.3	2	45.9	1	37.5	2
Encounter deaths	1.7	3	2.7	6	5.1	4	5.5	4
Police activities	41.4	1	40.0	1	30.6	2	38.9	1
Agony of sufferers	3.4	2	7.3	3	9.2	3	12.5	3
Government views	3.4	2	3.6	5	2.0	6	-	

Contd...

Category	Dailies							
	The Hindu		The New Indian Express		Eenadu		Vaartha	
	%	Rank Order	%	Rank Order	%	Rank Order	%	Rank Order
Political parties' views	1.7	3	2.7	6	3.1	5	4.2	5
People's reaction	1.7	3	0.9	7	2.0	6	-	
Human rights/ courts	-		-		-		-	
Human rights organizations	3.4	2	4.6	4	1.0	7	1.4	6
Peace talks	1.7	3	0.9	7	1.0	7	-	
N =	(58)		(110)		(98)		(72)	

Note: Figures in parentheses are totals.

Table–32
Percentage Distribution of Space of Local News Items by Subject Categories

Category	Dailies							
	The Hindu		The New Indian Express		Eenadu		Vaartha	
	sp	Rank Order	sp	Rank Order	sp	Rank Order	sp	Rank Order
Naxalite activities	45.9	1	41.2	1	60.1	1	41.5	1
Encounter deaths	0.5	9	1.9	6	2.8	5	8.5	4
Police activities	33.6	2	34.8	2	19.6	2	34.2	2
Agony of sufferers	6.3	3	9.4	3	8.5	3	13.4	3
Government views	5.3	4	6.0	4	1.8	7	-	
Political parties' views	0.7	8	1.9	7	1.9	6	2.0	5

Contd...

Category	Dailies							
	The Hindu		*The New Indian Express*		*Eenadu*		*Vaartha*	
	sp	*Rank Order*	*sp*	*Rank Order*	*sp*	*Rank Order*	*sp*	*Rank Order*
People's reaction	1.9	6	1.1	9	1.2	8	-	
Human rights/ courts	-		-		-		-	
Human rights organizations	1.4	7	2.2	5	0.5	9	0.4	6
Peace talks	4.4	5	1.4	8	3.6	4	-	
N =	100.0 (1412.46)		100.0 (1890.00)		100.0 (2306.88)		100.0 (1684.80)	

Note: Figures in parentheses are totals.

Table 33 provides data about the coverage of local issues on the front page. *Eenadu* published 28 local news items out of a total of 419 news items on the front page. *The New Indian Express* published 25 local news items out of a total 282 news items on the front page. On the other hand, *The Hindu* and *Vaartha* reported only 10 and 9 news items respectively on local issues. A majority of the news items that were reported in the local issues of all the four newspapers were only on Naxalite activities and police activities.

Table–33
Percentage Distribution of Frequency of News Items by Subject Categories to Local News in Front Page

Category	Dailies							
	The Hindu		*The New Indian Express*		*Eenadu*		*Vaartha*	
	%	*Rank Order*	*%*	*Rank Order*	*%*	*Rank Order*	*%*	*Rank Order*
Naxalite activities	90.0	1	68.0	1	3.6	1	66.7	1
Encounter deaths	-		8.0	3	3.6	-	22.2	2

Contd...

Category	*Dailies*							
	The Hindu		*The New Indian Express*		*Eenadu*		*Vaartha*	
	%	*Rank Order*	%	*Rank Order*	%	*Rank Order*	%	*Rank Order*
Police activities	10.0	2	16.0	2	28.6	2	11.1	3
Agony of sufferers	-		4.0		3.6		-	
Government views	-		-		3.6		-	
Political parties' views	-		-		-		-	
People's reaction	-		-		3.6		-	
Human rights/ courts	-		-		-		-	
Human rights organizations	-		-		-		-	
Peace talks	-		4.0	-	3.6		-	
N =	100.0 (10)		100.0 (25)		100.0 (28)		100.0 (9)	

The analysis of the coverage of local news in the inside pages of the sample dailies revealed interesting findings (Table 34).

Table–34
Percentage Distribution of Frequency of News Items by Subject Categories to Local News in Inside Pages

Category	*Dailies*							
	The Hindu		*The New Indian Express*		*Eenadu*		*Vaartha*	
	fr	*Rank Order*	*fr*	*Rank Order*	*fr*	*Rank Order*	*fr*	*Rank Order*
Naxalite activities	31.2	2	28.2	2	42.9	1	33.3	2
Encounter deaths	2.1		1.2		5.7	4	3.2	5

Contd...

Category	*Dailies*							
	The Hindu		*The New Indian Express*		*Eenadu*		*Vaartha*	
	fr	*Rank Order*	*fr*	*Rank Order*	*fr*	*Rank Order*	*fr*	*Rank Order*
Police activities	47.9	1	47.1	1	31.4	2	42.8	1
Agony of sufferers	4.2		8.2	3	11.4	3	14.3	3
Government views	4.2		4.7	5	1.4		-	
Political parties' views	2.1		3.5	6	4.3	5	4.8	4
People's reaction	2.1		1.2		1.4		-	
Human rights/ courts	-		-		-		-	
Human rights organizations	4.2		5.9	4	1.4		1.6	
Peace talks	2.1		-		-		-	
N =	100.0 (48)		100.0 (85)		100.0 (70)		100.0 (63)	

The two English dailies *The Hindu* and *The New Indian Express*, the Telugu daily *Vaartha* gave more coverage to 'police activities' in the local news as compared to *Eenadu*. However, *Eenadu* gave more news items and extent of space to Naxalite activities. In terms of frequency, the theme 'Agony of sufferers' received the highest percentage in *Vaartha* (14.3%) followed by *Eenadu* (11.4%). *The New Indian Express* (8.2%) and *The Hindu* (4.2%) while *The New Indian Express* gave more priority to 'The Human rights organizations' than other three dailies.

State News

Tables 35, 36 and 37 provide data about the coverage of state issues.

Table–35
Distribution of Frequencies of State News Items and Space by Subject Categories

Category	*Dailies*							
	The Hindu		*The New Indian Express*		*Eenadu*		*Vaartha*	
	fr	*sp*	*fr*	*sp*	*fr*	*sp*	*fr*	*sp*
Naxalite activities	268	6465.69	203	3837.12	388	11411.28	409	12873.12
Encounter deaths	99	1947.96	87	1481.76	104	2942.46	123	3369.60
Police activities	181	3410.19	126	2025.52	313	6388.2	288	6248.84
Agony of sufferers	12	359.1	13	300.72	40	937.44	36	907.40
Government views	103	2697.66	90	1964.48	177	4456.62	179	4715.36
Political parties' views	45	958.86	24	371.28	88	1249.09	79	1233.96
People's reaction	7	97.65	5	105.28	10	246.78	17	322.40
Human rights/ courts	8	211.05	2	77.84	11	137.16	5	101.40
Human rights organizations	29	512.82	17	236.88	34	451.98	39	707.20
Peace talks	8	331.38	13	376.32	24	781.38	19	748.28
N =	760	16992.36	580	10777.2	1189	29002.32	1194	31227.56

In reporting state news, all the four newspapers allocated the highest percentage of space to the news items related to Naxalite activities (first rank) followed by the themes, 'Police activities' (second rank), 'Government views' (third rank), 'Encounter deaths' (fourth rank) and Political Parties' views (fifth rank). *The New Indian Express* provided more space (3.5%) to theme 'peace talks' among the four dailies (Table 37).

Table-36
Percentage Distribution of Frequencies of News Items to State News by Subject Categories

Category	*Dailies*							
	The Hindu		*The New Indian Express*		*Eenadu*		*Vaartha*	
	%	*Rank Order*	%	*Rank Order*	%	*Rank Order*	%	*Rank Order*
Naxalite activities	35.3	1	35.0	1	32.6	1	34.2	1
Encounter deaths	13.0	4	15.0	4	8.7	4	10.3	4
Police activities	23.8	2	21.7	2	26.3	2	24.1	2
Agony of sufferers	1.6	7	2.2	7	3.3	6	3.0	7
Government views	13.6	3	15.5	3	14.9	3	15.0	3
Political parties' views	5.9	5	4.1	5	7.4	5	6.6	5
People's reaction	0.9	9	0.9	8	0.8	10	1.4	9
Human rights/ courts	1.0	8	0.3	9	0.9	7	0.4	10
Human rights organizations	3.8	6	2.9	6	2.8	9	3.3	6
Peace talks	1.0	8	2.2	7	2.0	8	1.6	8
N =	100.0 (760)		100.0 (580)		100.0 (1189)		100.0 (1194)	

Table 38 provides data about the coverage of state issues on the front page. In reporting state news, all the four newspapers allocated the highest percentage of news items on 'Naxalite activities'. Significantly, *Eenadu* published 39.5 per cent news items on this theme, while *Vaartha* gave 34.7 per cent of coverage to the same theme. The two English dailies, *The Hindu* and *The New Indian Express* gave prominence to the theme 'Naxalite activities' by assigning

Table–37
Percentage Distribution of Space of News Items to State News by Subject Categories

Category	*Dailies*							
	The Hindu		*The New Indian Express*		*Eenadu*		*Vaartha*	
	sp	*Rank Order*	*sp*	*Rank Order*	*sp*	*Rank Order*	*sp*	*Rank Order*
Naxalite activities	38.1	1	35.6	1	39.3	1	41.2	1
Encounter deaths	11.5	4	13.8	4	10.1	4	10.8	4
Police activities	20.1	2	18.8	2	22.0	2	20.0	2
Agony of sufferers	2.1	7	2.8	7	3.2	6	2.9	6
Government views	15.9	3	18.2	3	15.4	3	15.1	3
Political parties' views	5.6	5	3.5	6	4.3	5	4.0	5
People's reaction	0.6	10	0.9	9	0.9	9	1.0	9
Human rights/ courts	1.2	9	0.7	10	0.5	8	0.3	10
Human rights organizations	3.0	6	2.2	8	1.6	10	2.3	8
Peace talks	1.9	8	3.5	5	2.7	7	2.4	7
N =	100.0 (16992.36)		100.0 (10777.2)		100.0 (29002.32)		100.0 (31227.56)	

Note: Figures in parentheses are totals.

38.2 per cent and 35.4 per cent respectively on the front page. But, the three dailies, *The Hindu, The New Indian Express* and *Eenadu* gave second place to 'Encounter deaths' while *Vaartha* placed this theme in the third rank.

Table-38
Percentage Distribution of Frequency of News Items by Subject Categories to State News in Front Page

Category	*Dailies*							
	The Hindu		*The New Indian Express*		*Eenadu*		*Vaartha*	
	fr	*Rank Order*	*fr*	*Rank Order*	*fr*	*Rank Order*	*fr*	*Rank Order*
Naxalite activities	38.2	1	35.4	1	39.5	1	34.7	1
Encounter deaths	26.6	2	22.7	2	19.1	2	18.1	3
Police activities	12.0	4	14.0	4	15.5	4	17.8	4
Agony of sufferers	0.9		1.3		2.5	5	2.6	
Government views	16.0	3	21.8	3	17.4	3	18.9	2
Political parties' views	0.9		0.4		1.6		2.3	
People's reaction	-		-		-		0.5	
Human rights/ courts	1.3		0.9		0.8		0.7	
Human rights organizations	1.8		0.9		1.4		2.6	
Peace talks	2.2		2.6		2.2		1.8	
N =	100.0 (225)		100.0 (229)		100.0 (362)		100.0 (392)	

Note: Figures in parentheses are totals.

On the other hand, the category 'Government views' figured in second place in *Vaartha*, and third place in *The Hindu*, *The New Indian Express* and *Eenadu*. The category 'police activities' obtained rank of four, in all the four newspapers but with different proportions of frequencies. Coming to the coverage of people's reactions it is highly dismal in *Vaartha* (0.5%) and the other three news dailies did not feature even a single news item under this category on the front page.

Table 39 provides the data about coverage given to the state news on the inside pages. It can be seen from Table 39, that the four newspapers differed in their priorities, in terms of frequency to different themes. Considering the frequency of news items, the three newspapers, viz., *The Hindu, The New Indian Express*, and *Vaartha* gave first place to 'Naxalite activities' theme. But *Eenadu* gave first place to the theme 'police activities', while the other three newspapers gave second place to this theme. The category 'Government views' ranked third place in all the four newspapers. As regards the category 'Encounter deaths' it is fourth rank in *The New Indian Express* and fifth rank in the other three dailies. Similarly, the category 'political parties views' received fourth rank in the two Telugu dailies and in *The Hindu*, while it received fifth rank in *The New Indian Express*.

Figure–8
Distribution of News Items by Regional Focus

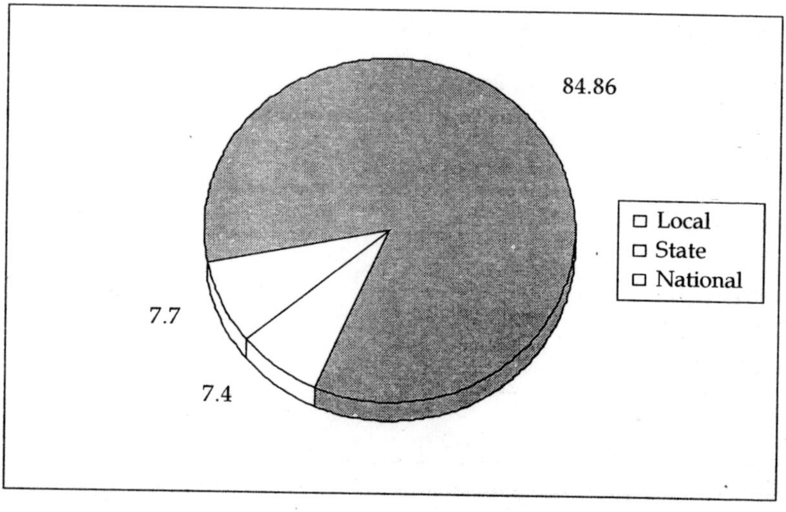

National News

Table 40 indicates the nature of coverage given to national news. As can be seen from Table 40, *Vaartha* spared more news items (117), as national issues followed by *Eenadu* (107), *The New Indian Express* (60) and *The Hindu* (42).

Table–39
Percentage Distribution of Frequency of News Items by Subject Categories to State News in Inside Pages

Category	*Dailies*							
	The Hindu		*The New Indian Express*		*Eenadu*		*Vaartha*	
	fr	*Rank Order*	*fr*	*Rank Order*	*fr*	*Rank Order*	*fr*	*Rank Order*
Naxalite activities	34.0	1	34.8	1	29.6	2	34.0	1
Encounter deaths	7.3	5	9.9	4	4.2	5	6.5	5
Police activities	28.8	2	26.8	2	31.1	1	27.2	2
Agony of sufferers	1.9		2.8		3.7		3.2	
Government views	12.5	3	11.4	3	13.8	3	13.1	3
Political parties' views	8.0	4	6.6	5	9.9	4	8.7	4
People's reaction	1.3		1.4		1.2		1.9	
Human rights/ courts	0.9		-		1.0		0.2	
Human rights organizations	4.7		4.3		3.5		3.6	
Peace talks	0.6		2.0		2.0		1.5	
N =	100.0 (535)		100.0 (351)		100.0 (827)		100.0 (802)	

Note: Figures in parentheses are totals.

Two themes–Naxalite activities, and government views figured prominently under the National news in all the four newspapers. The theme 'Naxalite activities' received greater coverage at National level news, followed by news relating to 'Government views' and 'police activities' in that order.

Table–40
Distribution of National News Items by Frequency and Space by Subject Categories

Category	*Dailies*							
	The Hindu		*The New Indian Express*		*Eenadu*		*Vaartha*	
	fr	*sp*	*fr*	*sp*	*fr*	*sp*	*fr*	*sp*
Naxalite activities	18	393.75	23	337.68	44	804.6	38	820.56
Encounter deaths	3	31.5	5	34.16	6	34.56	7	52.52
Police activities	7	157.5	10	87.92	7	73.44	13	192.4
Agony of sufferers	-	-	-	-	3	45.36	-	-
Government views	11	282.87	21	346.08	36	660.96	44	973.44
Political parties' views	3	34.65	1	11.2	9	199.8	12	260.52
People's reaction	-	-	-	-	-	-	-	-
Human rights/ courts	-	-	-	-	-	-	-	-
Human rights organizations	-	-	-	-	2	10.8	2	14.56
Peace talks	-	-	-	-	-	-	1	8.32
N =	42	900.27	60	817.04	107	1829.52	117	2322.32

As can be seen from Table 41, the coverage of National news in all the four newspapers differed remarkably in terms of frequency given to the themes. *The Hindu, The New Indian Express* and *Eenadu* gave 42.9 per cent, 38.3 per cent and 41.2 per cent of frequencies respectively to the theme Naxalite activities while in *Vaartha* it is second rank with 32.5 per cent. Similarly, the two English dailies *The Hindu* (7.1%) and *The New Indian Express* (8.3%) gave fourth place to the theme 'Encounter deaths'. But, in Telugu dailies *Eenadu* (5.6%) and *Vaartha* (6.0%), gave fifth rank to this theme.

On the other hand, 'the Government views' category took second place in the three dailies, viz., *The Hindu* (26.2%), *The New Indian Express* (35%) and *Eenadu* (33.7%) while *Vaartha* (37.6%) ranked the theme to the first place. The theme 'political parties' views' received lowest coverage by *The New Indian Express* (1.7%), while the Telugu daily *Vaartha* (10.2%) gave more coverage than other two dailies, viz., *The Hindu* (7.1%) and *Eenadu* (8.4%).

Table–41
Percentage Distribution of Frequencies of News Items to National News by Subject Categories

Category	*Dailies*							
	The Hindu		*The New Indian Express*		*Eenadu*		*Vaartha*	
	%	*Rank Order*	*%*	*Rank Order*	*%*	*Rank Order*	*%*	*Rank Order*
Naxalite activities	42.9	1	38.3	1	41.1	1	32.5	2
Encounter deaths	7.1	4	8.3	4	5.6	5	6.0	5
Police activities	16.7	3	16.7	3	6.5	4	11.1	3
Agony of sufferers	-		-		2.8	6		
Government views	26.2	2	35.0	2	33.7	2	37.6	1
Political parties' views	7.1	4	1.7	5	8.4	3	10.2	4
People's reaction	-		-		-			
Human rights/ courts	-		-		-			
Human rights organizations	-		-		1.9	7	1.7	6
Peace talks	-		-		-		0.9	7
N =	100.0 (42)		100.0 (60)		100.0 (107)		100.0 (117)	

Note: Figures in parentheses are totals.

Table–42
Percentage Distribution of Space of News Items to National News by Subject Categories

Category	*Dailies*							
	The Hindu		*The New Indian Express*		*Eenadu*		*Vaartha*	
	Space	*Rank Order*	*Space*	*Rank Order*	*Space*	*Rank Order*	*Space*	*Rank Order*
Naxalite activities	43.7	1	41.3	2	44.0	1	35.3	2
Encounter deaths	3.5	5	4.2	4	1.9	6	2.3	5
Police activities	17.5	3	10.8	3	4.0	4	8.3	4
Agony of sufferers	-		-		2.5	5	-	
Government views	31.4	2	42.3	1	36.1	2	41.9	1
Political parties' views	3.9	4	1.4	5	10.9	3	11.2	3
People's reaction	-		-		-		-	
Human rights/ courts	-		-		-		-	
Human rights organizations	-		-		0.6	7	0.6	6
Peace talks	-		-		-		0.4	7
N =	100.0 (900.27)		100.0 (817.04)		100.0 (1829.52)		100.0 (2322.32)	

Note: Figures in parentheses are totals.

Table 43 provides data about the distribution of frequency of National news on the front page in the sample dailies. As can be seen from Table 43, *Vaartha* spared more news items (39), followed by *Eenadu* (29), *The New Indian Express* (28) and *The Hindu* (15). The two themes 'Naxalites activities' and 'Government views' prominently figured under the National news in the four newspapers. 'The Naxalite activities' received 12 news items in *The Hindu*, 14 news items in *The New Indian Express*, 16 news items in *Eenadu* and 14 news items in *Vaartha*. The other theme 'Government views' received more news items in *Vaartha* (20), followed by *Eenadu* (9). *The New Indian Express* (8) and *The Hindu* (2).

Table–43
Distribution of Frequency of News Items by Subject Categories to National News in the Front Page

Category	*Dailies*							
	The Hindu		*The New Indian Express*		*Eenadu*		*Vaartha*	
	fr	*Rank Order*	*fr*	*Rank Order*	*fr*	*Rank Order*	*fr*	*Rank Order*
Naxalite activities	12	1	14	1	16	1	14	2
Encounter deaths	-		3		2		1	
Police activities	-		3		-		1	
Agony of sufferers	-		-		-		-	
Government views	2	2	8	2	9	2	20	1
Political parties' views	1	3	-		2		3	3
People's reaction	-		-		-		-	
Human rights/ courts	-		-		-		-	
Human rights organizations	-		-		-		-	
Peace talks	-		-		-		-	
N =	15		28		29		39	

Table 44 indicates the nature of coverage given to National news in inside pages by the sample dailies. As can be seen from Table 44, the two Telugu dailies *Eenadu* and *Vaartha* spared 78 news items each followed by English dailies, *The New Indian Express* (32) and *The Hindu* (27). The Telugu news daily *Vaartha* gave equal priority to the themes 'Naxalite activities' (30.7%) and 'Government views' (30.7%). The theme received first rank in *Eenadu,* second rank in *The New Indian Express* and third rank in *The Hindu.*

Table–44

Percentage Distribution of Frequency of News Items by Subject Categories to National News in Inside Pages

Category	*Dailies*							
	The Hindu		*The New Indian Express*		*Eenadu*		*Vaartha*	
	fr	*Rank Order*	*fr*	*Rank Order*	*fr*	*Rank Order*	*fr*	*Rank Order*
Naxalite activities	22.2	3	28.1	2	35.9	1	30.7	1
Encounter deaths	11.1	4	6.3		5.1	4	7.6	4
Police activities	26.0	2	21.9	3	9.0	3	15.3	2
Agony of sufferers	-		-		3.8		-	
Government views	33.3	1	40.6	1	34.6	2	30.7	1
Political parties' views	7.4		3.1		9.0	3	11.3	3
People's reaction	-		-		-		-	
Human rights/ courts	-		-					
Human rights organizations	-		-		2.6		2.5	
Peace talks	-		-		-		1.2	
N =	100.0 (27)		100.0 (32)		100.0 (78)		100.0 (78)	

In *The Hindu,* 'Government views' (33.3%) and 'police activities' (26.0%) issues received more number of news items, while in *The New Indian Express,* Government views (40.6% and Naxalite activities (28.1%) received greater more coverage. But the two Telugu daily

Table–45

Number of Violent Deaths Reported in Sample Dailies

Years		*The Hindu*						*The New Indian Express*						*Eenadu*						*Vaartha*					
	PAGE	*Naxalites*	*Police*	*Politicians*	*Informers*	*Coverts*	*Civilians*	*Naxalites*	*Police*	*Politicians*	*Informers*	*Coverts*	*Civilians*	*Naxalites*	*Police*	*Politicians*	*Informers*	*Coverts*	*Civilians*	*Naxalites*	*Police*	*Politicians*	*Informers*	*Coverts*	*Civilians*
1999	F	14	9	2	-	-	9	31	13	4	-	-	8	20	9	4	-	-	8	25	9	5	-	-	8
	I	10	1	-	2	-	3	1	1	-	-	-	12	6	2	2	-	-	8	5	2	1	-	-	3
2000	F	49	34	1	-	-	1	49	38	1	-	-	-	66	36	1	-	-	1	59	36	1	-	-	1
	I	19	1	-	2	-	-	29	-	1	-	-	-	25	1	1	-	-	1	15	-	1	2	-	-
2001	F	32	23	1	7	-	3	44	29	3	4	-	5	72	26	5	-	13	23	40	30	1	3	16	17
	I	32	1	3	5	-	1	8	2	2	8	3	1	2	2	1	2	1	1	22	-	1	-	-	-
2002	F	47	8	2	-	-	1	33	18	2	-	-	27	36	22	3	1	-	21	29	14	2	-	-	-
	I	2	1	1	2	-	-	15	-	-	-	-	-	6	3	1	1	-	6	8	4	2	1	-	6
2003	F	11	3	1	-	5	-	11	5	1	3	3	-	39	3	7	2	3	5	35	3	1	-	3	6
	I	19	1	4	1	-	2	21	-	1	2	-	-	3	5	4	2	-	3	8	2	5	-	-	2
2004	F	5	29	3	-	-	-	3	28	1	-	-	-	9	31	2	-	-	1	11	31	3	-	-	3
	I	4	-	-	1	1	1	4	-	-	-	-	-	3	2	1	1	-	-	-	-	-	-	-	-

Contd...

Years		The Hindu						The New Indian Express						Eenadu						Vaartha					
	PAGE	Naxalites	Police	Politicians	Informers	Coverts	Civilians	Naxalites	Police	Politicians	Informers	Coverts	Civilians	Naxalites	Police	Politicians	Informers	Coverts	Civilians	Naxalites	Police	Politicians	Informers	Coverts	Civilians
2005	F	50	11	4	2	-	12	48	15	11	-	-	14	39	31	7	1	-	16	48	18	5	-	-	11
	I	19	1	-	5	1	-	10	8	-	3	-	-	26	4	5	7	1	16	16	2	6	3	2	9
2006	F	60	17	1	-	-	27	43	25	-	-	-	58	51	11	1	-	-	61	57	13	1	-	-	69
	I	2	1	-	1	-	25	19	9	1	-	-	-	25	25	-	1	-	1	27	23	-	-	-	12
TOTAL		375	141	23	28	7	85	369	191	28	20	6	125	428	213	45	18	18	172	405	187	35	9	21	147
Grand Total		659						739						894						804					

F = Front Page I = Inside page

Vaartha put equal focus on two themes, viz., 'Government views' and 'Naxalite activities'. Another theme, 'police activities' received a consensus rank order of two in *The Hindu* and *Vaartha* and a consensus rank order of three in *The New Indian Express* and *Eenadu*. The 'Encounter deaths' issue on the other hand received fourth place in all the four sample dailies.

Most distinctly, the themes 'people's reactions' and 'Human rights/courts' not received a single news item in all the four dailies. But, the two Telugu dailies *Eenadu* and *Vaartha* covered 2 news items each on Human rights organizations.

Number of Deaths

Table 45 shows the details of deaths of Naxalites and police personnel during the study period that were reported in the front page and inside pages. Across the four dailies, *The New Indian Express* and *Vaartha* reported more deaths of Naxalites on the front page in 1999 as compared to *The Hindu* and *Eenadu*. In 2000, the two Telugu dailies reported more deaths of Naxalites on the front-page as compared to the two English dailies. However in 2006, *The Hindu* reported more deaths of Naxalites on the front page as compared to other three dailies.

5

Naxalite Movement: News Coverage of Specific Themes

The present chapter discusses 10 categories with 30 sub-themes related to Naxalite movement. The coverage of these issues in the sample dailies are discussed in terms of frequency of news items and the extent of space given to these sub-themes on the front page as well as inside pages. Further, the direction of treatment given by the sample dailies to the news items while giving coverage to these issues is also analyzed.

Naxalite Activities

The theme 'Naxalite activities' figured 1528 news items in the four news dailies during the study period. The highest number of news items on this theme figured in *Eenadu* (477), followed by *Vaartha* (474), *The Hindu* (310) and *The New Indian Express* (267) (See Table 47). The subject category Naxalite activities divided into 7 sub-themes, viz., ambush (130), raids (327), destruction (258), kidnaps (33), attacks on informers (65), attacks on coverts (28) and communication (687) figured news items in the four newspapers. The theme, Naxalites Communication dominated across all the four dailies both in terms of frequency of news items and extent of space. *Vaartha* allocated the highest percentage (52.7%) of news items to the theme, while *Eenadu* allocated (46.5%) followed by *The Hindu* 37.8 per cent and *The New Indian Express* 36.7 per cent. It is followed by news relating to raids and destruction caused by Naxalite activities, which are given second and third priorities in *The New Indian Express, Eenadu* and *Vaartha* respectively, while in *The Hindu,* the theme destruction received second rank and raids received third rank. The theme, ambush received fourth rank in all four newspapers (Table 47).

Table–46
Distribution of Frequency of News Items by Subject Categories in the Sample Dailies

Category	Theme	*The Hindu*		*The New Indian Express*		*Eenadu*		*Vaartha*	
		Front Page	*Inside Pages*	*Front Page*	*Inside Pages*	*Front Page*	*Inside Pages*	*Front Page*	*Inside Pages*
1. Naxalite activities	Ambush	24	8	25	4	27	14	19	9
	Raids	32	32	34	27	51	56	44	51
	Destruction	15	53	18	38	22	48	22	42
	Kidnaps	4	3	5	3	3	4	2	9
	Attacks on informers	5	14	2	11	6	15	1	11
	Attacks on coverts	1	2	1	1	7	2	10	4
	Communi-cation	26	91	27	71	58	164	58	192
2. Encounter deaths	Naxalites	54	43	50	36	69	42	66	55
	Police	-	-	-	-	-	-	-	-
	Both	6	-	7	2	3	1	8	5
3. Police activities	Counter measures	6	27	10	21	13	29	15	40
	Welfare measures	-	7	1	6	1	14	1	7
	Communi-cation	22	150	28	114	50	243	56	210
4. Agony of sufferers	Naxalite families	1	3	-	2	2	9	2	13
	Police families	1	6	3	5	3	18	4	14
	Targeted families	-	2	1	8	1	8	1	3
	Innocent victims	-	1	-	2	4	7	3	5
5. Govern-ment views	Central	3	12	9	13	14	29	23	29
	State	34	62	48	40	58	107	67	98
	Other states	1	4	1	4	1	6	2	4

Contd...

Category	Theme	The Hindu Front Page	The Hindu Inside Pages	The New Indian Express Front Page	The New Indian Express Inside Pages	Eenadu Front Page	Eenadu Inside Pages	Vaartha Front Page	Vaartha Inside Pages
6. Political parties' views	Congress	1	16	-	8	1	34	5	26
	BJP	1	7	1	3	2	19	2	16
	Communists	-	10	-	5	-	16	-	14
	TDP	-	13	-	7	4	19	2	17
	TRS	1	-	-	4	1	4	3	9
7. People's reaction against	Naxalites	-	6	-	5	-	9	2	6
	Police	-	2	-	1	1	2	-	9
8. Human rights/ courts	Human rights/ courts	3	5	2	-	3	8	3	2
9. Human rights organi-zations	Human rights organi-zations	4	27	2	20	5	32	10	32
10. Peace talks	Peace talks	5	4	7	7	9	16	7	13
Total		250	610	282	468	419	975	438	945

Table–47
Percentage Distribution of Frequencies of News Items to Naxalites Involved Themes

Naxalite Involved Themes	The Hindu fr	The Hindu Rank Order	The New Indian Express fr	The New Indian Express Rank Order	Eenadu fr	Eenadu Rank Order	Vaartha fr	Vaartha Rank Order
Ambush	32 (10.3)	4	29 (10.9)	4	41 (8.6)	4	28 (5.9)	4
Raids	64 (20.7)	3	61 (22.9)	2	107 (22.4)	2	95 (20.0)	2

Contd...

Naxalite Involved Themes	Dailies							
	The Hindu		*The New Indian Express*		*Eenadu*		*Vaartha*	
	fr	*Rank Order*	*fr*	*Rank Order*	*fr*	*Rank Order*	*fr*	*Rank Order*
Destruction	68 (21.9)	2	56 (20.9)	3	70 (14.7)	3	64 (13.5)	3
Kidnaps	7 (2.3)	6	8 (3.0)	6	7 (1.5)	7	11 (2.3)	7
Attacks on informers	19 (6.1)	5	13 (4.9)	5	21 (4.4)	5	12 (2.5)	6
Attacks on coverts	3 (0.9)	7	2 (0.7)	7	9 (1.9)	6	14 (2.9)	5
Communication	117 (37.8)	1	98 (36.7)	1	222 (46.5)	1	250 (52.7)	1
N =	310 (100.00)		267 (100.00)		477 (100.00)		474 (100.00)	

Figures in parentheses indicate percentages to total.

Figure-9
Percentage Distribution of Frequencies of News Items Related to Naxalites Themes

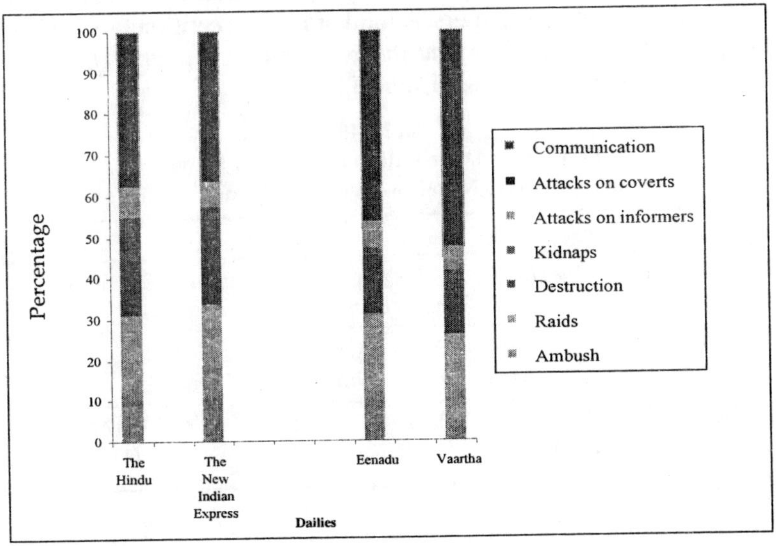

The Hindu and *The New Indian Express* gave seventh rank to 'attacks on coverts', *Eenadu* and *Vaartha* gave the sub-theme 'kidnaps' the seventh rank.

Further analysis on the correlation in terms of coverage given to the different sub-themes by the four newspapers showed that the two Telugu dailies *Eenadu* and *Vaartha* had close association in their coverage. Similarly, the two English dailies *The Hindu* and *The New Indian Express* also had close association in their coverage (Table 48).

Table–48
Correlation Coefficients of Frequencies of Naxalite Activities News Items by Themes among Four Sample Dailies

	The Hindu	*The New Indian Express*	*Eenadu*
The Hindu			
The New Indian Express	0.99		
Eenadu	0.96	0.96	
Vaartha	0.93	0.93	0.99

P<0.01

With regard to the analysis of allocation of space to Naxalite activities news in the four sample dailies, the data show that, *Vaartha* allocated larger share of space to 'Naxalite activities' as compared to the other three newspapers. A total of 14392.5 centimeters column of space was allocated by *Vaartha,* followed by *Eenadu, The Hindu* and *The New Indian Express* (Table 49).

Table–49
Percentage Distribution of Space of News Items to Naxalite-involved Themes

Naxalite Involved Themes	*Dailies*							
	The Hindu		*The New Indian Express*		*Eenadu*		*Vaartha*	
	Space	*Rank Order*	*Space*	*Rank Order*	*Space*	*Rank Order*	*Space*	*Rank Order*
Ambush	1049.58 (13.9)	4	924 (18.6)	3	1838.7 (13.5)	3	1647.88 (11.5)	3

Contd...

Naxalite Involved Themes	Dailies							
	The Hindu		*The New Indian Express*		*Eenadu*		*Vaartha*	
	Space	*Rank Order*	*Space*	*Rank Order*	*Space*	*Rank Order*	*Space*	*Rank Order*
Raids	1274.49 (16.9)	2	1165.36 (23.5)	2	2863.08 (21.0)	2	2336.88 (16.2)	2
Destruction	1240.47 (16.5)	3	770.56 (15.6)	4	1240.38 (9.1)	4	1378.52 (9.6)	4
Kidnaps	173.88 (2.3)	6	127.68 (2.6)	5	126.36 (0.9)	7	184.6 (1.3)	6
Attacks on informers	236.88 (3.1)	5	106.4 (2.1)	6	267.84 (2.0)	6	162.24 (1.1)	7
Attacks on coverts	63.63 (0.8)	7	43.12 (0.9)	7	335.34 (2.5)	5	392.08 (2.7)	5
Communi-cation	3469.41 (46.2)	1	1816.64 (36.7)	1	6929.82 (51.0)	1	8290.36 (57.6)	1
N =	7508.34 (100.00)		4953.76 (100.00)		13601.52 (100.00)		14392.56 (100.00)	

Thus the four dailies differed in their priorities, in terms of space devoted to different sub-themes. Considering allocation of space, *Vaartha* gave the highest amount of space to theme 'Naxalites involved Communication' (57.6%). The other three dailies *Eenadu* (51.0%), *The Hindu* (46.2%) and *The New Indian Express* (36.7%) also gave the first rank to this theme. The raids theme on the other hand, obtained second rank in all the four dailies.

The sub-theme 'ambush' received rank order of three in *Eenadu* (13.5%), *Vaartha* (11.5%) and *The New Indian Express* (18.6%) while in *The Hindu* (13.9%) it is ranked fourth. The other theme 'destruction' received third rank in *The Hindu* and fourth rank in three newspapers – *The New Indian Express, Eenadu* and *Vaartha.* The four dailies differed in terms of space devoted to themes 'kidnaps', 'attacks on informers' and 'attacks on coverts'.

Further analysis on the correlation in terms of coverage given to the different sub-themes by the four newspapers showed that the two Telugu dailies *Eenadu* and *Vaartha* had close association in their

Figure–10
Percentage Distribution of Space of News Items Related to Naxalites Themes

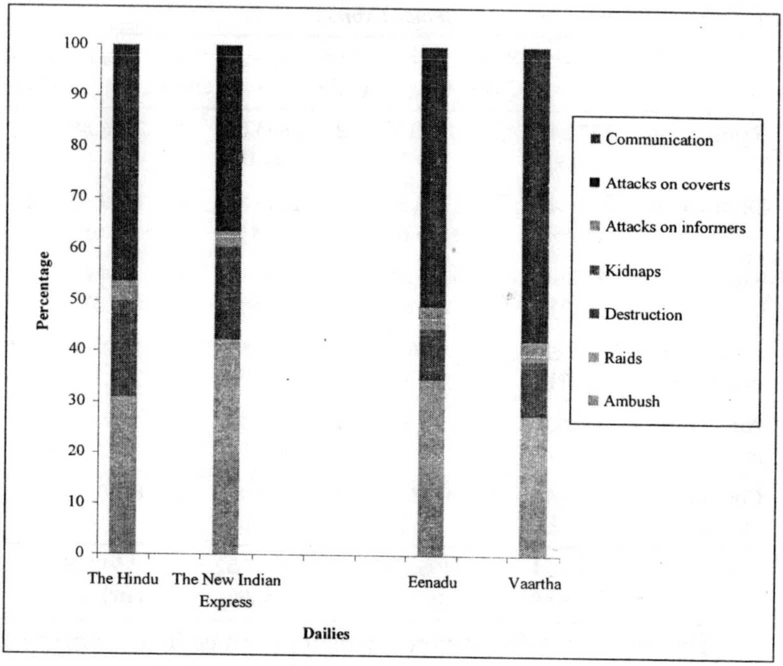

coverage. Similarly, the two English dailies *The Hindu* and *The New Indian Express* also had close association in their coverage (Table 50).

Table–50
Correlation Coefficients of Frequencies of Naxalite Activities News Items by Themes among Four Sample Dailies

	The Hindu	*The New Indian Express*	*Eenadu*
The Hindu			
The New Indian Express	0.95		
Eenadu	0.97	0.9	
Vaartha	0.97	0.89	0.98

P<0.01

Table 51 provides data about the distribution of frequency of news items and the extent of space devoted on the front and inside the pages, to sub-themes of Naxalite activities in the sample dailies.

It is evident that more news items figured on the front page of the sample dailies on sub-theme, namely, 'ambush'. The category of communication received first place in two Telugu dailies *Eenadu* and *Vaartha* with 58 news items each. However other two English dailies *The Hindu* and *The New Indian Express* gave second place to 'communication' theme. The category of raids received first rank in two English dailies, while the two Telugu dailies *Eenadu* and *Vaartha* allocated second place to it, followed by the theme destruction which received fourth rank in all the four dailies. *The Hindu* devoted only one news item on the theme 'attacks on coverts' and five news items on the theme 'attacks on informers', on the front page. *The New Indian Express* allocated only 2 news items with a total of 15.6 column cms to 'attacks on informers' and 'attacks on coverts' was given only one news item with a column length of 25.2 cms. *Eenadu* devoted only three news items to the theme 'kidnaps' and six news items to 'attacks on informers' and 7 news items to 'attacks on coverts' on the front page. *Vaartha* allocated only 2 news items with a total of 67.6 cms, of column to kidnapping while and 'attacks on informers' was given only one news item with a column length of 16.1 cms. As many as 10 news items were allocated to 'attacks on coverts' in *Vaartha*.

In the inside the pages, newspapers place all types of news items keeping in view of their importance. Accordingly, the news stories are displayed with a view to capturing the attention of the readers. The English and the Telugu dailies which have been under study followed the rules of predictability in displaying the stories.

The four newspapers revealed an interesting difference in the allocation of frequency of news items and the extent of space in the inside pages to different sub-themes under the 'Naxalites activities' category.

Table 51 shows that in *The Hindu*, communication (91), destruction (53), raids (32), attacks on informers (14) themes received more number of news items while in *The New Indian Express* communication (71), destruction (38), raids (27), attacks on informers (11) received less coverage. But, the two Telugu papers *Eenadu* and

Figure–11
Trend Line of News Sub-theme 'Destructions' by Year and Newspaper

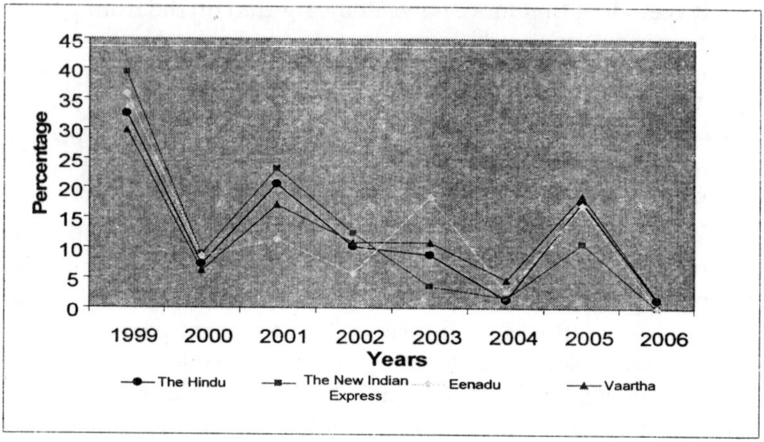

Vaartha put the focus on four sub-themes in *Eenadu* 'communication' (164), 'raids' (56), 'destruction' (48) and 'attacks on informers' (15) issues received more number of news items while in *Vaartha*, communication (192), raids (51), destruction (42), and attacks on informers (11) received greater coverage. Most distinctly, the sub-themes ambush, kidnaps, attacks on coverts received less coverage in all four newspapers on inside the pages.

Encounter Deaths

Regarding actions of the state, especially killings of Naxalites in encounters the news reports did not follow the sensationalist tradition, instead followed a stereotyped format. A majority of the reports on encounters fit this format.

The theme 'encounter deaths' figured 447 news items with area of space (10147.38 column cms., among the four newspapers during the study period. The highest number of news items figured in *Vaartha* (134) in terms of space, *Vaartha* devoted highest area of space (3565.12 col.cm) followed by *Eenadu* (115, 3042.36 col.cm), *The Hindu* (103,1987.02col.cm) and *The New Indian Express* (95, 1552.88 col.cm.) (See Table 52 and 53).

The subject category divided into 3 sub-themes viz., 'Naxalite deaths', 'police deaths' and 'both'.

Table–51
Distribution of Frequencies of News Items and Space by Themes of Naxalite Involved Themes in Front and Inside Pages

Naxalite Involved Themes	Dailies															
	The Hindu				The New Indian Express				Eenadu				Vaartha			
	Front Page		Inside Pages		Front Page		Inside Pages		Front Page		Inside Pages		Front Page		Inside Pages	
	fr	Space	fr	Space	fr	Space	fr	Space	fr	Space	fr	Space	fr	Space	fr	Space
Ambush	24	603.54	8	446.04	25	841.12	4	82.88	27	1584.36	14	254.34	19	1323.4	9	324.48
Raids	32	775.53	32	498.96	34	747.04	27	418.32	51	2040.66	56	822.42	44	1503.32	51	833.56
Destruction	15	299.25	53	941.22	18	323.68	38	446.88	22	622.62	48	617.76	22	600.6	42	777.92
Kidnaps	4	117.81	3	56.07	5	94.08	3	33.6	3	98.28	4	28.08	2	67.6	9	117
Attacks on informers	5	48.51	14	188.37	2	15.68	11	90.72	6	145.26	15	122.58	1	16.12	11	146.12
Attacks on coverts	1	30.24	2	33.39	1	25.2	1	17.92	7	276.48	2	58.86	10	274.56	4	117.52
Communication	26	778.05	91	2691.36	27	567.28	71	1249.36	58	2330.64	164	4599.18	58	2221.96	192	6068.4
N =	107	2652.93	203	4855.41	112	2614.08	155	2339.68	174	7098.3	303	6503.22	156	6007.56	318	8385

Table-52
Percentage of Distribution of Frequencies of News Items to Encounter Deaths by Themes

Encounter Deaths	*Dailies*							
	The Hindu		*The New Indian Express*		*Eenadu*		*Vaartha*	
	fr	%	*fr*	%	*fr*	%	*fr*	%
Naxalites deaths	97	94.2	86	90.5	111	96.5	121	90.3
Naxalites and Police (both)	6	5.8	9	9.5	4	3.5	13	9.7
N =	103	100.00	95	100.00	115	100.00	134	100.00

Table-53
Percentage of Distribution of Space of News Items to Encounter Deaths by Themes

Encounter Deaths	*Dailies*							
	The Hindu		*The New Indian Express*		*Eenadu*		*Vaartha*	
	Space	%	*Space*	%	*Space*	%	*Space*	%
Naxalites deaths	1867.95	94.0	1372.56	88.4	2937.06	96.5	3118.44	87.5
Naxalites and Police	119.07	6.0	180.32	11.6	105.3	3.5	446.68	12.5
N =	1987.02	100.00	1552.88	100.00	3042.36	100.00	3565.12	100.00

The sub-theme 'Naxalite deaths' dominated across all the four dailies both in terms of frequency of news items and extent of space. The least covered sub-theme in all the dailies appears to be both (Naxalites and Police deaths). It may be noted that not even one news item has figured in the sample dailies on police deaths.

Table 54 provides data about the distribution of frequency of news items and the extent of space devoted on the front and inside pages of sample dailies. It may be mentioned that, more news items figured in the front pages of the sample dailies. The sub-theme 'Naxalite deaths' received 69 news items in the *Eenadu*, followed by *Vaartha* 66, *The Hindu* 54 and *The New Indian Express* 50. In terms of

Table-54
Distribution of Frequency of News Items and Space by Themes of Encounter Deaths

Encounter Deaths	*Dailies*															
	The Hindu				*The New Indian Express*				*Eenadu*				*Vaartha*			
	Front Page		*Inside Pages*		*Front Page*		*Inside Pages*		*Front Page*		*Inside Pages*		*Front Page*		*Inside Pages*	
	fr	*Space*	*fr*	*Space*	*fr*	*Space*	*fr*	*Space*	*fr*	*Space*	*fr*	*Space*	*fr*	*Space*	*fr*	*Space*
Naxalites deaths	54	1292.76	43	575.19	50	943.04	36	429.52	69	2262.06	42	675	66	2187.12	55	931.32
Naxalites and Police	6	119.07	-	-	7	140	2	40.32	3	94.5	1	10.8	8	328.64	5	118.04
N =	60	1411.83	43	575.19	57	1083.04	38	469.84	72	2356.56	43	685.8	74	2515.76	60	1049.36

Note: The theme, police deaths did not receive any coverage in the four newspapers.

space, *Eenadu* allocated 2262.0 cm of column to this theme, followed by *Vaartha* (2187.1 cms. of column.), *The Hindu* (1292.7 cms. of column) and *The New Indian Express* (943.04 cms. of column). Encounter death of Naxalites received 55 news items in the inside pages of *Vaartha*, followed by *The Hindu* (43), *Eenadu* (42) and *The New Indian Express* (36). Most distinctly, the sub-theme 'Naxalites and Police deaths' received less coverage in all the four dailies.

Figure–12
Trend Line of News Sub-theme 'Encounters' by Year and Newspaper

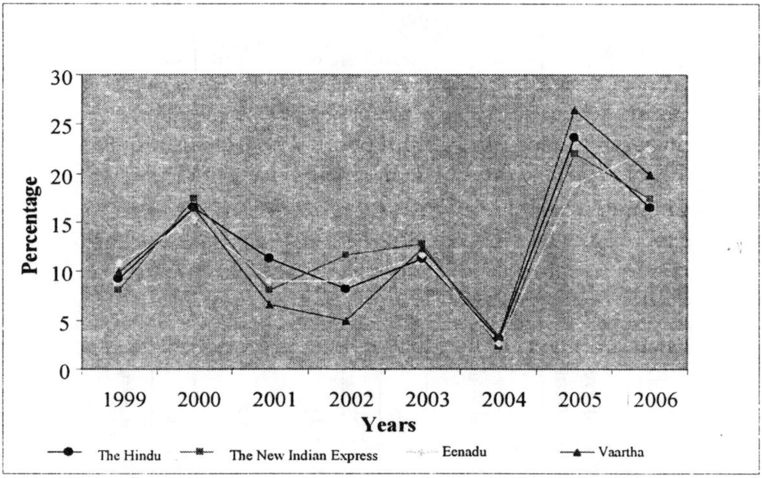

Police Activities

The theme, 'police activities' means police involved in various activities. The theme received 1071 news items in the four news dailies during the study period. The highest percentage of news items figured in *Eenadu* (32.7) followed by *Vaartha* (30.7), *The Hindu* (19.8) and *The New Indian Express* (16.8). The subject category 'police activities' divided into 3 sub-themes, viz., 'counter measures', 'welfare measures', and 'communication'. The data reveal that *Eenadu* gave the highest number of news items (83.7%) under the 'communication' theme, followed by *The Hindu* (81.1%), *Vaartha* (80.9%) and *The New Indian Express* (78.9%). The sub-theme 'welfare measures,' received less than 5 per cent of news items and space in all the four dailies. (See Table 55)

Table–55
Percentage of Distribution of Frequencies of News Items to Police Involved Themes

Police Involved Themes	*Dailies*			
	The Hindu	*The New Indian Express*	*Eenadu*	*Vaartha*
	fr	*fr*	*fr*	*fr*
Counter measures	15.6	17.2	12.0	16.7
Welfare measures	3.3	3.9	4.3	2.4
Communication	81.1	78.9	83.7	80.9
N =	(212)	(180)	(350)	(329)

In terms of coverage, *The New Indian Express* published the highest number of news items (17.2%) on 'counter measures', while *Vaartha* gave (16.7%) of news items and 20.3 per cent of space, followed by *The Hindu* (15.6%) of news items and 12.8 per cent of space, and *Eenadu* 12 per cent of news items and 13.5 per cent of space (see Table 56).

Table–56
Percentage Distribution of Space of News Items to Police Involved Themes

Police In-Volved Themes	*Dailies*							
	The Hindu		*The New Indian Express*		*Eenadu*		*Vaartha*	
	Space	*%*	*Space*	*%*	*Space*	*%*	*Space*	*%*
Counter measures	517.86	12.8	451.92	16.3	934.2	13.5	1429.48	20.3
Welfare measures	142.38	3.5	83.44	3.0	212.22	3.1	160.68	2.3
Communi-cation	3381.84	83.7	2235.52	80.7	5766.66	83.4	5428.28	77.4
N =	4042.08	100.0	2770.88	100.0	6913.08	100.0	7018.44	100.0

Mostly, news related to 'police activities' was spread in different inside pages. Relatively, fewer stories were published on the front page. In a newspaper-wise analysis, *Eenadu* published the maximum

Table–57

Distribution of Frequencies, Space and Location of News by Sub-themes to Police Involved Themes in the Sample Dailies

Police Involved Themes	*Dailies*															
	The Hindu				*The New Indian Express*				*Eenadu*				*Vaartha*			
	Front Page		*Inside Pages*		*Front Page*		*Inside Pages*		*Front Page*		*Inside Pages*		*Front Page*		*Inside Pages*	
	fr	*Space*	*fr*	*Space*	*fr*	*Space*	*fr*	*Space*	*fr*	*Space*	*fr*	*Space*	*fr*	*Space*	*fr*	*Space*
Counter measures	6	122.85	27	395.01	10	126.56	21	325.36	13	410.4	29	523.8	15	525.2	40	904.28
Welfare measures	-	-	7	142.38	1	23.52	6	59.92	1	27	14	185.22	1	31.2	7	129.48
Communication	22	498.33	150	2883.51	28	624.4	114	1611.12	50	1502.28	243	4264.38	56	1482	210	3946.28
N =	28	621.18	184	3420.9	39	774.48	141	1996.4	64	1939.68	286	4973.4	72	2038.4	257	4980.04

news items on the theme 'communication' in the inside pages, followed by *Vaartha, The Hindu* and *The New Indian Express* lead stories were also published on the first page. Most distinctly, the sub-theme' welfare measures' received less coverage in terms of frequency and space in all the four dailies. *The Hindu* did not publish not even a single news item on the sub-theme 'welfare measures' (see Table 57). *Eenadu* published considerable number of news items (15) and space (212.2 col.cms.) on 'welfare measures'. The sub-theme, 'counter measures' received more coverage in *Vaartha* both in terms of number of news item 15, 40 and space 525.2, 904.2 col.cms. on front and inside pages respectively.

Agony of Sufferers

Table 58 shows that the theme 'agony of sufferers' figured 132 news items in the four news dailies during the study period. The highest number of news items figured in *Eenadu* (52) followed by *Vaartha* (45), *The New Indian Express* (21) and *The Hindu* (14).

Table–58

Percentage Distribution of Frequencies of News Items to Agony of Sufferers Themes

Agony of Sufferers	*Dailies*							
	The Hindu		*The New Indian Express*		*Eenadu*		*Vaartha*	
	fr	%	*fr*	%	*fr*	%	*fr*	%
Naxalites families	4	28.5	2	9.5	11	21.2	15	33.3
Police families	7	50.0	8	38.1	21	40.3	18	40.0
Targeted families*	2	14.4	9	42.9	9	17.3	4	8.9
Innocent victims	1	7.1	2	9.5	11	21.2	8	17.8
N =	14	100.00	21	100.00	52	100.00	45	100.00

* Targeted families that figure in the 'hit list' prepared by Naxalites.

The subject category 'agony of sufferers' divided into 4 sub-themes, viz., 'Naxalites families' (32), 'Police families' (54), 'Targeted families' (24) and 'Innocent victims' (22) figured news items in the four newspapers.

'Police families' theme dominated across all three dailies both in terms of frequency and space. *Eenadu* allocated the highest number (40.3%) of news items to the theme followed by *Vaartha* (40%) and *The Hindu* (50%).

Next, the news relating to Naxalite families and targeted families, are given second and third priorities in the Telugu news dailies and the English newspaper *The Hindu*. But in *The New Indian Express* the theme 'targeted families' received 9 news items and the theme 'Naxalites families' received 2 news items. The sub-theme 'innocent victims' received more coverage in terms of frequency (11) in *Eenadu* followed by *Vaartha* (8). The two English newspapers gave less coverage to this theme.

In the analysis of allocation of space to the theme 'Agony of sufferers' in the four sample dailies (Table 59), the data show that, *Eenadu* allocated a larger share of space to it as compared to the other three newspapers. A total of 1178.8 column centimeters of space allocated by *Eenadu*, followed by *Vaartha* (1133 col.cm.), *The New Indian Express* (478.2 col.cm.) and *The Hindu* (447.9 col.cm.).

Table-59
Percentage Distribution of Space of News Items to Agony of Sufferers Themes

Agony of Sufferers	*Dailies*							
	The Hindu		*The New Indian Express*		*Eenadu*		*Vaartha*	
	Space	*%*	*Space*	*%*	*Space*	*%*	*Space*	*%*
Naxalites families	138.6	30.9	21.28	4.5	199.26	16.9	336.44	29.7
Police families	187.11	41.8	188.72	39.5	430.38	36.5	421.2	37.2
Targeted families	98.91	22.1	201.04	42.0	326.7	27.7	89.96	7.9
Innocent victims	23.31	5.2	67.2	14.0	222.48	18.9	285.48	25.2
N =	447.93	100.00	478.24	100.00	1178.82	100.00	1133.08	100.00

The Hindu devoted more space to the theme 'police families' (41.8%) followed by 'Naxalite families' (30.9%), and 'Targeted families' (22.1%). *The New Indian Express* allocated more space (42%) to 'Targeted families' while *Vaartha* and *Eenadu* devoted more space to 'police families' with 37.2 per cent and 36.5 per cent respectively. *The Hindu* devoted less space to 'innocent victims' (5.2%), on the other hand, *The New Indian Express* devoted less space to 'Naxalite families' (4.5%) which *Eenadu* devoted 16.9 per cent while *Vaartha* gave less space (7.9%) to 'Targeted families'.

Table 60 reveals the trend in the coverage of news related to sub-themes, in terms of frequency and space on the front and inside pages. *The Hindu* which reported 2 news items on the front page during the study period did not allocate even a single news item to the themes 'targeted families' and 'Innocent victims'. But, *The New Indian Express* published 4 news items on the front page. The two themes Naxalite families and innocent victims not covered on the front page. The two Telugu news dailies gave an equal coverage to the sub-theme on the front page.

With regard to the news coverage on 'police families', *Eenadu* gave priority in terms of frequency (18) and space (412.5 col.cms.) on the inside pages, whereas the other Telugu newspaper *Vaartha* received 14 news items and allocated 327 col.cm., space to this theme. The two other English newspapers – *The Hindu* and *The New Indian Express* did give less coverage to this theme.

As regards the theme 'Naxalite families' figures more news items (13) in *Vaartha*, followed by *Eenadu* (9), *The Hindu* (3), and *The New Indian Express* (2) on the inside pages 'Targeted families' related news received higher coverage in *Eenadu* both in terms of frequency of news items (8) and space (285 col.cms.) as compared to the other three dailies.

Government Views

The subject category 'Government views', figured 669 news items in the four dailies during the study period. The highest number of news items of this theme figured in *Vaartha* (223) followed by *Eenadu* (215). *The Hindu* (116) and *The New Indian Express* (115). (See Table 61).

The subject category 'Government views' is divided into 3 sub-themes viz., Central (132), State (514) and other State Governments (23) news items figured in the four newspapers.

Table–60
Distribution of Frequencies, Space and Location of News by Sub-theme Agony of Sufferers in the Sample Dailies

Agony of Sufferers	*Dailies*															
	The Hindu				*The New Indian Express*				*Eenadu*				*Vaartha*			
	Front Page		*Inside Pages*		*Front Page*		*Inside Pages*		*Front Page*		*Inside Pages*		*Front Page*		*Inside Pages*	
	fr	*Space*	*fr*	*Space*	*fr*	*Space*	*fr*	*Space*	*fr*	*Space*	*fr*	*Space*	*fr*	*Space*	*fr*	*Space*
Naxalite families	1	32.76	3	105.84	-	-	2	21.28	2	43.2	9	123.66	2	143.52	13	192.92
Police families	1	11.34	6	175.77	3	64.96	5	123.76	3	17.82	18	412.56	4	94.12	14	327.08
Targeted families	-	-	2	98.91	1	34.72	8	166.32	1	41.58	8	285.12	1	31.2	3	58.76
Innocent victims	-	-	1	23.31	-		2	67.2	4	70.2	7	152.28	3	116.48	5	169
N =	2	44.1	12	403.83	4	99.68	17	378.56	10	172.8	42	973.62	10	385.32	35	747.76

Table–61
Percentage Distribution of Frequencies of News Items to Government Views by Themes in the Sample Dailies

Government Views	*Dailies*							
	The Hindu		*The New Indian Express*		*Eenadu*		*Vaartha*	
	fr	%	*fr*	%	*fr*	%	*fr*	%
Central	15	12.9	22	19.1	43	20.0	52	23.3
State	96	82.8	88	76.5	165	76.7	165	74.0
Other states	5	4.3	5	4.4	7	3.3	6	2.7
N =	116	100.00	115	100.00	215	100.00	223	100.00

'State Government views' dominated across all the four dailies both in terms of frequency of news items and extent of space. The two Telugu dailies–*Eenadu* and *Vaartha* allocated 165 news items each. The English daily *The Hindu* gave more number of news items (82.8%) and space 2535.1 col.cms. to the theme compared to *The New Indian Express* 76.5 per cent news items and 1977.3 col.cms. space.

Table–62
Percentage Distribution of Space of News Items to Government Views by Themes in the Sample Dailies

Government Views	*Dailies*							
	The Hindu		*The New Indian Express*		*Eenadu*		*Vaartha*	
	Space	%	*Space*	%	*Space*	%	*Space*	%
Central	398.16	13.0	383.6	15.8	916.92	17.8	1072.24	18.8
State	2535.12	83.0	1977.36	81.6	4167.72	80.8	4520.88	79.5
Other states	121.59	4.0	63.28	2.6	73.98	1.4	95.68	1.7
N =	3054.87	100.00	2424.24	100.00	5158.62	100.00	5688.8	100.00

The theme 'Central Government's views' received interestingly coverage in terms of frequency of news items in all the four newspapers, while *The Hindu* gave 12.9 per cent to the theme. *The New Indian Express* gave slightly more percentage (19.1%) to the same theme. The two Telugu newspapers *Eenadu* and *Vaartha* dedicated 20 per cent and 23.3 per cent respectively to the theme.

Table–63
Distribution of Frequencies, Space and Location of News by Sub-themes in Government Views in the Sample Dailies

Government Views	*Dailies*															
	The Hindu				*The New Indian Express*				*Eenadu*				*Vaartha*			
	Front Page		*Inside Pages*		*Front Page*		*Inside Pages*		*Front Page*		*Inside Pages*		*Front Page*		*Inside Pages*	
	fr	*Space*	*fr*	*Space*	*fr*	*Space*	*fr*	*Space*	*fr*	*Space*	*fr*	*Space*	*fr*	*Space*	*fr*	*Space*
Central	3	52.29	12	345.87	9	175.28	13	208.32	14	475.2	29	441.72	23	588.64	29	483.6
State	34	929.25	62	1605.87	48	1221.92	40	755.44	58	1900.8	107	2266.92	67	2075.84	98	2445.04
Other States	1	6.3	4	115.29	1	4.48	4	58.8	1	10.8	6	63.18	2	26.52	4	69.16
N =	38	987.84	78	2067.03	58	1401.68	57	1022.56	73	2386.8	142	2771.82	92	2691	131	2997.8

As compared to other themes, the coverage of 'other State Government views' was relatively less.

Table 63 indicated the distribution of frequency and space to different sub-themes on the front and inside pages.

As can be seen, the four sample newspapers gave more priority to 'the State Government views'. Among the four newspapers, *Vaartha* gave the highest number of news items (67) and space 2075.8 col.cms. followed by *Eenadu* (58), *The New Indian Express* (48), *The Hindu* (34) in terms of space, 1900.8 col.cms. 1221.92 col.cms., 929.2 col.cms. allocated in the descending order.

The theme 'Central Government's views' received interesting coverage in terms of frequency and space in all the four newspapers. While *The Hindu* gave only 3 news items and 52.2 col.cms. of the space the Telugu newspaper *Vaartha* devoted higher coverage (23 news items and 588.6 col.cms.) to this theme on the front page.

Political Parties' Views

Table 64, shows the distribution of the subject category 'political parties' views'. *Eenadu* (100) published the highest number of news items on political parties' views out of a total of 271 news items in the four newspapers put together. The *Vaartha* (94) came up in the second place followed by *The Hindu* (49) and *The New Indian Express* (28).

Table-64

Percentage Distribution of Frequencies of News Items to Political Parties' Views by Themes in the Sample Dailies

Political Parties' Views	*Dailies*							
	The Hindu		*The New Indian Express*		*Eenadu*		*Vaartha*	
	fr	*%*	*fr*	*%*	*fr*	*%*	*fr*	*%*
Congress	17	34.8	8	28.6	35	35.0	31	33.0
BJP	8	16.3	4	14.3	21	21.0	18	19.1
Communists	10	20.4	5	17.8	16	16.0	14	14.9
TDP	13	26.5	7	25.0	23	23.0	19	20.2
TRS	1	2.0	4	14.3	5	5.0	12	12.8
N =	49	100.0	28	100.0	100	100.0	94	100.0

The subject category 'political parties' views' divided into 5 sub- themes, viz., Congress, BJP, Communists, TDP and TRS. Among all the themes Congress Party related news constitute major chunk (33.5%) followed by TDP (22.8%), BJP (18.8%) and TRS (8.1%).

Among the two English dailies, *The Hindu* gave prominence to the themes Congress, BJP, Communists and TDP in terms of frequency while *The New Indian Express* gave priority to the theme TRS.

In contrast, *Vaartha* devoted highest percentage of news items (12.8%) and space (18.5%) to the theme TRS, while *Eenadu* devoted the highest percentage of news items (35%) among the four dailies.

Table 65 shows the percentage allocation of space to different themes. The theme TDP ranked first in the two English dailies, *The Hindu* and *The New Indian Express* which dedicated space 36.2 per cent and 27.4 per cent respectively to the theme while the theme Congress, received first place across the two Telugu dailies *Vaartha* and *Eenadu* with a percentages 35 per cent and 30.6 per cent respectively. *The New Indian Express* allocated more space (20.3%) to the theme 'Communists'. The Telugu newspaper *Eenadu* gave more space to the theme 'TDP' than *Vaartha*.

Table–65
Percentage Distribution of Space of News Items to Political Parties' Views by Themes in the Sample Dailies

Political Parties' Views	*Dailies*							
	The Hindu		*The New Indian Express*		*Eenadu*		*Vaartha*	
	Space	*%*	*Space*	*%*	*Space*	*%*	*Space*	*%*
Congress	339.57	33.8	95.76	22.9	456.30	30.6	535.6	35.0
BJP	181.44	18.1	71.12	17.0	272.16	18.2	285.48	18.7
Communists	112.14	11.2	85.12	20.3	171.72	11.4	117.52	7.7
TDP	362.88	36.2	114.8	27.4	428.76	28.7	306.8	20.1
TRS	6.93	0.7	52.08	12.4	164.16	11.0	282.88	18.5
N =	1002.96	100.0	418.88	100.0	1493.1	100.0	1528.28	100.0

The four sample dailies dedicated more space on inside pages only (Table 66). Coming to the theme 'People's reactions' against to Naxalites/Police.

The Hindu and *The New Indian Express* reported only 8 and 6 news items respectively throughout the study period. The two other Telugu newspapers *Vaartha* and *Eenadu* did give slightly more coverage (17 and 12 news items respectively) to the themes.

In contrast, under these themes, not even a single news item figured in *The Hindu* and *The New Indian Express* on the front page. Thus the theme 'people's reactions against Naxalites' received more coverage in terms of frequency of news items in *Eenadu* (9) , *Vaartha* (6), *The Hindu* (6) and *The New Indian Express* (5).

'People's reactions against police' theme received higher coverage in *Vaartha* both in terms of news items (9) and space (169 col.cms.) as compared to the other three dailies.

The Hindu devoted only 3 news items to the theme 'Human rights/courts' and 4 news items to 'Human rights organizations' and 5 news items to the theme 'peace talks', on the front page. *The New Indian Express* allocated 2 news items to 'Human Rights/courts' and 2 news items to 'Human rights organizations' and 'peace talks' was got 7 news items.

Vaartha dedicated 10 news items with a total col.cms. of 253.2 to 'Human rights organization'. While the other themes 'Human rights/courts' and 'Peace talks' received insignificant coverage.

Eenadu allocated only 3 news items with a total of 42.6 col.cms. to 'Human rights/courts' and 'Human rights organizations' was given only 5 news items, with a column length of 162.5 cm. As many as 9 news items were allocated to 'peace talks' in *Eenadu*.

The English daily *The New Indian Express* gave less coverage to Human rights/courts theme as compared to other newspapers.

Directional Analysis

In the present study, an attempt was made to assess the direction of treatment given to the 10 subject categories. As stated earlier in Chapter-II, the coefficient of imbalance was used to find out the degree of treatment given to different subject categories by the sample

Table–66
Distribution of Frequencies, Space and Location of News by Sub-themes in Political Parties Views in Sample Dailies

Political Parties' Views	*Dailies*															
	The Hindu				*The New Indian Express*				*Eenadu*				*Vaartha*			
	Front Page		*Inside Pages*		*Front Page*		*Inside Pdges*		*Front Page*		*Inside Pages*		*Front Page*		*Inside Pages*	
	fr	*Space*	*fr*	*Space*	*fr*	*Space*	*fr*	*Space*	*fr*	*Space*	*fr*	*Space*	*fr*	*Space*	*fr*	*Space*
Congress	1	22.68	16	316.89	-	-	8	95.76	1	24.3	34	432	5	118.04	26	417.56
BJP	1	27.72	7	153.72	1	40.32	3	30.8	2	112.32	19	159.84	2	131.04	16	154.44
Communists	-	-	10	112.14	-	-	5	85.12	-	-	16	171.72	-	-	14	117.52
TDP	-	-	13	362.88	-	-	7	114.8	4	89.64	19	339.12	2	62.92	17	243.88
TRS	1	6.93	-	-	-	-	4	52.08	1	99.9	4	64.26	3	114.92	9	167.96
N =	3	57.33	46	945.63	1	40.32	27	378.56	8	326.16	92	1166.94	12	426.92	82	1101.36

dailies. For this purpose, a three point scale, namely, favourable, unfavourable and neutral, was adopted to assess the direction of treatment of the themes.

As can be seen from Table 67, the four sample dailies published more number of unfavourable news items, viz., *The Hindu* (469), *The New Indian Express* (406), *Eenadu* (620) and *Vaartha* (711). The chi-square analysis showed that the coverage given to the different issues did not differ significantly (X^2=4.97 df=6).

Between the two English dailies, *The Hindu* put more emphasis on the negative coverage of Naxalite movement related news items (-0.082) throughout the study period, whereas, of the two Telugu dailies *Vaartha* gave a critical treatment to the majority of Naxalite movement related news by emphasizing more on negative references (-0.092). Although *The New Indian Express* covered less number of Naxalite movement related news, the coverage of the stories was with an emphasis on negative references (-0.083). But *Eenadu* also is not an exception to this and was critical in covering the news themes (-0.056).

Table–67
Directional Analysis of Coverage of the Total Naxalite Related News Items in all the Sample Dailies

Dailies	*Direction of Coverage*				*Coefficient of Imbalance*
	n	*f*	*uf*	*ne*	
The Hindu	860	339	469	52	-0.082
The New Indian Express	750	290	406	54	-0.083
Eenadu	1394	442	620	332	-0.056
Vaartha	1383	462	711	210	-0.092
N =	4387	1533	2206	648	

n = number of news items; f = favourable; uf = unfavourable, ne = neutral

X^2=4.97 df=6 ns

Tables 68 and 69 show the direction of treatment given to the coverage of the subject categories. *The Hindu* reported more number of stories on 'Naxalite activities' (212) unfavourably as compared to

The New Indian Express. *The Hindu* covered more number of favourable stories on 'police activities' (166) and 'Government views' (62) whereas *Vaartha* covered more number of favourable news stories on 'Government views' (87). *Vaartha* covered more number of unfavourable stories on 'Government views' (94) as compared to *Eenadu*.

Table-68
Directional Analysis of the Naxalite Related News Items by Newspapers

Category	*Dailies*											
	The Hindu			*The New Indian Express*			*Eenadu*			*Vaartha*		
	f	*uf*	*ne*	*f*	*uf*	*ne*	*f*	*uf*	*ne*	*f*	*uf*	*ne*
Naxalite activities	78	212	20	73	174	20	144	231	102	147	258	69
Encounter deaths	2	101	-	1	94	-	4	86	25	-	131	3
Police activities	166	30	16	136	29	15	158	88	104	162	98	69
Agony of sufferers	4	9	1	6	12	3	22	29	1	14	30	1
Govt. views	62	49	5	57	45	13	69	87	59	87	94	42
Political parties' views	13	30	6	6	21	1	17	55	28	22	55	17
People's reaction	1	7	-	-	6	-	1	11	-	-	17	-
Human rights/ courts	3	4	1	-	2	-	5	5	1	3	1	1
Human rights organizations	4	25	2	4	18	-	12	22	3	16	23	3
Peace talks	6	2	1	7	5	2	10	6	9	11	4	5
N =	339	469	52	290	406	54	442	620	332	462	711	210

f= favourable; uf = unfavourable; ne= neutral.

Table-69
Theme-wise Coefficients of Imbalance of Naxalite Movement News Items in the Sample Dailies

Category	Dailies			
	The Hindu	*The New Indian Express*	*Eenadu*	*Vaartha*
Naxalite activities	-0.29	-0.24	-0.08	-0.12
Encounter deaths	-0.94	-0.96	-0.53	-0.95
Police activities	0.50	0.44	0.09	0.09
Agony of sufferers	-0.22	-0.16	-0.07	-0.23
Government views	0.05	0.05	-0.03	-0.01
Political parties' views	-0.21	-0.40	-0.210	-0.20
People's reactions	-0.85	-	-0.76	-
Human rights/courts	-0.06	-	-	0.24
Human rights organization	-0.54	-0.52	-0.16	-0.09
Peace talks	0.29	0.07	0.06	0.19

The four sample dailies reported more number of unfavourable stories on 'political parties views', viz., *The Hindu* (30), *The New Indian Express* (21) , the two Telugu newspapers *Eenadu* and *Vaartha* reported 50 each news items unfavourably on 'political parties views'. The four newspapers published more number of unfavourable news stories on 'encounter deaths'.

Over all, it appears that *The Hindu* gave more positive coverage to 'Police activities' (0.50) theme as compared to other three newspapers (Table 69). The sub-theme 'Government views' received a positive coverage in *The Hindu* and *The New Indian Express* and negative coverage in the two Telugu newspapers. The sub-theme 'peace talks' received positive coverage in all the four newspapers.

6

Summary and Conclusion

Since Naxalite movement is an off-shoot of communist philosophy, the discussion on Naxalite movement interpolates with communism. Since the inception of the movement, Naxalites took up the struggle on the armed front to achieve their goals. However, the movement completed four decades of its existence; it is continuing the armed struggle against the rich and the government. In relation to the academic discussion of the movement, various studies only focused on the genesis of the Naxalite movement and its impact on socio-economic aspects. Since Naxalite movement has been 40-year old, none of the studies in India analyzed the movement in relation to newspaper coverage. Only one study in specific done in Andhra Pradesh by Stevenson (1998) analyzed the role of newspapers qualitatively in insurgency with particular reference to Andhra Pradesh. Thus, the present study assumed significance in the context that the very few academic studies attempted to analyze the media contents or the coverage given to the Naxalite movement quantitatively. Therefore, the present study makes an attempt to content-analyze newspapers in English and Telugu by systematically and methodically by categorizing news contents, editorials, cartoons, and edit page articles by drawing an appropriate sample during the eight-year study period (1999-2006). The purpose of the present study is to ascertain the differential coverage given to Naxalite activities as well as Naxalite movement related news in certain selected newspapers. Four newspapers were selected for this purpose, two each in English and Telugu. Content analysis was used to compare the news content of the sample newspapers and to draw inferences about the coverage given to the phenomenon under study in the sample newspapers.

The specific objectives of the study are:

1. To find out the frequency and the extent of space allocated to different categories of news covering naxalite related issues in the front page and inside pages of the sample dailies.
2. To find out and make a comparative analysis in terms of frequency and space of the differences in the coverage of various categories of the Naxalite related news in the specific English and Telugu newspapers.
3. To find out the differences in the frequency and space devoted to the Naxalite themes related to local, state and national items, and to find out the direction of treatment given by the sample newspapers to the Naxalite related news.
4. To make a comparative analysis of the frequency of coverage of Naxalite movement related editorials, letter-to-the editor, Articles, Photos and cartoons which appeared in the sample newspapers.

Research Design

Sample Framework

A purposive sample consisting of four leading daily newspapers (two English and two Telugu) were taken. The papers in English were *The Hindu, The New Indian Express* and in Telugu *Eenadu* and *Vaartha*. The prime consideration in the selection of these newspapers was the prominence as reflected in their circulation and their regional representation. While *The Hindu* and *The New Indian Express* are considered elite dailies in English, the other two are premier Telugu newspapers in Andhra Pradesh. The important considerations that went into the selection of the two different language dailies.

1. English being the associate official language and the main medium of intellectual exchange among the elite in the country, the English dailies are read by the majority of policy makers, decision-makers and administrators.
2. The language newspapers are read by the masses and reach the majority of the population in the region.

The universe for this study comprises all the editions of the four selected dailies published during the calendar years i.e., January 1,

1999 to December 31, 2006. This study was based on the complete census during the eight years time span—not a random sample. From a preliminary analysis it was concluded that a small sample of issues would result in unfair representation of Naxalite movement related news coverage. Through out the year, news of Naxalite movement is distributed in various proportions. If a random sample were taken, the risk of missing important instances of Naxalite movement coverage would be high. Therefore, hundreds of newspaper issues had been sampled.

The leading English Daily *The Hindu* and the leading regional language (Telugu) daily *Eenadu*, were taken as a 'base' daily newspapers. Two steps were adopted to select the editions (dates) to constitute the study. In the first step, the researcher identified 100 major incidents for study period from January 1, 1999 to December 31, 2006. In the second step, the researcher examined the consequences of major incidents. Actions and reactions, follow up news coverage were considered for analysis. There were 320 editions per daily and a total of 1280 editions for four sample dailies came up for analysis, and found 7071 news stories (all units). The units of analyses for this study consisted of the news items, editorials, articles, letters-to-the editor, photos and cartoons published in the front page and inside pages of four selected dailies.

Keeping in view of the objectives of the study, 10 main subject categories were identified. They are: 1. Naxalite activities, 2. Encounter deaths, 3. Police activities, 4. Agony of sufferers, 5. Government views, 6. Political party views, 7. Peoples reaction, 8. Human rights/courts, 9. Human rights organizations and 10. Peace talks. Further, the coverage of the 10 subject categories was analyzed basing on the geographical dimension. Thus the news items were divided on the basis of geographical dimensions into three regions such as local, state and national. All the main subject categories were in turn divided in sub-categories.

Major Findings

Naxalite Activities and Newspapers

Over all, the analysis of newspapers showed that the Naxalites activities had received nearly 35 per cent or above of coverage in terms of frequency of news items and space across the four dailies. Although Naxalite activities involved violent incidents such as raids, destructions, abductions, the newspapers considered them as news worthy instead being a part of Naxalite movement. For example, *The New Indian Express*, on March 2, 2005 published the following news report to highlight the Naxalite violence:

> **Maoists hack 8 villagers**
>
> Kurnool, March 1: Maoists today hacked to death eight villagers and chopped the limbs of two others new interior Vempenta village of Kurnool district in a pre-dawn strike. The killings are being seen as retaliation to the burning of nine Dalits of the same village seven years ago by upper caste men.

The reason for giving such coverage for the Naxalite activities seems to be that the newspapers treated the theme as a law and order problem in the state as the Naxalites were vitiating the peaceful environment. When an event took place involving the government or the police or the Naxalites, newspapers were publishing them on the front page like crime news. Although newspapers were aware of the fact that the Naxalite movement was an ideological struggle, newspapers reported the incidents routinely without discussing the implications of the event on the public. One plausible reason could be that though the Press viewed the Naxalite movement as an ideological struggle, and the ideology of the movement was only violence to achieve the goals set by the Naxalites for themselves. Hence the entire movement was confined to event reporting. Second, most of the journalists working in newspapers lacked an in-depth study of the ideology. Another significant point to be noted is that while the Naxalites were fighting the government on the grounds of ideology, the news items mostly centered on the conflict, between the government officials and the Naxalites.

Further, conflict is treated as the important news value as taught in journalism textbooks, the newspapers under the study covered it as a conflict between two parties. In the coverage of conflict, majority of news items in terms of frequency dealt with the deaths, arson and abductions of government officials as if these events took place on their own being isolated from the movement. Furthermore, the Naxalites considered such violent events as part of their communication to the public at large and in particular, their counterparts in other regions of the state or the country because the Naxalites do not have access to normal mode of communications as they are being intercepted by the police. The Naxalites organize protests to express their opposition to the public as well as the government. These events too are communicated in the form of violence. The intensity of the event has an underlining code to send a message to their counter-parts in the other regions. If Naxalite activities are seen in conjunction with the theme 'Naxalites communication', it can be inferred that the violence can be understood in relation to the Naxalite movement. Thus, the Naxalite communication received important coverage across all the four dailies both in terms of frequency of news items and extent of space. *Vaartha* allocated the highest percentage (52.7%) of news items to the theme, while *Eenadu* allocated (46.5%) followed by *The Hindu* 37.8 per cent and *The New Indian Express* 36.7 per cent. It is followed by news relating to raids and destruction caused by Naxalite activities, which are given second and third priorities in *The New Indian Express, Eenadu* and *Vaartha* respectively, while in *The Hindu*, the theme destruction received second rank and raids received third rank. The theme, ambush received fourth rank in all four newspapers.

It is evident that more news items figured on the front page of the sample dailies on sub-theme, namely, 'ambush'. The category of communication received first place in two Telugu dailies *Eenadu* and *Vaartha* with 58 news items each. However other two English dailies *The Hindu* and *The New Indian Express* gave second place to 'communication' theme. *The Hindu* devoted only one news item on the theme 'attacks on coverts' and five news items on the theme 'attacks on informers', on the front page. *The New Indian Express* allocated only 2 news items with a total of 15.6 column cms. to 'attacks on informers' and 'attacks on coverts' was given only one news item with a column length of 25.2 cms. Nevertheless, the intensity of violence increased in 1999 while it declined in 2000. In 2001, the violence increased again because many Naxalites were killed in encounters or police actions. In retaliation, the Naxalites indulged in violence in the form of destructions, raids or ambush of attacking police stations (see Table 70). Moreover, Naxalite violence escalated in 2004 on the eve of Assembly and Parliament elections as Naxalites were indulging in killings of political leaders particularly the Telugu Desam Party (TDP) and Bharatiya Janata Party. The Naxalites through press statements vowed that they would oppose the return of TDP to power as the TDP was implementing the policies of capitalism.

Nevertheless, newspapers could dig below the surface to uncover the causes of Naxalite movement or even simply to seek out dissidents' views and allow them to explain their grievances in their own words. Violence, defined as the exertion of physical force to injure, damage or destroy is the primary subject of news stories covered in the sample newspapers. This is not surprising as the Naxalite groups engage in violence which is reported in the headlines. The other important reason that the news stories with violence and headlines indicating violence appears to be an eye catching means to capture the market besides performing the function of informing the reader. Another weakness of the press, according to ideologues, is that it does an excellent job of events but fails to evince interest in the processes that led to the events. For instance, the following news report in *The Hindu* December 9, 1999 illustrates the point:

> **Naxalites go on rampage;**
>
> **Protest week begins on violent note**
>
> Hyderabad, December 8: The AP Police are bracing themselves for retaliatory violence by the People's War Group Naxalites as the protest week to be observed by the extremists again what they call the "cold blooded killing" of three PWG Central Committee members in Karimnagar began on a violent note on Wednesday. The "protest week" is to culminate in two day bandh on December 15 and 16.

Newspapers, Naxalites and State Government

The Naxalite movement in Andhra Pradesh completed 30 years by the turn of 1998 when the present study began in 1999. Primarily, the movement which began as an armed struggle against the landed gentry changed its ideology during the course of its existence, and considered the government as a "class enemy" *inter alia* the police force as an arm of the government. The governments with their incoherent policies changed their perceptions with the change of the Chief Ministers. Although they held peace talks with Naxalite leaders, they are meant to gain political mileage over their counterparts in the political circles. However, the ideology and attitudes of the Naxalites too changed with the splits in the groups and leaders.

Moreover, the Naxalite movement which took off as a struggle against the landed gentry assumed different dimensions. For instance, the Telugu Desam Government headed by Nara Chandra Babu, returned to power in 1999. In spite of vehement opposition to his rule from the Naxalites, he came to power even when he was implementing the World Bank policies and borrowing money from the World Bank. The Naxalites leaders were opposing the American supported or World Bank policies through press statements. Further, they advised the Government to shun the policies of the World Bank and described the State Government as "stooges" of the World Bank. Moreover, as the Naxalites were opposing the World Bank policies they expressed their vehement opposition through violence in the form of indulging in all kinds of violence to threaten the officials whenever they went to the villages to educate the masses on the government schemes. Therefore, the newspapers reported these incidents in the newspaper columns.

For instance, the Naxalites made an aborted bid on the life of Chandra Babu Naidu in 2004 by planting a landmine on the way when he was proceeding to Tirupathi. Because of the attack, the then Telugu Desam Government advanced the elections in order to gain mileage over the attack on Naidu. The Telugu Desam Party made the attack as an issue in the elections, and included the Naxalite violence in the election manifesto. The subject category 'state government views' dominated across all the four dailies both in terms of frequency of news items and extent of space. The two Telugu dailies – *Eenadu* and *Vaartha* allocated 165 news items each. The English daily *The Hindu* gave more number of news items (82.8%) and space 2535.1 col.cms. to the theme compared to *The New Indian Express* 76.5 per cent news items and 1977.3 col.cms. space. Obviously, the press supports and promotes the ideology of the State. As long as there is no ban on the PWG and its front organizations, the press gives coverage to its activities. But once, the ban is imposed, there is an unwritten ban on a section of journalists in some newspapers to write about Naxalite-related news. Ironically, even during such periods of undeclared ban on news on Naxalites, some newspapers encourage news only on Naxalites which can sell the newspaper. But the moment something is written against the State, the journalist earns the wrath of the management.

The mainstream press takes full advantage of the habit of the reader to go through the headlines owing to time constraints, and twists headlines or inserts misleading headlines. Moreover, the contents of the reports and the headlines do not corroborate with each other. It may be understood that there is a deliberate distortion by the Press as it sometimes says that the Naxalite movement has been decimated by the government. In case of a major offensive by the Naxalites, the Press reacts stating 'Naxalites are regrouping followed by another news story that 'Naxalites are 'building a Red Army' or 'running parallel governments' in rural areas. On reason attributable to the press is that it is highly commercial. The newspapers in the state, both English and the Telugu are market driven. Any news story with a sensational angle is published in news columns. For instance, the surrenders of the Naxalites to the government or the stories narrated by the surrendered Naxalites are highlighted in the front page.

> **22 Naxalites surrender before SP**
>
> Hyderabad, April 19: In a development that is bound to cheer up the police in North Telangana districts, twenty two Naxalites of the PWG, including four commanders of the local guerilla squads of the recently launched PGA surrendered themselves before the DGP, Mr. H.J. Dora here on Thursday (*The Hindu,* April 20, 2001).

While the press has failed to focus on the unresolved question of tribal welfare and hence the tribal uneducated or semi-educated youth are attracted towards the Naxalite movement. Therefore, the continued tribal exploitation provided a breeding ground for Naxalites. Newspapers have inadequately dealt with the inconsistency of political parties in dealing with the poll boycott call of Naxalites. The newspapers never pointed out that the State Government was wobbling on the issue of Naxalite movement. For example, the founder the Telugu Desam Party N.T. Rama Rao described the Naxalites as patriots. Later, in 1991, he said that he would neither seek Naxalite help nor would reject it. On the other hand, the Congress claimed that it was implementing land reforms and tribal welfare programmes, but the programmes being implemented by the Congress Government do not reach the target groups. In this sense, the press has not analyzed the reasons for the failure of welfare programmes to reach the tribal pockets. For instance, the sub-theme welfare measures received less coverage in terms of frequency and space in all the four dailies. *The Hindu* did not publish not even a single news item on the sub-theme 'welfare measures' (See Table 57). *Eenadu* published considerable number of news items (15) and space (212.2 col.cms.) on 'welfare measures'. The sub-theme, 'counter measures' received more coverage in *Vaartha* both in terms of number of news items 15, 40 and space 525.2, 904.2 col.cms. on front and inside pages respectively.

The reason is understandable. Over the years, the press has been successful in moulding public opinion to make people believe that violence has no place in a democracy. The umpteen murders which take place everyday, communal politics leading to riots, group clashes, personal hatred, and faction feuds are adequate testimony to that violence is a part of our society. Yet the Press considers such violence as part of the society, while exaggerating Naxalite violence as harmful to society. Even cartoons denigrate the Naxalites and the movement taken up by them. The photographs that appeared in the four dailies focused on the gory deaths of Naxalites or the victims of the Naxalites, and in the process, the newspapers depicted the Naxalite violence negatively. One such media theory argues that the media constructs reality in the minds of the reader or viewer, as in the case of Naxalite movement, the media has projected them negatively. DeFleur and Ball-Rokeach (1989: 259) observed that press's interpretations of events can radically alter people's interpretations of reality and their consequent patterns of action.

Police, Encounters and Newspapers

The subject category 'police activities' divided into 3 sub-themes, viz., 'counter measures', 'welfare measures', and 'communication'. The data reveal that *Eenadu* gave the highest number of news items (83.7%) under the police 'communication' theme, followed by *The Hindu* (81.1%), *Vaartha* (80.9%) and *The New Indian Express* (78.9%).

Mostly, news related to 'police activities' was spread in different inside pages. Relatively, fewer stories were published on the front page. In a newspaper-wise analysis, *Eenadu* published the maximum news items on the theme 'communication' in the inside pages, followed by *Vaartha, The Hindu* and *The New Indian Express* were also published on the first page. Regarding actions of the state, especially killings of Naxalites in encounters the news reports did not follow the sensationalist tradition, instead followed a stereotyped format. A majority of the reports on encounters fit this format.

The theme 'encounter deaths' appeared in 447 news items with area of space (10147.38 column cms.) among the four newspapers during the study period. The highest number of news items figured in *Vaartha* (134) in terms of space, *Vaartha* devoted highest area of space (3565.12 col.cm.) followed by *Eenadu* (115, 3042.36 col.cm.), *The Hindu* (103,1987.02 col.cm.) and *The New Indian Express* (95, 1552.88 col.cm.) (See Table 52 and 53).

Evidently journalists have become so insensitive to the killings of Naxalites and the police repression is also exemplified by the fact that the headlines both in the English and the Telugu dailies on encounters just give figures. In all such instances and regarding underground activity, the press carries only the police version in a manner justifying the police action. For encounter reports have become stereotyped: "Three Naxalites belonging to the People's War Group were killed in encounter here today. Police said, the Naxalites on seeing the police party opened fire and the police returned the fire. The firing continued for two hours and at the end, the police recovered the dead bodies of Naxalites." Most of these stories relied on police sources or human rights activists. On of the tenets of journalism emphasizes that the each report must be verified before publication. Ethics have been less observed as journalists in their haste to meet the deadline; they have stopped verifying facts thus violating one of the basic tenets of journalism verification or checking facts with the various sources or taking the version of the party/ institution or individual named in the new story. Seldom do newspapers provide more than cursory attention to the reasons for the actions/events. Instead the coverage focuses on facts and events which were presented as the movement as an unfolding drama to be chronicled, rather than as a manifestation of a several societal maladjustment that requires explanation. The result of this kind of coverage is two-fold. As various critics have noted, by covering 'protests' simply as events, without explaining the underlying causes, reporters fail to provide readers the information they need to understand the dissidents' grievances. The various segments of society remain sealed off from each other, and opportunities for increased understanding and remedial action are lost. Ideologues questioned the propriety of the police taking the initiative in publicizing every arrest and surrender and commenting on it in the press. This, they said, takes place much before the person is charged as an accused or produced before a Magistrate. Elaborating on the issue further, they said this raises questions concerning the freedom of the press, its rights to access to the news and the accountability of the police to the public and not the least, the people's right to know. Also another significant aspect attached to it, they said is the fairness of a criminal trial. This interest is endangered every time a police officer holds a press conference or meets pressmen and brags about the arrest or surrender of a leading Naxalite. The people undoubtedly have a right to know whom the police has arrested/ or taken them in as surrendered members, lest such things happen in secrecy. The press, on its part, is not only entitled but is bound as a surrogate of the public to ferret out the facts of the arrest/ surrenders.

Ideologues like Balagopal or Vara Vara Rao remarked that the mainstream Telugu newspapers including the two dailies under study viz., *Eenadu* and *Vaartha* glorify surrenders and publish them on their front pages. The State apparatus and its representative generally, specifically senior police officials manage the press during such surrenders by calling for press conferences and put out elaborate details of the various offences and ammunition seized by them from the Naxalites. The ideologues as well as the human rights activists pointed out that no reporter ever probed into the drama preceding the surrender.

On the other hand, the Naxalites argue that the mainstream press has suppressed and does not factually analyze the evils of capitalism. The capitalist media experts and intelligentsia have ensured that the evils of the capitalist system are not told to the people truthfully. Even if some facts are published, they should not be attributed to evils of capital system. From this point of view, the press has been containing the Naxalite movement as persistent negative coverage about kidnaps, landmine blasts; killings build a negative opinion on the ideology and the tactics among the masses.

Political Parties, Naxalites and Newspapers

The subject category 'political parties views' divided into 5 sub-themes, viz., Congress, BJP, Communists, TDP and TRS. Among all the themes Congress Party related news constitute major chunk (33.5%) followed by TDP (22.8%), BJP (18.8%) and TRS (8.1%).

Among the two English dailies, *The Hindu* gave prominence to the themes Congress, BJP, Communists and TDP in terms of frequency while *The New Indian Express* gave priority to the theme TRS. In contrast, *Vaartha* devoted highest percentage of news items (12.8%) and space (18.5%) to the theme TRS, while *Eenadu* devoted the highest percentage of news items (35%) to the Congress among the four dailies. The reason for giving such coverage to these rightist parties or centrist-rightist parties is that these parties criticize the Naxalite movement or they issue statements condemning the violence indulged in by the Naxalites. Interestingly, the Communist Parties have not received the news coverage in the four dailies. Two reasons seem to be taken into consideration. One, the left parties do not criticize the Naxalites, and second is that the press adopts different yardstick for covering the Left parties. The mainstream press adopts a method to black out or censor news and views favourable to the Naxalite movement. For example, if there is a price rise or other issues like retrenchment, closures, lock outs etc., or any other political development which affects people, the reactions of various shades of political opinion is available in the press prominently while the views of the Naxalite leaders or their sympathizers are not covered prominently. Even if they are given, their views are mostly projected in a manipulated manner by not giving prominence in terms of content, space and place in the newspaper. This suppression or manipulation by the mainstream press gives an impression that the Left wing groups and their leaders are apathetic to the problems of the people. Obviously, the reason is that journalists do not have the basic understanding of the inner party functioning and the ideology of the movement. So much so, every secret conclave of Naxalites becomes a plenary meeting. Also every performance of Gaddar, a noted balladeer who composes and sings songs on pro-Naxalites is reported as a cultural event attended by the elite and the moneyed class to relieve them from ennui. The ideology propagated by the songs and the issues taken up are never properly highlighted or debated in the press so as to sensitize people on the issues and concerns of the masses.

Conclusion

Over all, the study concludes that the mainstream newspapers under study have reported the Naxalite movement negatively as can be seen from the directional analysis. Even the agony of the sufferers is reported negligibly. Thus, the results of this study can be compared with the findings of the earlier study done by Stevenson (1998). In terms of observations, Stevenson's study found that the mainstream newspapers did not support the Naxalite activities. In the present study, it was found that the four newspapers wrote very few editorials and edit page articles on the Naxalite movement.

Similarly, the present study found that the welfare measures undertaken by Naxalites were not reported by the newspapers. Neither about the aim of the Naxalite movement as an armed struggle to deter the landed gentry or the government to enforce them passes laws favourable to the poor. The newspapers have an onerous task to represent the case of the poor and the voiceless in the society. It is suggested that the newspapers can view Naxalite movement by assessing it periodically to point out the mistakes in the movement. On the other hand, the government too must take appropriate steps to reduce the intensity of the movement. In this situation, the newspapers can play a mediatory role to resolve the conflict between the two parties. Either the government or the Naxalites work for the welfare of the people, if at all, the press can project the reality or advice the warring groups to restrain from violence. However, a peace process is usually long and complex and the direction it takes is often open to wide range of interpretation. News reports provide citizens with important clues about the political climate surrounding peace process. Therefore, the press can make concerted efforts to work for the resolution of the conflict if press covers the processes by giving a careful judgment to the issues.

APPENDIX-I

Profiles of Naxalite Leaders

In the following pages, profiles of prominent leaders who participated in the Naxalite Movement during the last 40 years have been presented.

Ashim Chatterjee

Ashim Chatterjee a fire-brand student leader of CPI (ML) in Calcutta. Broke away from Charu Mazumdar in 1971 after the failure of the attempts to build an armed movement in the Debra-Gopiballavpore area in West Bengal and due to opposition of CPI (ML), towards the liberation struggle of Bangladesh. Chatterjee formed the Bengal-Bihar-Orissa Border Regional Committee, CPI (ML) as a separate faction. His group joined the CPI (ML) as a separate faction of Satyanaryana Singh. Later Chatterjee formed the Communist Revolutionary League of India.

Asit Sen

He was trade unionist of Life Insurance Corporation (LIC). Sen in particular opposed sending students to the villages and spoke in favour of launching partial and economic struggles in the cities to make the workers conscious of their vanguard role. Sen was also critical of what he saw as the subjugation of the working class by the petty bourgeoisie in the movement. Asit Sen branded its Guevarism and individual terrorism as opposed to People's War and was having no popular support. He was one of the founding leaders of Maoist Communist Centre (MCC) in Bihar. He wrote an article entitled 'Marxism -Leninism and the though of Mao Tse—Tung are one' is *Liberation* November, 1969.

Chandra Pulla Reddy

He was Communist Politician from Andhra Pradesh. He was in the forefront of the Telangana struggle during 1946-51. He was one of the founding members of Andhra Pradesh Coordination Committee of Communist Revolutionaries (APCCCR). In 1971, he broke away from APCCCR and formed AIRCP. In 1973 Chandra Pulla Reddy merged with CPI ML–S.N. Singh faction. He wrote various articles which later came to be known as 'CP writings'.

Charu Mazumdar

Charu Mazumdar the chief ideologue of Naxalite's movement in India was born in 1918 in Siliguri, West Bengal. As a college drop out Mazumdar joined the Tebhaga movement in 1946. During the mid-1960's Mazumdar and Kanu Sanyal organized a leftist faction of CPI (M) in Northern Bengal. During 1965-66, he wrote various articles based on Marx, Lenin–Mao ideology, which later came to be known as 'Historic Eight documents'. In 1967 a militant peasant uprising took place at Naxalbari led by Mazumdar and Sanyal groups, and thus the group was known as Naxalites. The same year Mazumdar and Sanyal broke away and formed the All India Coordination Committee of Communist Revolutionaries (AICCCR) and found the CPI (ML) in 1969 with Mazumdar as its Secretary. He raised slogans like "power flows through the barrel of a gun", and "China's Chairman Mao is our Chairman." Mazumdar died in police custody at the Alipore central jail on July 28, 1972.

Devulapalli Venkateswara Rao

D.V. Rao popularly known as 'DV'. He was active in the Telangana armed struggle* and formulated the 'Andhra Thesis' of the CPI. In early days he worked as state secretariat member of CPI (M). Later he was expelled from the CPI (M). He took along with him the party weekly, '*Janashakti*' (Power of the People), which continued its publication till 1969. He was one of the founding members of the APCCCR. In December 1969, six out of nine state committee members of APCCCR were arrested at a hotel in Madras; among them were D.V. Rao and T.N. Reddy. Later APCCCR was merged in Unity

---

* The Telangana people's movement started in the early 1940s in the Hyderabad kingdom in South India as part of the all India states people's movement against the despotic monarchies.

Centre of Communist Revolutionaries of India (UCCRI). He was elected its Secretary of UCCRI. His most famous work was 'Marxism, Leninism, Mao Zedong thought is our world outlook'.

Dipankar Bhattacharjee

Dipankar Bhattacharjee was the General Secretary of the CPI (ML) – Liberation. Bhattacharjee succeeded Vinod Mishra as the leader of the party in 1998. Dipankar Bhattacharjee was born in Gowhati (Assam) in December 1960. Studied in Ramakrishna Mission Vidyalaya Narendrapur near Kolkata and stood first in Higher Secondary Examination in 1979, he joined the Indian Statistical Institute, Kolkata and became active in CPI (ML) politics.

He later worked as the General Secretary of the Indian People's Front and then as the General Secretary of the Party's Trade Union wing of All India Central Council of Trade Union (AICCTU). He was elected a member of Central Committee and Polit Bureau of CPI (ML) in December 1987. After the sudden demise of Vinod Mishra the General Secretary of the party in 1975, Dipankar was unanimously elected to the post.

Gaddar

Gaddar known as Gummadi Vittal Rao, is a revolutionary Telugu balladeer and a vocal Naxalite activist from the Andhra Pradesh. Born in 1949 in Toopran village of Medak district, he came from a poor dalit family. In 1969 Gaddar joined the struggle of separate Telangana state by forming a Burrakaatha Troupe (a kind of folk art in AP).

The art form was performed under the banner of Jana Natya Mandali since 1972. While continuing the performance, Gaddar took a banking recruitment exam and was selected for the post of a clerk at Canara Bank in 1975. He quit his bank job in 1984 to concentrate on Jana Natya Mandali.

After he voiced his protest against the killing of several dalits by upper caste landlords in Karamchedu village in Prakasam district in July 1985, the police raided Gaddar's house. He went underground through the forests of Andhra Pradesh, Maharashtra, Madhya Pradesh, and Orissa spreading the revolutionary ideology through folk arts. Gaddar and his groups adopted folk forms such as Oggukatha, Veedhi Bhagotham (vernacular ballets using a combination of song, dialogue and dance) for the purpose of revolution. Jana Natya Mandali was soon regarded as the cultural wing of the CPI ML (People's War).

Kanu Sanyal

Born in 1932 in West Bengal, he was one of the founding leaders of CPI (ML) formed in 1969. He announced the formation of the original CPI (ML) on Lenin's birthday in 1969 at a public rally in Calcutta. He came out with the seminal Terai report on Indian revolution. For seven years Sanyal was imprisoned in Jail in Andhra Pradesh, Sanyal was released from Jail in 1977, following the shift of government in India as well as in West Bengal. Jyoti Basu, the new CPI (M) Chief Minister, personally intervened to ensured Sanyal's release. After his release Sanyal rallied his supporters and formed the Organizing Committee of Communist Revolutionaries (OCCR). In 1985, Sanyal's faction along with five other groups, merged to form the communist organization of India (ML). Sanyal became the leader of CPI (ML). He is now General Secretary of a new CPI (ML), formed by merger of several splinter groups of the original party. He authored 'Report on the Peasant Movement in the Terai Region.'.

K.G. Satya Murthy

He attended the meeting of Andhra Pradesh revolutionaries in Guttikonda bilam, a small village in Guntur district in 1969. Charu Mazumdar attended as a Chief Guest in that meeting. Known as Sivasagar, he was a revolutionary poet and one of the chief architects of the People's War. He was number 2 in the party rank. In 1987, Satya Murthy was ousted from the party, following an internal dispute with Kondapalli Seetha Ramaiah. He was a dalit representative. Later he strongly criticized that PWG as caste dominated party.

Kondapalli Seetha Ramaiah

Born into a middle class family in Jonnavada village, Andhra Pradesh, Seetha Ramaiah joined the communists at a young age. He went on to become the Krishna district Secretary of CPI which was active during the Telangana rebellion with the division in CPI in 1964, Seetha Ramaiah withdrew from political life. He began working as a Hindi teacher at Fatima School in Warangal when he befriended K.G. Satya Murthy. Both men joined the CPI (ML). Seetha

Ramaiah became a member of the AP State Committee, CPI (ML) when the CPI (ML) had internal strife. He joined the Central Organizing Committee (COC), CPI (ML) in 1972. In August 1974, the AP State Committee of COC, CPI (ML) was organized, with Seetha Ramaiah as one of it three members. On April 26, 1977 Seetha Ramaiah was arrested in Nagpur, when police caught him with weapons in a vehicle. Though he was released on bail, he absconded and went underground. In 1977 he broke away from COC, CPI (ML), on April 22, 1980 he founded the CPI (ML) People's War. On January 2, 1982, he was arrested in Hyderabad at Begum pet railway station when waiting to board a train to Bombay. On January 1, 1984 he managed to escape from the prisoner's wing of the Osmania Hospital.

Following an internal dispute, which ended with the expulsion of K.G. Satya Murthy (number 2 in the party rank) and Byreddy Sathyanarayana Reddy, Seetha Ramaiah's hold over the party strengthened. In 1991, Seetha Ramaiah was ousted from the party. In 1993, he was caught by police in his home village. After few years in prison, he was acquitted and released on humanitarian grounds. During his final year, he abstained from political activity. He suffered from 'Parkinson's disease'. Kondapalli Seetha Ramaiah died in his granddaughter's house in Vijaywada on April 12, 2002. He was 87 years at the time of his death.

Muppala Lakshmana Rao alias Ganapathi

He is present General Secretary of CPI (Maoist). He was born in Village Beerpur in Sarangapur mandal in Karimnagar district of Andhra Pradesh. He worked as Teacher in Karimnagar district and deserted his job for higher education in Warangal. There, he met Maoist leaders Nalla Adi Reddy and Kondapalli Seetha Ramaiah and joined Naxalite movement. He was one of the early members of CPI (ML) People's War and grew as General Secretary of the party that is now called as CPI (Maoist).

Narayanan Kunikal

Kunikal was Maoist leader from Kerala, who represented from Kerala the first meeting of the AICCCR in November 1967. Kerala Maoists attacked the Tiruchelli and Pulpalli police stations in November 1968, and thereby obtained the support of the Kunikal Narayanan group. Leading role in these violent operations was played by Kunikal Narayanan, his wife Mandakini and daughter Ajitha.

Parimala Dasgupta

A well-known trade unionist of the State Electricity Board of West Bengal. He defeated and formed a rival coordination Committee at the state level. In a document, he criticized the CPI (ML) for neglecting the cities for refusing to participate in trade unions, and for ignoring the task of building class based mass organizations. This document also attacked the CPI (ML)'s method of guerilla warfare as 'Che Guevarism'. He branded the annihilation policy 'Guevarism' and 'individual terrorism' opposed to the idea of 'People's War' having no support among the people.

Santal Jangal

Being a young activist, Santal Jangal was leader of Kisan Sabha in early days. He was defeated by Tenzing Wangdi (Congress candidate), in the 1967 Assembly elections from Phansidewa constituency (ST reserved) in West Bengal. He was of peasant origin, had very little formal education, but had been organizing peasantry in their area, Naxalbari for a long time and had become extremely popular.

Satyanarayana Singh

Veteran trade unionist of Bihar industrial belt. He was a member of the Central Committee and leader of the Bihar unit of CPI (M) before he became a Naxalite. He had a sizable following in the industrial belt of Bihar, a good section of which he brought over to the Naxalites. He was one of the staunchest supporters of annihilation and also provided leadership to the abortive Mushahari uprisings. His dispute with Mazumdar led to his expulsion from CPI (ML) although Singh claims that most of the members the Central Committee of the party were with him on this issue. S.N. Singh in his report on Mushahari noted the presence of 'Pseudo-political criminals' or 'vagabonds' among leading activitists. (Dasgupta, 1974).

S.N. Singh was not opposed to the annihilation as such in fact; he implemented this policy in a small way in Mushahari and some other parts of Bihar. But he opposed killing rich peasants while Mazumdar considered these peasants.

He wrote various articles in '*Liberation*' i.e., 'Building up the proletarian party and agrarian revolution' and 'Mushahari and its lessons'.

Satyanarayana Vempatapu

He was born in Boorjuvalasa village, Bobbili Taluk of Srikakulam district. He came from a poor peasant family. He worked as teacher in Goyyupaka village, agency area of Parvathipuram in 1956-57. After he started a private management primary school in Kondabaradi village in 1958, he worked against the atrocities of landlords. Vempatapu Satyanarayana joined the armed struggle of Srikakulam Tribal Peasants Movement. He had never been arrested in total eight years of movement. He attended first Congress of CPI (ML) in Calcutta. Satyanarayana was killed shortly after July 11, 1970, allegedly in an encounter by police in the Bori hills near Parvathipuram.

Subrata Dutt

Subrata Dutt known as Jauhar was a revolutionary activist from the state of West Bengal. He was elected the General Secretary of CPI (ML) Party Central Committee reorganized at a meeting at Durgapur, West Bengal in 1975. He died in a police encounter in Bhojpur.

Sushital Roy Choudhury

He worked as a close associate of Charu Mazumdar. He worked on the editorial boards of '*Swadhinata*' and then of '*Desh Hitaishi*' before he became a Naxalite. In his years as an active functionary of the communist movement he acquired the reputation of a soft-spoken sincere person although he was not known outside party circle. After the formation of All India Coordination of Communist Revolutionaries (AICCCR) he acted its convener and after CPI (ML) was formed he became a leading member of its Polit Bureau and also the editor of *Liberation,* its organ.

Tarimala Nagi Reddy

Tarimala Nagi Reddy often called 'TN' was a Communist politician from A.P. Born in Tarimala in Anantapur district, he studied at Loyola College in Madras and at Banaras Hindu University in Varanasi. During his student days he involved in Nationalism and Marxism. Because of his activities, he was jailed in 1940, 1941 and 1946.

Nagi Reddy was elected to the Madras Legislative Assembly, as a Communist candidate in 1951. He was elected to the Lok Sabha from Anantapur in 1957 and to A.P. Legislative Assembly as CPI candidate from Puttoor in 1962. He was again elected to the Assembly as a CPI (M) candidate from Anantapur in 1967.

In 1968 he broke with CPI (M) and formed the Andhra Pradesh Coordination Committee of Communist Revolutionaries (APCCCR). He succeeded in attracting a large part of the CPI (M) cadre to APCCCR. During a brief period, APCCCR was part of All India Coordination Committee of Communist Revolutionaries (AICCCR). Nagi Reddy was however very critical of the Left adventurist line of the Charu Mazumdar, instead he promoted mass line. Thus, Reddy and APCCCR were expelled from AICCCR. In 1975, Unity Centre of Communist Revolutionaries of India (UCCRI-ML) was formed through the merger of APCCCR and three other groups. T.N. Reddy worked as a leader of APCCCR until his death in 1976. His most famous work was 'India Mortgaged'.

Varavara Rao

Varavara Rao, a known Telugu revolutionary poet, a public speaker and a literary critic was an emissary of the CPI (Maoist) during the latter's talks with State Government of Andhra Pradesh in 2002 and 2004. Varavara Rao was born on November 3, 1940 in a small village (Chinna Pendyala) in Warangal district of Andhra Pradesh, India. Started writing poetry and literary criticism from college days, he worked as a lecturer teaching Telugu literature to graduate and undergraduate students for about 40 years.

Rao founded 'Sahithi Mithrulu' (friends of literature) and launched *Srujana,* a forum for the promotion of modern Telugu literature in November 1966. He formed 'Thiragabadu' (rebel) poets groups along with his friends in January 1970. He was one of the founders of Viplava Rachayitala Sangham (Virasam-Revolutionary Writer's Association) on July 4, 1970 and consistently remained active being on the executive body of the organization. He is also the founder executive member of the All India League for Revolutionary Culture (AILRC) formed in 1983. He has been its General Secretary since 1993. Involved in 18 cases, he spent six years in jail intermittently since 1973, the last one being 'one thousand days and nights of solitary confinement' during 1985-89 in Secunderabad and Ramnagar conspiracy against state which is pending since 1986. The courts have acquitted him in all other cases.

As part of this revolutionary movement V.V. brought out seven anthologies. His post doctoral work (1991-94) was on the transformation of folk song into peoples' song in Telangana during 1968-88. His letters from jail were published simultaneously in two dailies *Andhra Prabha* (Telugu) and *The Indian Express* literary supplements from April 1988 to April 1989. His collections of the letters, 'Sahacharulu' (companions) were published in 1989. V.V. translated into Telugu Ngugi Wa Thiango's novel 'Devil on the Cross' and a 'Writer's Prison Diary Detained' into Telugu during his confinement in jail in 1985-89. Varavara Rao along with another revolutionary Gaddar acted as an emissary for CPI (ML) Peoples War when the TDP Government proposed peace talks with Peoples War in 2001. The talk's process went on between May and July 2002 and Varavara Rao and Gaddar pulled themselves out of the peace negotiations after a series of 'encounter' deaths.

Again in June 2004, Varavara Rao along with Gaddar and novelist G. Kalyana Rao acted as emissaries of CPI (ML) People's War in the peace talks initiated by the Congress Party. The peace talks which started in 2004 after a round of negotiations ended with the ban of CPI (Maoist), Virasam and other people's organization in August 2005.

Within 24 hours of the ban on Virasam, Varava Rao and Kalyana Rao were arrested on August 19, 2005 under AP Public Security Act and were sent to Chanchalguda Central Prison in Hyderabad. Since his arrest, seven new cases were filed against him. The court had struck down the case on Varavara Rao under Public Security Act on March 31, 2006 and he obtained bail for all other cases by the time. He was released from jail on bail on March 31, 2006 after a period of about seven and half months.

Vinod Mishra

Vinod Mishra popularly known as 'VM'. Born on March 24, 1947 in Meria Village of Chunal Block in Mirzapur district of Uttar Pradesh, Vinod's father Suryakesh Mishra was an office employee in an ordinance establishment at Jabalpur in Madhya Pradesh. After passing his school days at the Adarsh Banga Vidyalaya Inter College, he graduated from Kanyakubja Degree College and joined in Christ Church Degree College for his post-graduate degree in Mathematics. Grown up in a Leftist political milieu, young Vinod joined the

Regional Engineering College at Durgapur in 1966 as faculty in mechanical engineering.

He soon associated himself with the Leftist student's movement and following Naxalbari, this association turned him into a Naxalite. He established links with AICCCR and started political propaganda among students.

His brief note entitled "Fight against the Metaphysical view point of perfectionism" appeared towards the end of 1977 and the campaign was formally launched in January, 1978 with circular drafted by him, entitled "Strengthen the party organization." Vinod Mishra accompanied by Raghu visited China in 1979. They undertook extensive tours as state guests and exchanged experiences with Chinese leaders who were highly impressed by his activities. However, he politely refused to accept any material help including the Chinese comrades' offer for his kidney operation. His firm belief was all resources for the Indian revolution must be mobilized in India. Both CPC and the CPI (ML) kept the visit a closely guarded secret until after the latter came into the open.

APPENDIX–II

Chronology of Events

Table–70

Naxalbari Type Upsurges (1968-70)

S.No.	*Place*	*Region/District*	*State*	*Leadership*	*Details*
1.	Debra–Gopiballavpore (These are two police station areas)	Midnapore (bordering Bihar and Orissa)	West Bengal	Ashim Chatterjee, Santosh Rana	1. October 1, 1969 One thousand armed peasants attacked the house of notorious *jotedar*. 2. October 14, 1969 Squad of 12 guerillas killed *Jotedar*, by the end of the 1969 about 20 *Jotedars* were executed by the rebels. A report in the Indian press said in January 1970 that the Maoists controlled a zone of 200 villages in Debra and 300 villages in Gopiballavpore, 127 class enemies were annihilated in this period out of them, 94 were *jotedars*, 14 were police agents 10 policemen or paramilitary personnel and 9 others.
2.	Mushahari (a small block of 12 villages)	Muzaffarpur	Bihar	Satyanarayana Singh	April 1968 the movement started when peasants of the Gangapur village forcibly harvested by standing crops from the landlords land.
3.	Lakhimpur–Kheri	Terai (Close to the Nepal border)	Uttar Pradesh	Shiva Kumar Mishra and Mohinder Singh	The top Maoist of Uttar Pradesh S.K. Mishra was arrested on Novemebr 21, 1970, the Mohinder Singh group rebelled against Mazumdar leadership and the movement was split in late 1970. Each of the two groups reported two cases of annihilation of landlords between July 1971 and January 1972.

Contd...

S.No.	Place	Region/District	State	Leadership	Details
4.	Chamkaur Sahib Police station attack	Rupar, Gurudas districts	Punjab	Satyanarayana Singh	Land Seizure campaigns organized, the first major action took place on April 30, 1969, and Maoists attacked a police station in Chamkaur Sahib and injured a police official. The Mazumdar group claimed that they annihilated the Dy. Superintendent of Police in Patiala in August 1971. In September they snatched four rifles and two hundred rounds of ammunition from a police post in Sangrur district and killed a police official in raid. By March 1972, the Maoists had killed a total of 36 persons including land lords police men and police agents. The police had killed 24 rebels.
5.	Pulpalli, Manantody Tiruchelli	North Wynad, Canannore	Kerala	Kunikal Narayanan, Verghese, K.P.R. Gopalan, Philip Prasad, V.K. Balan	Sixty rebels led by Ajitha (Kunnikal's daughter) Philip and Verghese attacked a wireless police station in Pulpalli on the morning of November 24, 1968. They assaulted the sub-inspector and constables with country made guns and spears, killing a Havildar.
6.	Ganjam and Koraput	Mayurbhanj, Sundargarh	Orissa	D.B.M. Patnaik, Nagabhushan Patnaik, Radhamohan Das, Purshotham Pali, Gananath Patro, Rabidas	The first Squad action took place on August13, 1969, in the Pedamulaga village in the Gunupur region.
7.	Goalpara	Goalpara, Kamrup	Assam		The Maoists conducted economic campaign in 1968, launched squad actions in 1969 by April 1970 three landlords had been annihilated.

Table–71

Massive Attacks on Landlords and Moneylenders by Naxalites in Srikakulam Armed Struggle

S.No.	*Date*	*Village*	*Name of Victims*	*No. of Persons Participated*
1.	1968 November 24		Maddi Kamesu	
2.	1968 November 25	Pedagottili	Teegala Harichandra Rao, Teegala Lakshminaryana	1500 members
3.	1968 November 27	Duddukhallu	Rammurthy (Moneylender)	400 tribes
4.	1968 December 27	Modemkhallu	Unna Ramamurthy, Unna Jagannadha Rao	1000 members
5.	1969 March 10	Badevalasa	Chokkapu Tirupatamma, Chokkapu Narayanamma	30 members
6.	1969 March 24	Bathupuram	Varanasi Nityanandham	50
7.	1969 March 30	Tadisila	Namaluri Narayanamma	500 members
8.	1969 April 24	Sompeta-Padmapuram	Manipatruni Karunandh Patnaik	10 members
9.	1969 May 11	Ponkala Sompeta Circle	Govinda Naidu	7 members
10.	1969 May 16	Tumbali Kurupam	Dollu Appala Swamy, Mosangi Narasimhamurthy, Mosangi Sasirekha	
11.	1969 May 26	Loharjola, Kotturu (PS)	11 Houses	100 members
12.	1969 October 4	Kapuummulada	Sakalaabattula Krishna Murthy	100 members
13.	1969 October 13	Thodumu, Parvathipuram	Vendikanti Mahanti, Devaraylu	
14.	1969 November 2	Pedabuddidi, Parvathipuram Tehsil	Potnuru Satyanarayana	200 Adivasis

Table–72
Annihilation of Class Enemies by Naxalites in Srikakulam Armed Struggle

S.No.	Date	Place	Name of Victim	Attacked by
1.	1969 February 6	Potivada Village, Elvinpeta (Police Station)	Vittal Prasad alias Trinadha Rao	
2.	1969 February 26	Boddapadu	Battina Bhima Rao, Bondada Simhadri	Subba Rao Panigrahi Dalam
3.	1969 March 7	Pokkiri Village, Neelakantapuram (Police Station)	Alluvada Gumpa Swamy (Karanam)	200 Tribals
4.	1969 April 5	Gujjuvayi Sivada	Tadela Simhadri Naidu	
5.	1969 May 14	Mushidiwada, Visakhapatnam district	Pusapati Narasimha Raju	Nagabhushan Patnaik and 5 members of dalam and local dalits
6.	1969 May 19	Borivanka Village, Sompeta Circle	Balleda Venkateswara Sarma, Ballada Krishna Murthy	
7.	1969 June 20	Akkupalli Village, Srikakulam district	Komchada Bhuchandra Rao	Chowdari Tejeswara Rao, Pylavasu, Tumada Ganapathi and 80 members
8.	1969 July 18	Degalapoluru	Pratap Chandra Padi	-do-
9.	1969 July 21	Malliveedu village, Srikakulam district	Balaji Naidu S/o Netala Appalaswami Naidu	

Contd...

S.No.	Date	Place	Name of Victim	Attacked by
10.	1969 August 24	Kalalakondabaridi, Elwinpeta Police Station.	Aarika Sriramulu (Contractor)	Vempatapu Satyanarayana
11.	1969 November 9	Banjaru Yuvarajapuram Village	Saari Appanna	
12.	1970 January 18	Bhavanapuram Village	Vuna Savaraiah	
13.	1970 February 13	Ambati Kambaram Village	Sukutagowna	
14.	1970 February 20	Thallapalem, Nellore district	Puchhalapalli Venkatarami Reddy	
15.	1970 March 19	Nayakammaguda, Srikakulam district	Savara Nayakamma (Tribal Informer)	
16.	1970 April 8	Tharlapalli Village, Guntur district	A.Venkata Lakshmi Narasimha Rao	

Note: Totally 34 persons were killed by Naxalites in various incidents in the movement period.

Table-73
Encounter Killings in Srikakulam Movement

S.No.	Date	Place	Name of the Leader	Details	Number of Deaths
1.	1968 March 4	Peddakarja forests, Near Tadi Konda, Elvin Peta (Police station) Parvathipuram Taluk	Karrenna, Uyaka Geedari (Tribals)	Encounter between police and Naxalites	2
2.	1969 May 27 at 3 pm	Patha Kota forest, Near Jalanthra Kota, Sompeta	Panchadi Krishna Murthy	Six others including Niranjana Rao (age 14 years) were taken into custody and shot dead)	7
3.	1969 November 23	Kerasingi hills, Patapatnam, Tekkali Taluk	Dr. Chaganti Bhaskar, Thamada Ganapathy	Taken into custody that they were tortured and they ultimately die	4
4.	1969 December 22	Rangamatia hills, Mandasa	Subba Rao Panigrahi, Panchadi Nirmala, Ramesh Chandra Sahu	Taken into custody and tortured and shot dead	3
5.	1970 July 10	Borikondalu, Kurupam	Vempatapu Satyanarayana, Adibhatla Kailsam	Encounter	2
6.	1970 July 30	Ranarayu Kondalu, Mandasa	Dr. Devineni Mallikharjuna	Shot dead	3

Note: Mass Killings of over 350 revolutionaries by the State during 1968-76 in the so-called encounters.

Table–74
Major Encounter Killings

S.No.	Date	Place	Identity of Victims	Mode of Killing	No. of Deaths
1.	1985 April 1	Venkataraopet, Karimnagar district	Activists 3 Agri Laborers 2	Tied hands and shot dead	5
2.	1985 September 4	Boorugupakala, Visakhapatnam district	Activists	Tortured and shot dead	5
3.	1987 June 11	Cintabodi, Adilabad district	Activists	Shot dead at once	4
4.	1987 August 14	Illendu, Khammam	Activists	Arrested and shot dead	4
5.	1987 August 30	Abbapur, Warangal	Activists	Shot dead at once	4
6.	1987 November 25	Eleswaram, East Godavari district	Activists	Shot dead	5
7.	1991 February 22	Ahmadipur, Medak	Three activists and two landless share croppers	Taken into custody and shot dead	5
8.	1991 May 29	Kachinapalli, Khammam	One squad member, two elected representatives and two legal activists	One person killed in firing on an armed squad and the rest taken into custody and shot dead	5
9.	1991 December 4	Tulasipeta, Adilabad district	Three organizers and two tribal youth	Chased and killed	5

Contd...

S.No.	Date	Place	Identity of Victims	Mode of Killing	No. of Deaths
10.	1991 December 9	Bommakur, Warangal district	One organizer and three rural youth	Taken into custody and killed	4
11.	1991 December 18	Mukhadumpuram, Warangal district	Rural Youth	Taken into custody and killed	4
12.	1991 December 28	Masjidguda, Rangareddy district	Ghulam Rasool (Journalist) and one unemployed youth	Taken into custody and killed	2
13.	1992 January 6	Pagideru, Khammam district	13 Rural youth and one van driver	13 persons taken into custody from a van and shot dead. Van driver was later killed in a fake accident	14

Table–75
Top Leaders Killed by Naxalites

S.No.	Date	Name of Politician	Nature of Death
1.	1983 May	K. Kesavareddy, Ex. MLA (Cong) Huzurabad, Karimnagar district	Shot dead
2.	1984 February	B. Ramchandra Rao, RSS Leader Jagitiala, Karimnagar district	Shot dead
3.	1988 July	K. Ramadas, Ex. MLA (Cong) Kolhapur Mahabubnagar district	Murdered
4.	1988 November	Sappa Ramulu, MPP Adilabad district	Murdered
5.	1989 April	Daggubati Chenchu Ramaiah, F/o Dr. Daggupati Venkateswara Rao, Paruchuru, Prakasam district	Hacked to death

Contd...

S.No.	Date	Name of Politician	Nature of Death
6.	1989 June 10	Malhar Rao MPP (TDP), Tadicharla, Karimnagar district	Abducted and murdered
7.	1989 December	Raghavendra Reddy (BJP), Mahabubabad, Warangal district	Shot dead
8.	1990 August 7	Duggirala Venkta Rao, Ex. MLA (TDP), Gopalapuram	Shot dead
9.	1991 May 8	S. Chenna Reddy, Ex. MLA, Penugonda	Shot dead
10.	1991 December 5	T. Hayagrivachary, Ex. Minister, Hanumakonda	Shot dead
11.	1995 December 1	Magunta Subba Rami Reddy, Congress MP, Ongole, Prakasam district	Shot dead
12.	1998 January 25	L. Kishan Reddy, Ex. MLA, Nizamabad	Shot dead
13.	1998 July 10	P. Ramesh Reddy, Chairman DCCB, Adilabad	Shot dead
14.	1998 December 16	K. Narayna Reddy, Ex. MP (Cong)	Shot dead
15.	1999 April 13	Duddilla Sripada Rao, Former Speaker, AP State Assembly, MLA, Manthani, Karimnagar district	Shot dead
16.	1999 August 16	Budda Vengal Reddy, Ex. MLA (TDP) Atmakur, Kurnool district	Shot dead
17.	1999 September 15	P. Purshotham Rao, MLA, Sirpur	Shot dead
18.	2000 March 7	A. Madhava Reddy, Minister, Panchayat Raj, Government of AP and Home Minister earlier	Landmine at Ghatkesar
19.	2000 December 29	D. Ragyanayak MLA, Devarakonda, Mahaboobnagar district	Shot dead at Maddimadugu
20.	2005 August 15	C. Narsi Reddy, MLA, Makthal	Shot dead at an Independence day programme at Narayanapet

Table-76
Major Incidents of Police Personnel Killed by Naxalites in Landmine Blasts

S.No.	*Date*	*Place of Incident*	*Details*	*No. of Deaths*
1.	1981 April 20	Indervalli , Adilabad district	Mohd Ghouse PC (Raid)	1
2.	1985 September 2	Kazipet Rly Jn , Warangal district	N. Yadagiri Reddy, SI, Kazipet PS	1
3.	1986 November 6	Peddapalli , Karimnagar district	T. Buchireddy, DSP, Karimnagar	1
4.	1987 July 30	M. Bhimavaram Visakhapatnam district	HC- 2, PC-4 (Ambush)	6
5.	1987 August 18	Addala Thimmapur, Adilabad district	SI-2, PC-8 (Ambush)	10
6.	1989 February 1	Singapur, Adilabad district	SI, PC-6 (Attack with grenades)	7
7.	1991 June 15	Chalapaka, Eturunagaram, Warangal district	CI, SI, PC-4	6
8.	1991 August 3	Yanam Palli	SI, PC-7	8
9.	1991 December 19	Ramavaram, Karimnagar district	CI, SI-2, PC-3	6
10.	1992 February 7	Ramareddy Village, Nizamabad district.	LK Naik CRPF-3, HC-1, PC-2	6
11.	1992 August 29	Murtharam (M) Karimnagar district.	Veeradevyadav, Dy. Comndt. B.S.F., PC-6	7
12.	1992 September 4	Kalavalangaram, Khammam district	RI, RSI, ARSI, HC, PC-6	10
13.	1992 September 24	Viswanthagudem, Warangal district	SI (BSF), HC-2, PC-11	14
14.	1992 October 27	Donkarai, East Godavari district	SI, HC, PC-2	4
15.	1993 July 8	Bhupalapalli, Warangal district	ARSI, HC, PC-3	5
16.	1993 October 12	Bathupalli, Pocharam, Karimnagar district	HC, PC3	4

Contd...

S.No.	Date	Place of Incident	Details	No. of Deaths
17.	1993 November 14	Somasila – Kollapur, Mahabubnagar district	Paradesi Naidu, SP, Mahabubnagar, SI-2, HC-1, PC-5	9
18.	1993 January 27	K.S.Vyas, DIG, LB Stadium, Hyderabad	DIG (shot dead)	1
19.	1994 November 26	Peddampet, Karimnagar district.	Comnt, Commander, HC-2, PC, SI	6
20.	1994 November 29	Orugonda Busstand, Warangal district	HC-3, PC-5	8
21.	1996 October 7	Jakaram, Warangal district	CI, HC, PC-5	7
22.	1996 November 15	Sirpur Adilabad district	SI, HC-3, PC-9	13
23.	1997 January 8/9	Karkagudem, Khammam district	HC-3, PC-13	16
24.	1997 May 17	Laxmapur-Amnabad, Mahabubnagar district	SI, PC-4	4
25.	1997 August 8	Lothugedda, Visakhapatnam district	PC-7	7
26.	1998 February 22	Mulakuddur, Visakhapatnam district	PC-2, Tribals 7	9
27.	1998 June 10	Mothgudem, Warangal district	SI, PCs 9, Others 3	13
28.	1999 September 4	Sanjeeva Reddy Nagar, 'X' Roads, Hyderabad	Umeshchandra, IPS	1
29.	1999 December 2	Thumukumta, Veesenagandla Mandal, Mahabubnagar district	PC-3, Civilians 2	5
30.	2000 February 19	Darakonda Police Outpost, G.K.Veedhi, Visakhapatnam district	PC 7	7
31.	2000 February 20	Baster, Madhya Pradesh	ASP and 22 Policemen	24
32.	2001 April 18	Chintakarrapalem, Y. Ramavarm Mandal, East Godavari district		4

Table-77
Attacks on Civil Liberties and Cultural Activists

S.No.	Date	Name	Details	Place	Done by
1.	1985 January 12	Gopi Rajanna	Young Lawyer of Jagtial and activist of Karimnagar Unit of APCLC	Murdered at Jagtial Karimnagar district	BJP activists in collusion with the police
2.	1985 September 3	Dr. A. Ramanadham	Doctor and Senior Office bearer of APCLC	Shot dead at his clinic Warangal	Mufti police
3.	1986 November 7	Japalakshman Reddy	Senior Office bearer of APCLC		Police
4.	1989 August 31	Dr. Balagopal	General Secretary, APCLC	Abducted at Karim-nagar	Praja Bandu
5.	1991 December 7	Narra Prabhakar Reddy	Lawyer, Convener Warangal District Unit APCLC and Secretary Warangal Bar Association	Killed at his house, Warangal	Police
6.	1997 April 6	Gaddar	Revolutionary Singer & Cultural activist	Opened fire at Hyderabad	Green Tigers
7.	2000 November 23	T. Purushotham	Joint Secretary, APCLC	Hacked to death, Madhurapur Colony Dilsukh nagar, Saroor nagar PS, Hyderabad	Unknown persons

Contd...

S.No.	Date	Name	Details	Place	Done by
8.	2001 February 18	Md. Azam Ali	General Secretary, Nalgonda district unit APCLC	Hacked to death at Nalgonda	Unknown persons
9.	2003 November 6	Dr. G. Lakshman	President APCLC	Kidnapped at Tarnak, Hyderabad and tortured brutally and released	Tirumala Tigers (Nayeemuddin gang)
10.	2003 December 11	Bichcha Reddy	Human rights activists, APCLC, Mahabubnagar	Fatal accident at Mahabubnagar	
11.	2005 August 24	K. Kanaka Chari	Teacher and Rights activists, Executive Committee Member Patriotic and Democratic Movement (PDM)	Abducted and hacked to death	Narsa Cobras
12.	2005 September 10	Mannem Prasad	District President, Struggle committee for Annihilation of caste	Murdered at Singaraya Konda, Prakasam district	Nallamala Black Cobras

Table-78
Major Encounters

S.No	Date	Place	Identity of Victims	Mode of Killing	No. of Deaths
1.	1999 March 31	Chinta Kunta Near Narsapur town, Medak district	10 Naxalites including three women were killed	Tortured and shot dead	10
2.	1999 April 15	Sita Rampally near Siddi Pet, Medak district	Six Naxalites were killed	Round up and shot dead	6
3.	1999 May 9	Kanchamal, Kondapur, Lingampet Mandal, Nizamabad district	Six Naxalites were killed	Shot dead	6
4.	1999 December 2	Koyuru, Karimnagar district	Nalla Adi Reddy, Erram Reddy Santoshreddy, Seelam Naresh alias Murali CPI (ML) PW central committee members	Taken out of the Bangalore and shot dead	4
5.	2000 April 10	Dondapadu Guntur district	Kommireddy Viswamohan Reddy and Smt. Mariamma (Viswamohan Reddy is also a known writer and poet)	Shot dead	2
6.	2000 April 10	Burgumpadu, Patha Pinapaka, Khammam district	CPI (ML) Janashakti Naxalites–5	Shot dead	5
7.	2000 April 26	Thallavellemla Village, Chityala Mandal Nalgonda district	6 Naxalites including one women were killed Katta	Shot dead	6

Contd...

S.No	Date	Place	Identity of Victims	Mode of Killing	No. of Deaths
			Ramaswami alias Sagar Commander PW, Rachakonda Dalam		
8.	2000 April 27	Kowkonda, Warangal district	12 Naxalites were killed	Shot dead	12
9.	2000 November 1	Bhopalapally	Seven Women Naxalites were killed	Shot dead	7
10.	2001 June 19	Godukondla, Chintapalli Mandal Nalgonda district	8 Naxalites including 3 women	Shot dead	8
11.	2001 August 5	Chandurthi Rudrangi (M) Karimnagar district	Five Naxalites including one women Naxalite	Shot dead	5
12.	2002 March 11	Tupakulapalli, Eturu Nagaram, border of Warangal and Karimnagar district		Tortured and shot dead	11
13.	2002 June 24	Ulvanur Mavillavai Near Poloncha, Khammam district	Women Naxalites 2	Shot dead	2
14.	2002 July 2	Nerella, Dharmapuri Mandal Karimnagar	Top women Naxalites leader Padmakka alias Rajitha, Karimnagar, Nizamabad dist., West Division Secretary and Sagar	Shot dead	4

Contd...

S.No	Date	Place	Identity of Victims	Mode of Killing	No. of Deaths
15.	2002 July 26	Dameru Village Warangal Karimnagar border	Five Naxalites, including three women, Vijayendra Reddy alias Sreenu, G. Ramesh alias Naveen	Shot dead	5
16.	2002 November 11	Mahadeveapur forest area, Karimnagar district	Bhimla Nayak alias Karim-nagar- Sayam Warangal District Secretary CPUSI	Shot dead	7
17.	2002 November 17	Ilapuram border of Karim-nagar-Warangal district	Five Naxalites of PGA	Shot dead	5
18.	2003 May 14	Agarguda forest area, Bezuru Mandal, Adilabad district	Lalitha (District Secretary), Aruna (Member Military Platoon), Kuruna (Member Jananatya Mandali)	Short dead	2
19.	2003 October 24	Bollapalli, Guntur district	Lathakka alias Radhakka, Koumudi	Shot dead	2
20.	2004 January 25	Peeleru, Chitturu district	Three top leaders including a state military commission member Errasatyam and Sivanand	Arrested and shot dead	2
21.	2005 March 7	Manala Kommanpalli mandal, Nizamabad district	Ramesh, Secretary West Division, Suneetha (Wife of Ramesh), Sreenu Commander, Sobha (Wife of Sreenu)	Tortured and shot dead	10

Contd...

S.No	Date	Place	Identity of Victims	Mode of Killing	No. of Deaths
22.	2005 March 19	Boorgupeta, Venkatapuram mandal, Warangal district	Yadanna, Dist. Secretary of Warangal and Khammam, Maoist Cadre 3	Shot dead	4
23.	2005 July 1	Siddipeta, Karimnagar district	Top Janashakti Leader Riaz and Three other Naxalites	Shot dead	4
24.	2005 August 22	Barukonda, Vanguru mandal, Mahabubnagar district	CPI (Maoist) Nalgonda Secretary Diwakar alias Rar, Courier -1	Shot dead	2
25.	2006 April 28	Seshachalam Sundupalli mandal, Kadapa district	State Committee members-2, women members-6	Shot dead	9
26.	2006 June 16	Nallamala forest Pullala Cheruvu mandal, Prakasam district	Mattam Ravi Kumar State Committee member	Shot dead	1
27.	2006 June 27	Pedda Jalabanda, Near Sangadigundala, Nallamala forest area, Mahabubnagar district	Mahesh Commander Kalvakurthi dalam, women cadre 6	Shot dead	8
28.	2006 July 23	Devaboyinapenta, Nallamala forest, Prakasam district	Maoist AP State Committee Secretary Burra Chinnaiah alias Madhav along with Seven Maoists (including 5 women)	Encounter	8

Contd...

S.No	Date	Place	Identity of Victims	Mode of Killing	No. of Deaths
29.	2006 September 15	Tadvai forest area, Warangal district	Karimnagar East division, Maoist Committee Secretary, Madhu was killed along with women cadres Nirmala, Padma, Prameela	Shot dead	4
30.	2006 October 6	Forest area of Nallamala, Anantapur district	Sudharsan alias Samala Venkateshu Nallamala forest division committee secretary	Shot dead	1
31.	2006 October 7	Gorlagoyee, Mampa (Ps) Koyuru Mandal, Visakhapatnam district	Kadari Ramu alias agency RK (Senior member East division)	Shot dead	1
32.	2006 November 10	Pallela Vaaripalle reserve forest area, Gopavaram mandal, Kadapa district	Obulesu, Maoist state committee member and Rayalaseema Maoist committee secretary, Prasanthi (Obulesu's wife) Mallikarjuna Ananthapur district Secretary and cadres 6 members	Shot dead	9

Table-79
Major Abductions by Naxalites

S.No.	*Date*	*Incident*
1.	1987 December 27	PWG Naxalites abducted a group of IAS Officers from Gurthedu forest area in East Godavari district, Andhra Pradesh., viz., 1. S.R. Sankaran, Principal Secretary, Government of AP 2. M.V.P.C. Sastri, Dist. Collector, East Godavari 3. V.M. Manohar Prasad, Special Officer for Tribal Areas 4. T. Vijaya Kumar, Project Director, ITDA 5. R. Subrahmanyam, Sub-Collector, Rampachodavaram 6. S. Narsimha Rao, Dy. Collector, Kakinada
2.	1989 December 23	The Naxalites abducted Telugu Desam Party leader Mandava Venkateswara Rao, MLA, Dachapalli from Ramamadugu village.
3.	1991 May 10	P. Sudhir Kumar, Andhra Pradesh State Youth Congress President, Son of Former Union External Affairs Minister P. Shivashankar, abducted by the PWG Naxalites in broad day light from the residence in Himayatnagar, Hyderabad.
4.	1992 February 10	P. Bala Raju, MLA. Chintapalli and G. Sreenivasulu, IAS and Seven others were abducted by Naxalites from Koyuru forest Visakhapatnam district.
5.	2001 October 26	Marthanda Rao, rich contractor and relative of Union Minister of State Ch. Vidya Sagar Rao from residence in Korem village, Boinapalli mandal, Karimnagar district.
6.	2002 August 23	Naxalites abducted 5 police constables from the Anakapalli police station, Visakhaptnam district, one was (Chittibabu) subsequently killed while the remaining four were released.
7.	2002 December 19	Two Policemen of the Dachepalli Police Station in Guntur district were abducted from Takkellapadu village.
8.	2003 April 2	PWG Naxalites forced out four policemen including a Sub-Inspector, from a Stationery bus near Katama Raju Tanda in Peddaraveedu village on the fringes of the Nallamal forests in Prakasam district.

Table–80
Naxalites Major Attacks on Police / Security Forces

S.No.	Date	Place	Details	Nature of Death	No. of Deaths
1.	1999 September 4	Sanjeeva Reddy nagar Cross Roads, Hyderabad	Umesh Chandra, IPS	Short dead	1
2.	1999 December 1	Thumukunta, Veesenagandla mandal, Mahabubnagar district	SI-1, PC-2, Private Zeep driver-1, Cleaner-1	Landmine	5
3.	2000 February 19	Darakonda Police outpost G.K. Veedhi, Visakhapatnam district	ARSI-1, PC-6	Attack	7
4.	2001 April 18	Chintakarrapalem, Y. Ramava-ram mandal, East Godavari district	Police-4	Landmine	4
5.	2001 August 20	Bandla Motu-Remidicherla Village, Guntur district	Police-10	Landmine	10
6.	2001 September 9	Sunnampalli near Maaredumilli, Rajahmundry, Bhadrachalam State high way, East Godavari district	Ansari Hawaldhar, CRPF, Suresh Yadav, V.K. Sahu, Ravindra Kumar Behra, Heera Singh, CRPF Jawans	Landmine	5
7.	2002 July 23	Adigoppula, Durgi mandal Guntur district	RSI-4 Greyhound Constables-3	Landmine	4

Contd...

S.No.	Date	Place	Details	Nature of Death	No. of Deaths
8.	2002 November 18	Chintagudem between Tupakula gudem and Eturunagaram	Passengers-20	Blowup RTC bus	20
9.	2003 January 5	Dachepalli, Guntur district	Police–3	Landmine	3
10.	2005 March 11	Chilakalurpet, Guntur district	R. Prasad, CI, HC-1, PC-1, Homeguard–1, Civilians 3	Hacked to death	7
11.	2005 April 27	Ongole, Prakasam district	Maheshchandra Ladda, narrowly escaped, one civilian dead	Claymore mine	1
12.	2005 December 25	Kooneru Railway Station, Vizianagaram district	RPF-4, (Escorting Raigarh passengers train)	Attack	4

Table-81
A.P. Government's Policy Towards Naxalites
(Chronology of the Events that Led to Re-imposition of Ban on the Naxalites

S.No.	*Date*	*Details*
1.	1968 November 25	Srikakulam armed struggle begins.
2.	1969 June 7	A.P. State Government declare Parvathipuram agency, Palakonda and Patapatnam areas are disturbed areas under the Act Andhra Pradesh (Suppression of disturbance) Act, 1948. Three taluks in Warangal district and parts of Manthani taluk in Karimnagar district and several areas of Khammam district have also been declared disturbed areas.
3.	1970 January 16	'Parvathipuram Conspiracy Case' registered. A charge sheet was filed against 140 Naxalites.
4.	1975 July 4 – 1977 March 31	Emergency – Repression on ultra leftists and others then A.P. Chief Minister Jalagam Vengal Rao carried out massive combing operations leading to numerous human rights violations.
5.	1976	Besides, two taluks of East Godavari were notified as 'disturbed'.
6.	1976 August 3	The Judgement was pronounced convicting 17 leading Naxalites.
7.	1978 September 7	The famous Jagtial march was organized in A.P., in which thousands of people take part.
8.	1978 October 20	Andhra Pradesh Chief Minister Dr. Marri Chenna Reddy declared 'Sircilla' and 'Jagtial' were disturbed areas. This act giving police 'draconian' powers.
9.	1981 April 20	Police firing on Gonds in Inderavelli, Adilabad district (13 Gonds and one police constable were dead).
10.	1983	Telugu Desam Party founder N.T. Rama Rao started of his tenure with a romantic offer of' Laal salaam'(Red salute) to the Naxalites.

Contd...

S.No.	Date	Details
11.	1985	Andhra Pradesh Government establishes Special Task Force (STF), which later became the elite anti extremist commando force The Grey Hounds.
12.	1989-90	A.P. Chief Minister Marri Chenna Reddy lifts all curbs on Naxalite groups; Naxalites operate freely for about a year.
13.	1992 May 21	Crack down begins after Chief Minister N. Janardan Reddy imposes ban on People's War and Six front organizations. (In the wake of the assassination of former Prime Minister Rajiv Gandhi).
14.	1994	N.T. Rama Rao (TDP) returns to power wavering stand continues.
15.	1995 June 21	N.T. Rama Rao Government lifts the ban on the condition that the Naxalites should not report to violence.
16.	1996 July 22	Ban re-imposed by Chief Minister Chandra Babu Naidu (TDP) government and renewed every year subsequently.
17.	2002 January 15	Committee of concerned citizens (CCC) urges the People's War (PW) and Government to have talks.
18.	2002 May 10	P.W. announces unilateral ceasefire for one month.
19.	2002 June 8, 9	TDP Government says it is willing to talk.
20.	2002 July 19	P.W. called off the talks in protest against the allegedly killing of their cadres in 'fake encounters'.
21.	2004 June 12	Dr. Y.S. Rajasekhara Reddy (Congress) government announce ceasefire.
21.	2004 June 21	Maoists respond by declaring truce for three months.
22.	2004 July 7	Chief Minister Dr. Y.S. Rajasekhara Reddy meets Union Home Minister Shivraj Patil, centre gives its go ahead for talks.

Contd...

S.No.	Date	Details
23.	2004 July 24	Y.S.R. Government (Congress) allows the ban to lapse to facilitate talks with Maoist leaders.
24.	2004 September 23	Government invites Maoist leaders for talks.
25.	2004 October 15	Government and Maoist representatives begin talks.
26.	2004 October 18	First round of talks conclude.
27.	2004 October 31	Police Violate the ceasefire agreement with encounter of Mangannapeta forest area Warangal district.
28.	2005 January 15	CPI (Maoists) State Secretary Ramakrishna announces withdrawal from talks.
29.	2005 August 15	Sri Narsi Reddy, M.L.A. of Makthal and eight others shot dead in Mahabubnagar district.
30.	2005 August 17	Ban re-imposed on Maoists.

Table–82
Violence in Andhra Pradesh

Year	*Naxalites Killed*	*Civilians Killed*	*Security Force Personnel Killed*
1968	2	1	0
1969	76	32	3
1970	28	27	0
1971	7	17	1
1972	27	26	0
1973	12	7	0
1974	4	8	1
1975	19	9	1
1976	19	13	0
1977	2	3	0
1978	0	8	0
1979	0	19	0
1980	7	21	0
1981	2	18	1
1982	4	22	0
1983	2	26	0
1984	0	42	2
1985	38	29	6
1986	19	28	5
1987	29	53	24
1988	55	59	3
1989	51	97	13
1990	24	192	4
1991	102	218	50
1992	249	178	58

Contd...

Year	*Naxalites Killed*	*Civilians Killed*	*Security Force Personnel Killed*
1993	139	134	37
1994	106	106	21
1995	75	113	8
1996	157	155	47
1997	168	206	51
1998	275	198	35
1999	214	121	38
2000	219	91	33
2001	120	150	41
2002	87	90	15
2003	175	136	15
2004	52	69	7
2005	161	186	22
2006	133	37	10
Total	2859	2945	552

Source: Compiled and compared with the reports of Ministry of Home, Government of India, and Institute for Conflict Management, New Delhi and APCLC.

APPENDIX–III

Profiles of Newspapers

In the following pages, profiles of newspapers that have been selected for the purpose of analysis have been presented.

THE HINDU

The Hindu, a national daily, published simultaneously from 12 centers, viz., Chennai, Coimbatore, Bangalore, Madurai, Hyderabad, New Delhi, Visakhapatnam, Thiruvananthapuram, Kochi, Vijayawada, Mangalore and Tiruchirapalli is connected with high speed data lines for news transmission across the country. The paper is known for its seriousness and has a reputation for objectivity and credibility in the coverage of news. It was the first to introduce a facsimile edition in the country while launching its Coimbatore edition. *The Hindu* was also the first newspaper in the country in the early 60s to avail of a chartered plane service to reach its readers in far-flung areas.

The paper was started on September 20, 1878 as a weekly, became a daily in 1889 as a regular newspaper in English at Madras (Chennai) by two young men G. Subrahmanya Aiyer and M.Venkataraghavachariar. Running a newspaper in those days was not an easy task as journalism did not have a strong footing in India. Financial problems led to termination of agreement between these two young men, and in 1905 the paper was sold to S. Kasturi Ranga Iyengar.

Despite financial constraints and stringent laws of the then British Government, Kasturi Ranga Iyengar managed the newspaper successfully. After his death in 1923, his two sons Kasturi Srinivasan and Kasturi Gopalan took over the paper.

Kasturi Srinivasan became the editor and fought the British Government relentlessly. He continued to be the editor till 1959. Srinivasan's stewardship was the golden era of the paper when it forged ahead and established its reputation and fame not only in India but also abroad.

With the death of Srinivasan, his brother's sons G. Narasimham and G. Kasturi took over the management of the paper and G. Narasimham become the Editor. When he passed away in 1977, G. Kasturi occupied the editor's chair. He quit the paper in 1989 over a dispute with the associate editor of the paper N. Ram. The dispute arose between Kasturi and Ram over the publication of documents on the Bofors gun deal. It was alleged that in the Bofors gun deal, top government functionaries as well as political leaders were paid huge sums of money as commission for settlement of the deal between the Government of India and the Bofors Company of Sweden. N. Ram along with Ms. Chitra Subramanyam the Geneva Correspondent of the paper dug out a lot of documents from various sources and published them in the paper. Kastrui who opposed the publication resigned. Consequently, in 1991 deputy editor N. Ravi, Ram's younger brother replaced G. Kasturi as Editor. Nirmala Lakshman Kasturi Srinivasan's granddaughter became Joint Editor of *The Hindu* and her sister, Malini Parthasarathy, Executive Editor. Later, N. Ram was appointed on June 27, 2003 as the editor-in-chief.

In 2003, the Jayalalitha government of the state of Tamil Nadu filed cases against *The Hindu* for 'breach of privilege' of the state legislative body. The move was widely perceived as a government's assault on freedom on the press. However, *The Hindu* emerged unscathed from the ordeal, scoring both political and legal victories as it instantly commanded the support of the journalistic community throughout the country.

The Hindu launched the Visakhapatnam edition on May 10, 1990. At the time of launching this edition, *The Hindu* Wrote, "In addition to its comprehensive coverage of national and international news, *The Hindu* will provide from its new base more extensive reportage of news on the political, economic, social and cultural activities in the different districts and regions of the State."

As on December 2006, the circulation of the paper crossed one million copies. *The Hindu* publishes weekly supplements on Business Review, Education plus (on Monday), Education, Book Review (on Tuesday), Job Opportunities (on Wednesdays), Science, Engineering, Technology and Agriculture (on Thursdays), Friday Features covering Cinema, arts, music and entertainment, Young World, an exclusive children's supplement. 'Quest', a supplement by children for children, appears once a month. Metro plus, a supplement for metro news (Monday to Thursday and Saturday), Weekly Magazine covering social issues, art, literature, gardening, travel, health, cuisine, hobbies etc., 'Open Page' a supplement for reader to express their views on various subjects (on Sundays).

The Hindu is known for its wide coverage of news on Science and Technology, international issues and sports. The paper started the digital edition or e-paper. At present three editions of the Newspaper - Chennai, Hyderabad and Delhi are available in digital form at the first stage. They are available for viewing at 6 am Indian Standard Time (IST) every day.

THE NEW INDIAN EXPRESS

Indian Express is the single largest chain newspaper in English in India, published from 19 centers viz., Ahmadabad, Baroda, Bangalore, Belgaum, Bhubaneswar, Chandigarh, Coimbatore, Delhi, Hyderabad, Cochin, Kozhikode, Madras, Madurai, Mumbai, Nagapur, Pune, Thiruvananthapuram, Vijayawada and Visakhapatnam.

Indian Express is owned by Ramnath Goenka who was the first to start chain newspaper in India known as 'Express Group' of newspapers. With the death of Ramnath Goenka in 1991, the ownership of the paper was shared by his grandsons Vivek Goenka and Manoj Kumar Santhalia.

Indian Express was founded in 1931 by Dr. P. Varadarajulu at Madras and was later taken over by S. Sadanand of *The Free Press Journal*. When Sadanand was unable to run the newspaper on account of financial problems, he sold the paper to Ramnath Goenka. Through the freedom struggle, *Indian Express* played a key role in disseminating news about the national struggle; K. Swaminathan was the first editor of the newspaper between 1932 and 1939. Later, he was succeeded by G. Ramachandran who served the paper as its editor from 1945 to 1947. Goenka put forth all his energies in making the paper one of the finest Indian dailies. Prominent editors such as Khasa Subba Rao, Pothan Joseph, J. Natarajan, Prem Bhatia, H.Y. Sharada Prasad, and S. Mulgoankar worked in the paper and shaped it to earn a prominent place among the English dailies in the country.

Indian Express and freedom of press: In 1975, Emergency was imposed on the country by Mrs. Indira Gandhi, the then Prime Minister to curb internal disturbance. Pre-censorship was imposed on the newspapers. Indian Express supported the main opponent of Mrs. Gandhi, Jayaprakash Narayan, who was mobilizing people to dethrone an allegedly corrupt government. As a result, the newspaper was subjected to a lot of hardship by the Government. The survival of the newspaper became a problem. Bhattacharjee (1995) one of the former editors of the newspaper, noted that "The Express could not have survived if the courts and many officials had not registered the extra legal measures of the government."

Ramnath Goenka pooled up all the resources to fight for the freedom of the press by opposing the censorship laws until the Emergency was lifted in 1977. Palkiwala (1995) Commented thus: He (Goenka) acted on his conviction that the press should never be a Poodle of the Establishment but should act as the watchdog of democracy. He believed that a courageous and independent press is the noblest servant of society, along with a courageous and independent judiciary.

In the post- emergency period, the paper was served by many top editors of the country like S. Nihal Singh, B.G. Verghese, Suman Dubey, Arun Shourie, Prabhu Chawla and H.K.Dua, during the editorship of Arun Shourie between 1988 and 1991; the paper carried many investigative stories including the Bofors scandal and exposed man corrupt politicians.

The Visakhapatnam edition of *Indian Express* was launched in 1984 with the aim of reaching the readers in Visakhapatnam and neighbouring state, Orissa. *The Indian Express* management split in 1997.

The New Indian Express weekly and fortnightly supplements on career, women's life, lifestyle, school magazine, Health with *New Indian Express*, Education Express, Youth Express, Movie scope, weekend and The New Sunday Express Magazine.

EENADU

Eenadu, the largest circulated Telugu daily is published from 23 Centers, viz., Visakhapatnam, Hyderabad, Vijayawada, Tirupathi, Anantapur, Karimnagar, Rajahmundry, Suryapet, Guntur, Nellore, Srikakulam, Kurnool, Tadepalligudem, Warangal, Cuddapah, Mahaboobnagar, Bangalore, Delhi. The chief editor of the paper is Ch. Ramoji Rao, the proprietor of the Nizamabad, Khammam, Ongole, Chennai, Mumbai *Eenadu* group of publications.

Eenadu is popular for its innovative presentation and coverage of news and experiments with its lay out. Launched on August 10, 1974 with an insignificant circulation of 4,500 copies at the time of its inception at Visakhapatnam, *Eenadu* currently established itself as the largest circulated daily not only in Andhra Pradesh but also in the country. According to the Audit Bureau of Circulation *Eenadu* has a circulation of over 13.8 lakhs by December, 2006.

With the success of the Visakhapatnam edition in 1974, *Eenadu* expended its base in the state by establishing many editions subsequently. The Hyderabad edition was set up on December 17, 1975, following by another edition at Vijayawada in 1978. Within four years of its inception, *Eenadu* carved a niche for itself in the field of Telugu journalism. On June 20, 1982, *Eenadu* launched its fourth edition from Tirupathi. With the new edition, *Eenadu* appointed staff reporters at all the district headquarters with tale printer lines. Till 1982, the Telugu newspapers were giving importance to national news by publishing news agency dispatches on the front page while the state and district news was relegated to inside pages. *Eenadu* changed the trend and focused on state news by giving prominent place on the front page.

On January 25, 1989, *Eenadu* introduced the district supplement known as 'mini' edition. Each district supplement consisting of 8 to 12 pages is published multi colour tabloid form, catering to the needs of the local people. Today, these district supplements have become so successful in the state that the other newspapers have started imitating it.

These 'minis' have been successful in more than one way. For readers they give detailed news about happenings in the districts. In Hyderabad and Visakhapatnam, *Eenadu* has gone one step further by providing zonal news in the city. Each city is divided into three zones and a 'mini' supplement is published for that zone in a city, concentrating on local news. Because of these editions, *Eenadu* employed news contributors all over the state, over 90 per cent of the circulation is catered to by *Eenadu's* own modes of transport.

In order to cater to the segmented readers, *Eenadu* started various features. Raithay Raju (Farmer is the King) launched in 1985, August, it has evolved into a bridge to the farmer and his world. Pratibha (Talent), a weekly feature for the benefit of students was introduced in 1989, January to discuss topics related to education. A daily four page broad sheet pullout for women, 'Vasundhara' was introduced on September 24, 1992 which discusses issues exclusively related to women. *Eenadu* started Business page, Pelli Pandiri (a matrimonial column), Cinema, Chaduvu (Education), Sukhibhava (health), Champion (sports), e-nadu (technology), Siri (Savings), Eetharam (youth), Hai Bujji (Children) special features were introduced in main edition. Another important feature '*Eenadu Aadivaram*', A special Sunday Magazine, specially created for the Telugu readers, *Eenadu Aadivaram* was a 32 page magazine with 16 colour pages. Wholesome, entertaining and informative. A cover story for the weekend, articles and views that best reflected Telugu tastes. Uncommon and unusual people, events, anecdotes, were also Aadivaram's forte. Most important feature 'cartoons', Sridhar cartoons are the main asset of the *Eenadu*.

VAARTHA

Sanghi Industries started the *Vaartha,* Telugu daily from the A.B.K. publications banner on February 1, 1996. The founder of organization is Girish Sanghi. He is the Chairman and Managing Director of the Company. Whose investment is Rs. 2,400 crores. It has interests that span diverse activities, such as textile, polyesters, plantations, yarn, highways communications, cement, zip fasteners and adhesive tapes. A.B.K. Prasad was its first editor and the paper started publication from nine centers with an initial circulation of 3.5 lakhs. Sophisticated computer technology, satellite link, hot line facility to the composing centers, Pagination and composition of newspaper in the centre itself facilitates the newspaper in giving up to date news. The paper gave importance to sensational news and scandals. Later K. Ramachandra Murthy was worked as editor of the newspaper. In depth reports and editorials of A.B.K. Prasad and K. Ramachandra Murthy were the main assets of the newspaper. It is being published from 16 centers: Hyderabad, Vijayawada, Visakhapatnam, Rajahmundry, Cuddapah, Nizamabad, Ongole, Warangal, Anantapur, Kurnool, Karimnagar, Mahaboobnagar, Khammam, Nellore, Tirupathi and Nalgonda. At present Tankasala Ashok is the editor of the newspaper. The newspaper has the following divisions:

(i) Main Paper, *(ii)* Tabloid (city and district), *(iii)* Cheli, *(iv)* Sunday Magazine.

Main paper covers all the national and international news. The main paper also presents some advertisements in its. Tabloid covers city and district news. Cheli completely focuses on women and children. This edition also provides information about health, legal matters and other such matters. This edition has a separate page called 'Tera' (Screen). Where we can get sizable information about movies and film stars. Sunday magazine provides comprehensive information on all kinds of topics. It gives interviews of famous people in the society. It also gives comprehensive of burning questions of the hour.

Vaarthas bouquet of features includes Cheli (A women's Best Friend). Thus every day feature provides her with everything that would allow her to be the best she can. Important issues that effect women are covered along with a Plethora of special interest information, personality development, beauty tips, household tips, childcare, fashion career, success stories and so on.

Mogga (Bud): This is where young talent is spotted and encouraged young and budding writers are encouraged to write stories, articles and personal experiences. The feature includes everything of interest for the all round growth of a child. Puzzles, general knowledge, art, sports, science, history, values and personalities.

Naadi (Pulse): A daily feature that is devoted to health and Medicare.

Palle (Village): A weekly column that focuses on agricultural and rural issues possibly a first for any newspaper in the country. Horticulture, flori, pisi, seri cultures, cottage and rural industries are covered, analyzed and tips offered to improve performance.

Vanijya Vaartha (Business News): The world of business and finance is comprehensively covered in this daily two page section.

Vruthi (Occupation): For those looking for a bright future, Vruthi provides the right direction, it offers youth the opportunity for all round development of their personality through effective counseling on education.

Aata (Sport): Sports coverage was never so expansive or informative.

APPENDIX–IV

Major Incidents

The researcher identified 100 major incidents for study period from January 1, 1999 to December 31, 2006. The list of major incidents is given below:

Year 1999	*Incident*
April 1	Chinta Kunta Encounter–(Near Narsapur Town, Medak district), 10 Naxalites including three women were killed.
April 14	Former AP Assembly Speaker D. Sripada Rao was shot dead by Naxalites, near Annaram Village, Karimnagar district.
April 16	Sita Rampally Encoutner (Medak district). Six Naxalites were killed.
May 10	Kanchamal–Kondapur Encounter, Lingampet Mandal, Nizamabad district - Six Naxalites were killed in an encounter.
August 12	TDP former MLA Budda Vengal Reddy gunned down in Atmakur, Kurnool district.
September 5	Naxalites gundown IPS Offer Umesh Chandra at the Sanjeeva Reddy Nagar, Cross Roads in Hyderabad.
September 15	TDP leader, MLA from Sirpur P. Purushothama Rao and three gunmen were killed by Naxalites.
December 2	Three Police Personnel and two civilians were killed in a landmine triggered by Naxalites near Thumukunta of Veesanagandla mandal, Mahaboobnagar district.
December 3	Koyuuru Encounter–Three top PWG leaders fall to police bullets.
December 16	Naxalites killed Madhya Pradesh State Transport Minister Kavre in Balaghat district of Madhya Pradesh.

Year 2000	*Incident*
February 20	Seven Police personnel were killed in an attack by Naxalites on a Darakonda police outpost between G.K. Veedhi and Sileru in the agency of Visakhapatnam district.
February 21	23 Policemen including an ASP were killed in a landmine blast in Bastar, State of Madhya Pradesh.
March 4	13 persons including 11 Naxalites and two police personnel were killed in an encounter at Kachanara Village in Jahanabad district.
March 8	Andhra Pradesh Panchayat Raj Minister A. Madhava Reddy was killed in a landmine blast set-off by the Naxalites on the outskirts of Hyderabad.
April 4	8 Chief Ministers Conference of Naxalites hit states.
April 11	Kommireddy Viswamohan Reddy and Smt. Mariamma were killed by police in an encounter in Dondapadu in Guntur district (Viswamohan Reddy is also a known writer and poet). Burgumpadu-Patha Pina Paka Encounter: 5 Naxalites were killed by police encounter in Khammam district.
April 27	Chityala Encounter–6 Naxalites, including one woman were killed by police encounter.
April 28	Kowkonda encounter: 12 Naxalites were killed by police encounter.
November 2	Bhopalapally Encounter: Seven Woman Naxalites were killed by Police.
November 24	APCLC leader T. Purushotham hacked to death.
Year 2001	*Incident*
February 12	The District Collector of Warangal and his driver injured in an attack by Naxalites.
February 18	APCLC Leader Azam Ali hacked to death.
March 10	15 Naxalites were killed in an exchange of fire in Mirzapur district of Uttar Pradesh.
March 23	Naxalites attack on Srisailam and Sunnipenta police stations in Kurnool district.
April 19	Four Police personnel were killed in a landmine blast in Chintakarrapalem village in Y. Ramavaram mandal of East Godavari district.

June 10	Ten Naxalites were killed in three encounter incidents.
June 17	Four informer/coverts, shot dead by Naxalites.
June 20	Eight Naxalites including three women were shot dead in an encounter at Godukondla village, Chintapalli mandal, Nalgonda district.
August 6	Four Naxalites were killed in an encounter near Chandurthi village, Rudrangi mandal Karimnagar district.
August 11	Naxals attack on Kalimela and Motu Police Stations in Orissa.
August 21	Seven Police personnel were killed in a landmine blast triggered by Naxalites at Bandla Motu village in Guntur district.
September 10	5 CRPF Personnel were killed in a landmine blast triggered by Naxalites at Sunnampalli near Maaredumilli, East Godavari district.
December 25	Naxalites attack on Hanma Konda Police Station.
December 30	Congress MLA Ragya Naik gunned down by the Naxalites in the interior Maddi Madugu village of Amrabad mandal of Mahaboobnagar district.
Year 2002	*Incident*
January 20	Peopleswar declared to readiness for the ceasefire and talks.
March 12	Eturu Nagaram Encounter: 6 Naxalites and a SI were killed in a firce encounter in the Eturu Nagaram forest area on the border of Warangal and Karimnagar districts.
June 5	Talks between Government and Naxalite party representatives.
June 25	Ulvanur–Mavillavai encounter: Two women Naxalites killed in encounter near Paloncha in Khammam district.
July 3	Nerella Encounter: A top women Naxalite leader (Padmakka) among 4 killed at Nerella in Karimnagar district.
July 20	Naxalites withdrawing from talks with Government.
July 24	Adigoppula Landmineblast: First Major PW Strike after pulling out of talks. Four Police personnel were killed in Adigoppula village in Guntur district.
July 27	Five Naxalites were killed in an encounter in Warangal–Karimnagar border.
August 2	6 Naxalites including two women members killed in two encounter incidents in Prakasam, Warangal districts.

August 12	7 CRPF men were killed in Naxal blast in Orissa.
August 24	Naxalites blasted Anakapalli and Chodavaram Police Stations and 4 Cops abducted.
November 12	7 Naxalites were shot dead in an encounter in Mahadevapur forest area in Karimnagar district.
November 18	Ilapuram encounter: 5 Naxalites were killed in an encounter near Ilapuram village located on border of Karimnagar-Warangal districts.
November 19	20 persons were killed as Naxals blow up RTC bus, near Chintagudem village between Tupakula gudem and eturu nagaram.
Year 2003	*Incident*
January 6	Three police personnel were killed in landmine blast triggered by Naxalites. Three Naxalites were killed in the subsequent encounter, in Dachepalli village, Guntur district.
May 15	Three Women Naxalites were killed in an encounter near Agarguda forest area, Bezuru mandal, Adilabad district.
June 12	Naxalites blast a police station at Addanki in Prakasam district.
October 2	Chief Minister of Andhra Pradesh N. Chandra Babu Naidu, a Minister, two MLAs escaped assassination attempt when a powerful landmine triggered by Naxalites at Alipiri, between Tirupathi and Tirumala in Chittoor district.
October 25	Security forces kill two top leaders (Latha and Koumudi) of the PWG in an encounter at Bollapalli in Guntur district.
November 7	APCLC leader Dr. Lakshman was kidnapped by some unidentified persons.
November 24	Naxalites of the PWG kill, five persons after branding them as 'coverts'
Year 2004	*Incident*
January 26	Three top leaders including a state Military Commission (SMC) member Erra Satyam killed in two Separate encounters in Chittoor and Kadapa districts.
March 19	Tribal Welfare Minister: Mani Kumari's husband Venkat Raju shot dead by Naxalites in Paderu.
April 9	28 Security personnel were killed in landmine blast in Singhbham in Jharkhand state.

June 16	Congress Government agrees to PWG's terms.
July 12	Two Naxalites of the PWG are killed in an exchange of fire between two groups (coverts attack) near Oddugudem in Warangal district.
July 22	Andhra Pradesh State Government has decided not extend the ban on people's war and its six frontal organisations has been allowed to lapse.
July 29	Martyrs Memorial Meeting Organised by Naxalite Party emissary in Warangal.
October 12	People's war leaders come over ground for talks with Government.
October 15	CPI (ML) PW and MCCI have merged to form a CPI Maoist.
October 16	First round talks between the government and Naxalites.
October 19	First round of talks with Naxalites concluded.
October 25	"Congress mishandling naxal issue", strongly criticized by L.K. Advani.
November 26	Exchange of fire between Naxalites and the police in Rudrangi village in Chandurthi mandal (first exchange fire during the truce period).
December 4	Second exchange of fire between the police and Naxalites in the Machapur area.
December 12	Third exchange of fire after the peace talks have began at Kodeshalakunta village in the Jakaram forest area in the Mulugu mandal.
December 15	Police raids continue says CPI (Maoist) call for 'counter-offensive'.
December 16	Four constables hurt in landmine blast in the G.K.Veedhi mandal, Visakhapatnam district.
Year 2005	*Incident*
January 6	CPI Maoist Cadres killed the Mungar SP, K.C. Surendra Babu and six other policemen in a landmine explosion near the Bhimbandh area in Bihar state.
January 9	A Women guerilla squad member of CPI (Maoist) Lalithakka was killed in an alleged encounter with the police in Prakasam district.

January 16	Six Naxalites including two women died in encounters in Prakasam and Mahabubnagar districts.
January 18	Maoists withdraw from talks.
January 21	Three Naxalites killed in Siricilla encounter.
February 7	State to consult centre on Naxalites issue.
March 2	Eight farmers hacked to death by Maoists in Vempenta, near Atmakur mandal, Kurnool district.
March 8	Manala encounter–Three women among 10 Maoists killed in an encounter near Manala in Nizamabad district.
March 12	CI and three policemen killed in naxal attack in Chilakaluripet police station, Guntur district.
March 20	Four Maoists killed in encounter Divisional Committee Secretary Yadanna among victims.
April 28	One dead in clay more blast Ongole SP Mahesh Chandra Ladda escape Maoist attack.
July 2	Top Janashakti leader Riaz and three other Naxalites killed in encounter.
August 16	The Congress MLA from Makthal C. Narsi Reddy and eight persons including one of his sons are killed by Maoists in Narayana peta in the Mahabubnagar district.
August 18	Ban clamped on Maoists.
August 23	CPI (Maoist) Nalgonda Secretary Diwakar alias Ravi killed in encounter.
November 14	Naxals attack on Jahnabad, free cadre from jail, five killed 20 Ranvir Sena Men kidnapped from prison.
December 26	Four RPF Personnel who were escorting Raigarh Passenger train were killed and five others were injured in an attack by CPI (Maoists) at Koneru Railway Station in the Vizianagaram district.
Year 2006	*Incident*
February 7	Nine Jawans killed by Maoists in Chhattisgarh.
March 1	25 persons were killed in landmine blast Erroban in Chhattisgarh.
April 29	Seshachalam encounter – Nine Maoists killed in Kadapa forests.

June 17	Top Maoist leader Matta Ravi Kumar killed in encounter in the Nallamala forest.
June 28	Eight Maoists killed in encounter at Nallamalla forest.
July 18	27 Salwajudvam activists killed by Naxalites in Chhattisgarh.
July 24	Maoists AP State Committee Secretary Madav and 7 Naxalites killed in the encounter.
September 9	In one of the biggest ever haul of weapons in the country the Andhra Pradesh police recovered 600 uncoaded rockets, 275 unassembled rockets, 27 rocket launchers were seized.
September 16	Six Maoists killed in two encounters in Warangal and Nalgonda districts Karimnagar East division. Maoist committee Secretary Madhu was killed along with three women cadres, Nirmala, Padma and Prameela.
October 7	Top Maoist leader, Nallamala forest division committee Secretary Sudharsan alias Venkatesu was killed in an encounter with the police in the forest area of Nallamala.
October 8	Kadari Ramu alias agency RK killed by police in an encounter.
November 11	Nine Maoists gunned down, top leader Obulesu and his wife among those killed in an encounter.

Total number of incidents: 100.

APPENDIX–V
Code Sheet

Name of the Paper   Number of Pages
Week: Date:

S.No. Subject Category	Direction	FRONT PAGE									INSIDE PAGES							EDITORIAL PAGE						
		NEWS									NEWS							Editorial		Car-toon	Edit articles		Letters-to-the editor	
		L		S		N		Photo	Cartoon PC	Cartoon MC	L		S		N		Photo	Nax.	Oth.		Nax.	Oth.	Nax.	Oth.
		fr	Sp	fr	Sp	fr	Sp	fr	fr	fr	fr	Sp	fr	Sp	fr	Sp	fr	fr/Sp	fr	fr	fr/Sp	fr	fr/Sp	fr
1. Naxalite activities																								
1. Ambush	f																							
	uf																							
	ne																							
2. Raids	f																							
	uf																							
	ne																							
3. Destruction	f																							
	uf																							
	ne																							
4. Kidnaps	f																							
	uf																							
	ne																							
5. Attack on informers	f																							
	uf																							
	ne																							
6. Attack on coverts	f																							
	uf																							
	ne																							

Contd...

7. Communication	f	
	uf	
	ne	
2. Encounter deaths		
1. Naxalites	f	
	uf	
	ne	
2. Police	f	
	uf	
	ne	
3. Both	f	
	uf	
	ne	
3. Police activities		
1. Counter measures	f	
	uf	
	ne	
2. Welfare measures	f	
	uf	
	ne	
3. Communication	f	
	uf	
	ne	
4. Agony of sufferers		
1. Naxalite families	f	
	uf	
	ne	

Contd...

2. Polices families	f
	uf
	ne
3. Targeted families	f
	uf
	ne
4. Innocent victims	f
	uf
	ne
5. Government views	
1. Central	f
	uf
	ne
2. State	f
	uf
	ne
3. Other States	f
	uf
	ne
6. Political parties views	
1. Congress	f
	uf
	ne
2. B.J.P.	f
	uf
	ne

Contd...

3. Communists	f	
	uf	
	ne	
	uf	
	ne	
4. TDP	f	
	uf	
	ne	
5. Others	f	
	uf	
	ne	
7. People's reactions		
1. Naxalites	f	
	uf	
	ne	
2. Police	f	
	uf	
	ne	
8. Human rights/ courts	f	
	uf	
	ne	
9. Human rights related organizations	f	
	uf	
	ne	
10. Peace talks	f	
	uf	
	ne	

Note: f: favourable, uf: unfavourable, ne: neutral; L: Local, S: State, N: National.

APPENDIX–VI

Correction Factor

Unit of Space Measurement

The standard unit of measurement adopted in the study was one centimeter of body type containing four agate lines with a column width of 25 ems., (12 ems. = 1 inch). The procedure in employing this unit was to first measure the various news stories in a newspaper with an ordinary centimeter rule. The news stories were measured and recorded in column centimeters regardless of the size of type or width of the (single) column. After calculating the total length of space devoted for each subject category in each newspaper under study was available in centimeters. The result was multiplied by a correction factor (k) to standardize the column centimeters for comparing of four newspapers. Because the four newspapers in the study had different column widths and different body type, a different correction factor was applied to each newspaper using the following formulae:

$$K = \frac{W}{25} \times \frac{L}{4 \times 10} \; where$$

W = width of the column in cms. L = average number of lines of body type per 10 centimeters.

In the study, *The Hindu* had a column width of 2.5 inches (1 inch = 12 ems.) equivalent to 30 cms. The other three newspapers –*The New Indian Express, Eenadu , Vaartha* had a column width of 1.7 inches, the equivalent to 20.4 cms.

To ascertain the average number of lines of body type per 10 centimeters, inside pages with typical type size and leading were measured. The average lines varied from paper to paper because of different body types and widths. On the average, *The Hindu* had 30 lines per 10 cms. while *The Indian Express* had 27 lines, *Vaartha* 25 lines and *Eenadu* had 26 lines.

The correction factor of each newspaper was calculated with the formulae mentioned earlier. The correction factor (k) of four newspapers is as follows:

The Hindu : $K = \frac{W}{25} \times \frac{L}{4 \times 10} = \frac{21}{25} \times \frac{30}{4 \times 10} = 0.84 \times 0.75 = 0.63$

The New Indian Express : $\frac{21}{25} \times \frac{27}{4 \times 10} = 0.84 \times 0.67 = 0.56$

Eenadu : $\frac{21}{25} \times \frac{26}{4 \times 10} = 0.84 \times 0.65 = 0.54$

Vaartha : $\frac{21}{25} \times \frac{25}{4 \times 10} = 0.84 \times 0.62 = 0.52$

Bibliography

Alisky, M. (1958). 'The Peruvian Press and the Nixon Incident', *Journalism Quarterly*, 35(4): 411-419.

Allen,T. & Seaton, J. (1999). *The Media of Conflict War Reporting and Representations of Ethnic Violence*, London: Zed Books.

Auter, P.J. & Moore, R.L. (1993). 'Buying from a friend: A Content Analysis of Two Tele Shopping Programmes'. *Journalism Quarterly*, 70(2): 425-436.

Balagopal, K. (September 6, 1997). 'Naxalite Terrorists and Benign Policemen', *Economic and Political Weekly*, 2253-2260.

Banerjee, S. (1980). *In the Wake of Naxalbari*, Calcutta: Allied.

Banerjee, S. (2003, November 1). 'Naxalites: Time for Introspection', *Economic and Political Weekly*, 4635-4636.

Bansal, K. (2002). 'International News Coverage in Four Indian Newspapers: A Content Analysis Study', *Media Asia*, 29(3):31-40.

Barcus, F.E. (1962). 'A Content Analysis of Trends in Sunday Comics 1900-1959', *Journalism Quarterly*, 38(2): 171-180.

Barnes, S. & Kaase, M. (1979). *Political Action*, Beverly Hills, CA; Sage Publications.

Bassiouni, M.C. (1981). 'Terrorism, Law Enforcement and Mass Media Perspectives, Problems and Proposals', *Journal of Criminal Law and Criminology*, 72(1).

Bassiouni, M.C. (1982). 'Media Coverage of Terrorism: The law and the public' *Journal of Communication*, 33(2):128-143.

Batlin, R. (1954). 'San Francisco newspapers' campaign coverage 1886-1952', *Journalism Quarterly*, 31(3) : 297-302.

Berelson, B. (1952). 'Content Analysis in Communications Research', Glancoe : Free Press.

Bethell, T. (1977). 'The Myth of an Adversary Press', *Harper's Magazine*, January, 33-40.

Bhargava, G.S. (1989). ' Naxalites in Andhra Pradesh', *Mainstream*, 71-76.

Bishara, A.B. & Shalom, K. (1985). 'Perspectives in Conflict: The Role of Palestinian Media in the West Bank, the Gaza Strip and East Jerusalem' *Journal of Communication*, 35(1):16-22.

Brigittee, L.N. (2000). 'Accomplice or Witness? The Media's Role in Terrorism', *Current History*: 174-178.

Bromley, D.G. & Shupe, A.D. (1979). *'Moonies' in America: Cult, Church and Crusade*, Beverly Hills: Sage.

Buckman, R.J. (1993). 'How eight weekly newsmagazines covered elections in six countries', *Journalism Quarterly*, 70(4): 780-792.

Burnet, M. (1971). *'The Mass Media in a Violent World'*, Symposium Proceedings: UNESCO.

Busby, L.T. & Greg, L. (1993). 'Feminism and advertising in traditional and non-traditional women's magazines 1950-1980s', *Journalism Quarterly*, 70(2): 247-264.

Bush, C.R. (1960). 'A System of categories for general news content', *Journalism Quarterly*, 37(2): 206-210.

Caruthers, S.I. (2000), *The Media War: Communication and Conflict in the Twentieth Century*. New York: St. Matrin's Press.

CCOMPOSA (2001). *'Resolution on the Present Political Situation'*, second annual conference of CCOMPOSA .http://www.cpnm.org/documents/ccomposa.htm.

Chadwick, B.A. Bahr, H.M. & Albrecht, S.L. (1984). *Content Analysis: In Social Science Research Methods* (pp. 239-257), New Jersey: Prentice-Hall.

Committee of Concerned Citizens (1997-2000), *Report of the Committee of Concerned Citizens*, Hyderabad.

Committee of Concerned Citizens (1999). *'In Search of Democratic Space'*, Report of the Committee of Concerned Citizens, Hyderabad.

Committee of Concerned Citizens (2002, April 23). *'An Appeal by Ten Senior Editors'*, Third Report of Committee of Concerned Citizens-1997-2002, Hyderabad.

Cornwell, E.E. Jr. (1959). 'Presidential news: The expanding public image', *Journalism Quarterly*, 36(3): 275-283.

Coulson, D.C. & Anne, H. (1995). 'The Louisville Courier—Journal's news content after purchase by Gannet', *Journalism and Mass Communication Quarterly* 72(1): 205-215.

Crozier, B. (1960). 'The Rebels: A study of post war insurrections'. London.

Dasgupta, B. (1974). *The Naxalite Movement*, Bombay: Allied.

Davis, H. & Rarick, G. (1964). 'Functions of editorials and letters-to-the editor', *Journalism Quarterly*, 41(1):108-109.

DeFleur, M. & Ball-Rokeach, S. (1989). *Theories of Mass Communication* (Fifth Edition), New York: Longman.

Devi Prasad, B. (1993 Feb.). '*The Newspapers Revisited, A Study of the Coverage of the 1991, Indian Elections*', Paper presented at the meeting of the Common Wealth Association for Education in Journalism and Communication (CAEJC), Hyderabad.

Devi Prasad, B. (2008). 'Content Analysis: A Method in Social Science Research', in D.K. Lal Das & V. Bhaskara Rao (eds.) *Research Methods for Social Work* (pp. 173-193), New Delhi: Rawat.

Devi Prasad, B. & Sampath Kumar, R.D. (1991). 'Opinion molding by the press: An analysis of the election related content of editorials and letters-to-& the editor', *Media Asia*, 18(1): 24-29.

Devi Prasad, B. Visveswara Rao, K. & Sampath Kumar, R.D. (1992). 'Civic concerns in an emerging city and its adjoining regions: A content-analytic study of critical letters to the 'Action Please' Column in Indian Express', *Nagarlok*, XXIV (2): 32-42.

Dieter Rucht, (1991). *Research on Social Movement, the State of the Art in Western Europe and the USA Campus*, Verlag: West View Press.

Dremers, O.P. & Nichols, S. (1987). *Precision Journalism: A Practical Guide*, New Delhi: Sage.

Duggal, V.K. (2005). 'Government's approach to Maoists attacks'. *Report from Union Home Secretary*, New Delhi.

Entaman, R.M. (1994). 'Representation and reality in the portrayal of Blacks on Network television News', *Journalism and Mass Communication Quarterly*, 71(3): 509-520.

Ganapathy *alias* Muppalla Lakshmana Rao (1998). 'Unification is the only way to advance the cause of the Indian revolution' in http://www.rediff.com/ news/1998/oct/07gana/html

George, A.L. (1959). *Propaganda Analysis*, Illinois: Row, Peterson and Company.

Ghosh, S. (1975). *The Naxalite Movement, a Maoist Experiment*. Calcutta: Allied.

Gitlin, T. (1980). *The Whole World is Watching: Mass Media in the Making and Unmaking of the New Left*, Berkley: University of California, 3-4: 21.

Gregg, J.E. (1965). 'Newspaper editorial endorsements and California elections 1948-1962', *Journalism Quarterly*, 44(4): 532-538.

Grey, D.L. & Brown T.R. (1970). 'Letters-to-the editor: Hazy reflections of public opinion', *Journalism Quarterly*, 47(2), 450-56.

Gupta, R.K. (2004). *The Crimson Agenda: Maoist Protest and Terror*, New Delhi: Wordsmiths.

Hachten, W.A. (1999). *The World News Prism: Changing Media of International Communication*, Ames: University of Lowa Press.

Hallin, D.C. & Gitlin, T. (1994). 'The Gulf war as popular culture and T.V. Drama'. In W.L. Bennett & D.L. Paletz (eds.) *Taken by Storm: The Media Public Opinion and U.S. Foreign Policy in the GulfWar* (pp. 149-163), Chicago: University of Chicago Press.

Hallin, D.C. (1986). *The Uncensored War*, New York: Oxford University Press.

Hallin, D.C. (1987). 'Hegemony: The American news media from Vietnam to El. Salvador: A study of ideological change and its limits', in D.Paletz (eds.), *Political Communication research* (pp. 3-25). Norwood NJ: Ablex.

Haskins, J.B. (1965). 'The editorial mix: One solution to a magazine editor's dilemma', *Journalism Quarterly*, 42(4): 557-562.

Head, S.W. (1952). 'Content Analysis of Television drama programmes', *Quarterly of Film, Radio, T.V.* 9(2): 175-192.

Holsti, O.R. (1969). 'Content Analysis', in G. Lindzey, and Aronson E. (eds.), *The Hand Book of Social Psychology*, Vol. II, (pp. 608-686), New Delhi:Amerind.

Inkeles, A. & Geiger, K. (1952). 'Critical letters-to-the editors of the Soviet-Press: Areas and modes of complaint', *American Sociological Review*. 17(6):694-703.

Inkeles, A. & Geiger, K. (1953). 'Critical letters-to-the editors of the Soviet-Press: Social characteristics and interrelation of critics and the criticized', *American Sociological Review*. 18(1):12-22.

Janis, I.L. & Fadner, R. (1965a). 'The coefficient of imbalance', in H.D. Lasswell, N. Leites & Associates (eds.) *Language of Politics: A Quantitative Semantics* (pp. 153-169), Cambridge: MIT.

Janis, I.L. (1965). 'The problem of validating content analysis', in H.D. Lasswell, N. Leites & Associates (eds.), *Language of Politics: A Quantitative Semantics* (pp. 55-82), Cambridge: MIT Press.

Johari, J.C. (1972). *Naxalite Politics in India.* The Institute of Constitutional and Parliamentary Studies, New Delhi: Research Publications.

Kamat, M.V. (2003, October 23). 'The Leftist menace in India', *The Free Press Journal.*

Kerlinger, F.N. (1973). *Foundations of Behavioural Research* (Second edition), New York: Holt, Rinehart and Winston.

Khan, M.I. & Kumar, K. (1993). *Studies in Modern Mass Media,* Vol. I, New Delhi: Kanishka, 34-35.

King, E.G. (1989). 'Exposing the 'Age of Lies': The propaganda menace as portrayed by magazines in the aftermath of World War-I', *Journal of American Culture,* 12(1): 35-40.

Knight, G. & Dean, T. (1982). 'Myth and the Structure of News', *Journal of Communication,* 32(2): 144-161.

Krippendorff, K. (1980). *Content Analysis: An Introduction to its Methodology,* California: Sage.

Lasswell, H.D. (1948). 'The Structure and Function of Communication in Society', in E. Bryson (eds.), *The Communication of Ideas,* New York: Harper and Brothers.

Lasswell, H.D. & Leites, N. (1965). *Language of Politics: Studies in Quantitative Semantics,* Cambridge: MIT.

Lee Seow, T. & Maslog, C.C. (2005). 'War or peace journalism? Asian newspaper coverage of conflict', *Journal of Communication,* 55(2): 311–329.

Lipsky, M. (1970). 'Protest in City Politics', in Doris, A. Garber (ed.), *Media Power in Politics,* New Delhi: Indo American Cooperative Publishing Reprint.

Lowry, D.T. & David, E.T. (1989). 'Part-time T.V. Portrayals of sex, contraception and venereal diseases', *Journalism Quarterly,* 66(2): 347-352.

Mallin, J. (1974). *Terrorism in Revolutionary Warfare: Strategic Review.*

McGoldrick. A. & Lynch, J. (2000). *Peace Journalism, How to do it Retrieved* on June 2, 2003 from http://www.transcend.org\pj manual.htm.

McCombs, M.E. (1981). 'The Agenda Setting Approach,' *Hand Book of Political Communcation,* (eds.) D.D. Nimmo & K.R. Sanders, Beverly Hills: Sage.

Mehta, D.S. (1979). *Mass Communication and Journalism in India.* Bombay: Allied.

Midgley, S. & Rice, V. (eds.) (1984). *Terrorism and the Media in the 1980s*

(Conference Proceedings), Washington: The Media Institute and Institute for Studies in International Terror.

Miller, S. (1975, spring). 'The Content of News Photos: Women's and Men's Roles', *Journalism Quarterly*, 52: 72.

Mohanty, M. (1977). *Revolutionary Violence: A Study of the Maoist Movement in India*, New Delhi: Sterling.

Molotch, H. (1979). 'Media and Movements', *The Dynamics of Social Movement* (eds.) Zald, M.N. & McCarthy, D. Cambridge: Plenum.

Murthy, D.V.R. (2000). 'Developmental News Coverage in the Indian Press: An Analysis of Four Dailies', *Media Asia*, 27(1), 24-53.

Murthy, D.V.R. (2001). *Developmental Journalism*, New Delhi: Dominant.

North, R.C. Holsti, O. Zaninovich, M.G. & Zinnes, D.A. (1963). *Content Analysis: A Handbook with Applications for the Study of International Crisis*, Evanston: North Western University Press.

Olson, B. (1994). 'Sex and the soaps: A comparative content analysis of health issues', *Journalism Quarterly*, 71(4): 840-850.

OPDR (2005). 'Fact finding report on Koyyuru encounter-1999', *Rights on Gallows and Repression on People:* A compilation of Organization for the Protection of Democratic Rights.

Parthasarathy, R. (1984). *Basic Journalism*, New Delhi: Macmillan.

People's War Group (1980). Unpublished State Committee report.

Rai, H. & Prasad, K.M. (1972). 'Naxalism: A Challenge to the Proposition of Peaceful Transition to Socialism', *Indian Journal of Political Science*, XXXIII, 4 October-December, 480.

Ram, Mohan (1969). *Indian Communism Split within a Split*, Delhi: Vikas.

Ram, Mohan (1971). *Maoism in India*, Delhi: Vikas.

Ram, Mohan (1973) 'Communist Movement in Telangana'. In Paul, R.B. & Macus, F.F. (eds.) *Radical Politics in South Asia* (pp. 280-321), Cambridge: MIT.

Ramakrishnan, Venkatesh (October 21, 2005). 'The Naxalite Challenge', *Frontline*.

Ramana, P.V. (2004). 'Left wing extremism in India'. In Dipankar Sengupta & Sudhir Kumar Singh (eds.) *Terrorism in South Asia*, (pp. 145-168), New Delhi: Authors Press.

Rao, K.A. (1996). *Naxalite Terrorism: Social and Legal Issues*, Madras: East West Books.

Reddy, K.S. (October 19, 2004). 'Naxalites their network', *The Hindu*.

Roy, Ashis Kumar (1975). *The Spring Thunder and After*, Calcutta.

Sahni, Ajai (October 21, 2005). 'Delusion of Peace', *Frontline*.

Saigal, Rahoul (March 19, 2005). 'Power Politics in the Red Corridor', *The Pioneer*.

Schmid, A.P. & De Graaf, J. (1982). *Violence as Communication: Insurgent Terrorism and the Western News Media*, London: Sage.

Singh, Prakash (1995). *The Naxalite Movement in India*, New Delhi: Rupa.

Singh, Prakash (February 2007). 'Naxalite Movement in India', *Yojana*.

Singh, Satyanarayana (1969). 'Building up the proletarian party and agrarian revolution', *Liberation*, 3(1).

Stevenson, K. (1998). *Press and Insurgency: A Study in Andhra Pradesh*, unpublished Ph.D. thesis, Mangalore University, Mangalore.

Subrahmanyam, V. (1994). 'Koyyuru Episode: The Real Questions', *Economic and Political Weekly*, XXIX (7).

The Task Force on Naxalism (April 3, 2005). 'Socio-Economic Factors behind growth of Naxalism', *The Hindu*.

Tichenor, J.P. George, A.D. & Clarice, N.O. (1994). 'Communication and Community Conflict'. In Doris, A. Graber (ed.) *Media Power in Politics* (96-106), New Delhi: Macmillan.

Toffler A. & Toffler H. (1994). *War and Anti-War: Survival at the Dawn of the 21st Century*, Boston: Little Brown.

Tuchman, G. (1978). *Making News*, New York: Free Press.

Vacin, G.L. (1965). 'A Study of letter writers', *Journalism Quarterly*, 42(2): 464-465.

Wang, J. (1996). 'The siren songs of consumption: An analysis of foreign advertisements in two mainland Chinese newspapers 1985-1993', *Gazette*, 56(3): 201-219.

Wanta, W. (1988 spring). 'The Effects of Dominant Photographs: An Agenda Setting Experiment', *Journalism Quarterly*, 65: 107-111.

Wilkinson, P. & Stewart, A.M. (1987). *Contemporary Research on Terrorism* (eds.) Aberdeen: University Press.

Wilkinson, P. (1994). *Terrorism: British Perspectives*, UK: Darthmouth.

Wolfsfeld, G. (1984 September). 'Collective Political Action and Media strategy: The Case of Yamit', *Journal of Conflict Resolution*, 28(3): 363-381.

Wolfsfeld, G. (1997). 'Promoting Peace through the News media: Some initial lessons from the peace processes', *Harvard International Journal of Press/Politics*, 2(2), 52-70.

Woodrum, E. (1984). 'Mainstreaming content analysis in Social Science: Methodological advantage, Obstacles and solutions', *Social Science Research*, 13(2): 1-19.

Wurth, H.S. (1983). 'Network News Coverage of Terrorism: The Early Years', *Terrorism*, 6(3): 403-521.

Index